NAPOLEON III

NAPOLEON III

W. H. C. Smith

Principal Lecturer in History,
Goldsmiths' College,
University of London

ST. MARTIN'S PRESS NEW YORK

TO MY PARENTS

Contents

Preface

THIS book was written as the result of a general interest in French nineteenth-century history and a particular interest in the person of Napoleon III. It is designed not only for students in the field but also for a wider public, and it is hoped that in spite of imperfections and limitations it will prove acceptable to both types of reader.

The character of Napoleon III is one which has aroused, and still arouses, strong feelings, and almost anything written about him is bound, therefore, to provoke a further outbreak of controversy. Since history is, however, only a temporary verdict and not a final judgement there is always room for another case either for the prosecution or for the defence. That is, in a sense, the real justification for producing this biography.

Throughout the book I have translated from the French where necessary, and I accept full responsibility for the translations and for any mistakes which may have occurred.

I have many acknowledgements to make—in England to the staff of the Public Record Office, in particular to Mr. K. Timings who was extremely helpful on many occasions. I would also like to thank my friend Mrs. Ilse Kaden for her interest and her help with translations from German. I must thank my Publishers for their patience and their courtesy, and above all, I must thank Miss J. Howe who had the thankless task of typing from my manuscript.

My colleagues in the History Department in Goldsmith's College have supported me by displaying constant interest in the progress of my book, and I should like at the same time to thank the College Library Staff for their work in obtaining for me many books and periodicals which I had difficulty in locating. I am further indebted to my own College and to the University of London Research Fund for grants which enabled me to go to France for the purpose of research. In the case of my own College I am also grateful to them for giving me leave of absence to go to France in 1968 to lecture at the *École Pratique des Hautes Études* of the Sorbonne in Paris. This appointment was as a result of a very kind invitation by M. Jean Tulard of the *École*

Pratique des Hautes Études, who was unfailingly kind and helpful during my stay in France. I might add that the events of May and June, 1968, enabled me to understand the revolutionary mentality in France somewhat better than I had before.

My thanks are also due to the staff of the *Archives Nationales* in Paris, in particular to Mme S. d'Huard who very generously discussed with me possible sources for investigation into the history of the Second Empire, and the staff of the Research Department of the *Ministère des Affaires Étrangères* who took great trouble in helping me to locate documents in a period of history when the sources are more than usually difficult to track down. M. Fleury, Secretary to H.I.H. Prince Napoleon, kindly allowed me to look at what remains of the former Library of Napoleon III and I am grateful to him. Above all my thanks in France go to my friend Mlle Andrée Mansuy whose constant interest, kindness and encouragement made me persist in a task which I sometimes felt would never be brought to completion.

I hope that all those to whom I am indebted will not feel that their help was wasted.

Prologue

ON 17th October, 1815, a small group of people disembarked from H.M.S. *Northumberland*, which had anchored at Jamestown, the principal port and town of the colony of St. Helena. The most important of the group was the man henceforward to be known, officially, as General Bonaparte, who had asked for English hospitality, and who could be said, after a fashion, to have got it.

Napoleon's sojourn at St. Helena until his death in 1821 was a tragicomedy, at times worthy of the traditions of the *commedia dell' arte*. Villainous jailers, faithful retainers, intrigues, scenes, espionage, even poison—none of the traditional elements was missing. The whole affair would be appalling were it not for the fact that it centred around Napoleon, whose extraordinary genius enabled him to manufacture something worthwhile out of apparently unpromising material.

"Manufacture" is, indeed, the operative word, for, captive among a captive audience, genius found its own way of working out the problem. As Emperor of the French, and virtual master of Europe, Napoleon had known who and what he was, and what he must do. Now he could be several people as his fancy and his genius dictated, and so he alternated between the Promethean-caged-eagle part and the long-suffering-martyr role. In between came moments of true self-revelation; querulousness, bad temper, and suppressed fury. Napoleon's character, in its many-sidedness, gave him the qualities needed to play the parts, and his genius directed them to advantage. Knowing that death would terminate the performance, Napoleon even managed to write a scenario for that, although the performance was delayed for twenty years after the actual funeral. Napoleon knew perfectly well that it was unlikely he would be forgotten : what mattered to him, therefore, was *how* he was remembered. Since the debate about him continues, the six years on St. Helena were certainly not wasted.

Among the many who thought about him one may, with safety, number the members of his own family. He had been good to them in the halcyon days. If he had been demanding, he had also been rewarding, and he had in many ways treated them better than they

deserved. Of them all, only Madame Mère emerges as really worthwhile and worthy of compassion. The rest were, at their best, indifferent
material—described by a modern writer as "Golden Millstones"— at
worst they had been a contributory factor in bringing down the
Empire.

Perhaps it was this disappointment with his brothers and sisters
which made Napoleon place such hope in his son ("My Son will avenge
me"), in the belief that the second generation might do better than the
first. It is probable that Napoleon never questioned the idea that there
would be a second Empire; he had seen to that by his actions both
before and after his fall. That great and perspicacious writer on Louis
Napoleon, F. A. Simpson, had noticed this. Historians saw, he
said,[11] . . . 'The Hundred Days,' as a mere epilogue to the great drama
of the First Empire's fall, not realizing that it was in point of fact a
prologue to the strange romance of the Second Empire's rise.[11] The only
problem was when, how and who? Here the historian has the advantage over contemporaries: he knows the answer. In Napoleon's case,

the life of his successor and his attempts, ultimately successful, to gain
the throne of his uncle are so bizarre as to compel the historian to say:
"it is really all true."

I

The Family Background

*"Tel enfant de hasard, rebut des échafauds,
Dont le nom est un vol, et la naissance un faux."*

V. Hugo: *Les Châtiments*

ON 4th January, 1802, Louis, the fourth of the Bonaparte brothers, was married. His bride was Hortense, daughter of the Empress Josephine by her first husband, the Vicomte de Beauharnais. The marriage was an arranged one and was from the outset disastrous. As the bridegroom himself said: "Never was there a ceremony so sad, never did two espoused people feel more sharply a presentiment of all the horrors of a forced and ill-assorted marriage." Louis gave no specific reasons for his fears that the marriage was doomed, but if it is true that he was homosexual and had contracted syphilis while serving in the Egyptian campaign of 1797-98, neither condition argued well for the happiness of his bride. Added to these problems, or perhaps caused by them, was Louis's temperament which with its moods and harshness made his wife's life a misery. Madame de Rémusat noted as early as 1806: "Her husband's tyranny was exercised in every particular—his character, quite as despotic as his brothers', made itself felt on his whole household."

Feelings had, however, nothing to do with procreation and Hortense bore Louis three sons: the first, born within ten months of the marriage in October, 1802, christened Louis Charles, died in 1807; the second Napoleon Louis, born in 1804, died in 1831; the third, Charles Louis Napoleon was born on 20th April, 1808.

Charles Louis had arrived at a high point in the Bonaparte fortunes and his baptism, on 2nd June, 1810, reflected the Imperial glories. The ceremony was performed by Cardinal Fesch his great uncle; his Godfather and Godmother were the Emperor Napoleon and the Empress Marie Louise. His maternal grandmother, the ex-Empress Josephine, had been retired from the Imperial scene since the divorce in 1809 and was not actually present at the ceremony at Fontainebleau.

The reason for the splendour of this Imperial occasion went beyond a mere desire for pomp. By the laws of succession to the Imperial throne dated the 28th *Floréal* Year XII and the 5th *Frimaire* Year XIII the Crown devolved on the children of Napoleon's brothers in default of direct descendants from the Emperor himself. This meant that Charles Louis was second in line of succession to his uncle, his elder brother being the heir presumptive, a circumstance which continued until Marie Louise produced Napoleon's own son in 1811.

It will have been remarked that Charles Louis's father was not present at the baptismal ceremony. Indeed, he was on the point of leaving the Dutch Kingdom which his brother had given him in 1806 and fleeing to Bohemia, worn out by the harassment to which he was subjected by Napoleon over his manner of ruling in Holland. Added to this, there was the personal problem in that Hortense and her husband had been estranged for some time and that she herself was conducting an *affaire,* well known in Parisian society with the Comte de Flahaut. Flahaut was an illegitimate son of Talleyrand, by whom Hortense produced her own bastard, born on 21st October, 1811, who was to be the future Duc de Morny.

The facts of the estrangement, and the absence of Louis at his son's baptism have led to the charge that Charles Louis was not his father's child, but the child of a Dutch admiral called Verhuell. This charge was given great publicity by Victor Hugo, once he had passed to the opposition at the beginning of the Second Empire. Before that, other candidates for paternity had been proposed, but there seems to be no basis in fact for this charge of bastardy, although it is a close-run thing arithmetically. Because of the death of their eldest son in 1807, Louis and Hortense had two fugitive reunions between 28th June and 6th July and between 12th August and 27th August. At some time in this period, Hortense became pregnant—a fact noticed in the official *Journal de l'Empire* in October of the same year.

Louis himself did not, except in moments of gross ill humour, ever deny his fatherhood—but Louis's character was so bizarre that not much attention need be paid to the outbursts of *ce n'est pas mon enfant.* As Hortense Cornu, a childhood companion of Charles Louis said, "He [Louis] was half mad and said [this], I believe, only to annoy his wife." In the long run, does it matter? Charles Louis Napoleon believed himself to be his father's son and his uncle's nephew and that is what counts. At the worst he can be merely accused of living out a fantasy—with some very real consequences.

Louis Napoleon was a delicate child, perhaps because he was born prematurely. From the very beginning of his life he suffered also from not having a settled home—partly due to the separation of his parents, which Napoleon finally authorized in 1810, and partly because the family fortunes were linked with the fate of the Empire. When the Empire fell, Louis Napoleon was seven, and it seems unlikely that he can have remembered much either of the institution or of his uncle, but the instability with which he was surrounded from birth must certainly have had an adverse influence on his character.

By nature timid, retiring, and easily moved either to crises of tears or of rage, Louis Napoleon was a difficult child to bring up—particularly without the influence of a father. Psychologists could probably make much of this paternal deficiency as revealing itself in many attitudes and responses of Louis Napoleon in later life, but the historian is hardly competent to carry through such an analysis. Whether or not Queen Hortense was ideally suited to the bringing up of a son, it is of no use to dispute, since she did, in fact, do so. Due to her easygoing nature, her regime differed greatly from that of her husband, in whose care was their elder boy, and even her choice of tutors left much to be desired. The Abbé Bertrand, who had charge of the boy until his twelfth year, was a man of culture and charm—but was also addicted to erratic hours and lacking in that quality of *gravitas* which the Romans had felt so essential to anyone in a position of responsibility. In short, he was lazy and took most things unseriously, neither trait being very suitable for a man in his position.

At the age of twelve, Louis Napoleon was provided with a new tutor, Philippe Le Bas, son of the *Conventionnel,* who had committed suicide the day of Robespierre's fall in July, 1794. The choice was an odd one for the stepdaughter of an Emperor. In the long run the experiment foundered on Le Bas's austere republican nature which, unlike the Abbé Bertrand's was distinctly tinged with *gravitas.* However, the break with Le Bas did not come until 1827, when the Prince was nineteen and beyond the range of personal preceptor. Until then, Le Bas seems to have inculcated some respect for work into his charge, as his results at the *gymnasium* at Augsburg bear out, for in February, 1822, his pupil came fourth in a class of seventy. But by 1827, when Le Bas left the prince, it seems that Louis Napoleon was more interested in athletics than he was in academic studies—and he had already begun to make an impression on the young women whom he met.

Le Bas's judgement on his pupil was at this stage harsh, and almost self-reproaching: "One must be resigned to emerging as a superficial man when one begins a worldly life at a far too early age." But a later commentator has been kinder to Le Bas than the tutor was to himself:

One cannot doubt that the affair ended so. But it remains beyond doubt that during those six years that they had been together, Louis had grown from a sickly and sentimental child into an independent and athletic young man; that his tutor's friendship stood for self-discipline and a devotion to study which enabled him to carry on for the next nine years some degree of self-education, and to make good use of the other six most formative years of his imprisonment (1840-46).[1]

One may doubt if Le Bas's influence was quite so far-reaching, important though it must have been. Le Bas considered athletics were overdone and in the end other forces helped to shape the Prince's character—not least his own actions in pursuit of his dream.

It is true that Le Bas implanted the idea of scholarship in the boy's mind, for Le Bas was a scholar by temperament as well as profession. But there was much of the auto-didact about Louis Napoleon and he never really bothered to master what he did not care to. The boy was sentimental and a dreamer; so was the man, for Louis Napoleon liked books and libraries; he even had aspirations to historical and literary productions, but the main-spring of his actions lay elsewhere in a portion of his make up which Le Bas could do little to control or mould. Here, perhaps, it was the verdict of a woman which was not only kinder, but more perceptive : "Curly, blond hair, features regular, although a little too heavy for his height, an air of kindness, sentimental, melancholic—which is extremely interesting." This was Valérie Masuyer, lady in waiting to Hortense, writing in 1830. This portrait of the romantic young prince in exile reveals an aspect of the prince which a man like Le Bas would not have considered of importance, but to an age saturated in Walter Scott and the romantic writers words like "sentimental" and "melancholic" were almost words of praise.

The surroundings in which the Prince spent his childhood were suitably romantic since he and his mother alternated between Bavaria and Switzerland, regions of lakes, mountains and forests. From 1817 until 1820, mother and son lived at Augsburg where Louis Napoleon attended the *gymnasium*; from 1820 until Hortense's decision to settle in Switzerland they alternated between Augsburg and Arenenberg. In 1823 Hortense finally settled in her Swiss home, where, on a promontory reaching out into Lake Constance, lay a small château which Hortense transformed into a "Gothic Villa." The scenery around the house was so "romantic," with lake, forests, and mountains in the distance, that it might have served as the setting for Lamartine's great poetic sigh *"Le Lac."*

Inside, the villa was steeped in past glories, and in these surroundings, even had he wanted to, Louis Napoleon could hardly avoid being impressed by the constant reminders of who and what he was. The house contained family portraits, furnishings, even conscious reconstruction of former homes, for the principal drawing room was a replica of that at Malmaison. To those who had known the Empire, every step must have been a reminder: to those who had not known it, every step must have been an inspiration. Apart from the décor, one should not underestimate Hortense's personal influence as an Imperial messenger when dealing with her son:

> You and your brother are assuredly heirs of Napoleon, after the king of Rome ... in our present condition, uncertain of what you may become, never weary with hoping. Keep your eyes peeled, look out for propitious moments. If France eludes you definitely, Italy, Germany, Russia and England still present resources for the future: everywhere "flights of fancy" arise which can raise the heirs of a great and illustrious man to the skies.[2]

These *caprices d'imagination* of which Hortense spoke were indeed to become vital factors in Louis Napoleon's attitude to his life.

Can one doubt but that they were encouraged by the establishment at Arenenberg of a colony of Beauharnais-Bonapartes, including Eugene, brother of Hortense, ex-King Jerome of Westphalia, and former officers of the Imperial Army? This group formed a nucleus of a miniature court of the Empire around which circled the visitors who were not only royal or martial, but even literary. Could Chateaubriand, Alexander Dumas and Casimir Delavigne resist the appeal of such a romantic household? Little wonder that charades were a favourite game.

All this, however, was a summer fancy; in late autumn, Hortense and her son went to Italy for the winter, only returning to Switzerland in late spring. Beyond the alps there were other reminders of the family, tangible as well as intangible. At Rome lived Madame Mere herself, Cardinal Fesch, Pauline (Princess Borghese) and Lucien Bonaparte, while ex-King Louis lived in Florence with his elder son Napoleon Louis.

The unromantic air of Florence, well ruled by its Hapsburg Grand Duke Leopold and saturated by antiquity, was not conducive to the growth of new fads and romantic fashions and this atmosphere had produced a great difference in outlook between the two brothers: a difference perhaps accentuated by the fact that one was a mother's and the other a father's son. Napoleon Louis had married his cousin, daughter of ex-King Joseph of Spain, and was engaged in building an industrial fortune in paper manufacture. His morose, dyspeptic father was no magnet either for literary brilliance or for ambulatory souvenirs of the Empire and so the elder Prince was not surrounded by the same swarm of Imperial bees as his younger brother. As luck would have it, he too was destined to be a child of his times—but this was not the result of planning.

However, this is to digress from a consideration of the early manhood of Louis Napoleon before he became politically active. His twenty-first year, 1829, found him: "A wild harum-scarum youth . . . apparently without serious thought of any kind, although even then he was possessed with the conviction that one day he would rule France." The comment is Lord Malmesbury's, but since it comes from the future Foreign Secretary's memoirs, one may say hindsight has dictated part of the judgement. In 1829, two lives stood between Louis Napoleon and his role of pretender, Napoleon's own son, the Duc de Reichstadt, living with his Hapsburg grandfather, the Emperor Francis at Vienna and his elder brother's. It is unlikely that Louis envisaged the disappearance of both. In fact, the Prince was without too many prospects and certainly without immediate employment. His only regular work was as a volunteer in the Swiss Army at its summer exercises at Thun, where the Commander, Colonel Dufour, was a Napoleonic veteran. Weary of being a part-time soldier, he made an attempt to take up a more permanent military career in the service of Nicholas I of Russia, but this had been vetoed by his father early in 1829 on the grounds that no cause could justify service under a foreign flag. So the summer of 1830 found Louis Napoleon at his customary occupation in the military camp at Thun, studying artillery and military tactics, presumably thinking of nothing more dramatic than the impending autumn visit to Italy with his mother. It was here that he heard the news of the revolution of 1830, which overthrew the Bourbons and put Louis Philippe on the throne of France.

In August he wrote to his mother: "The Tricolor floats at this moment over France. Happy are they who were among the first to give it back its brilliance." On a later date he wrote "How happy I would be to see the soldiers wearing the tricolor cockade!" It was not to be. The July Monarchy, although it revoked some of the edicts of exile did not free the Bonapartes from the law of banishment. During the July days, too many placards had appeared in the working-class areas of Paris proclaiming Napoleon II for the government of Louis Philippe to feel comfortable about re-admitting the family.

So, the change of dynasty had not changed the family's situation. Exile continued, and the ways of exile. In November, 1830. Louis Napoleon and Hortense set out for Italy on their normal autumn migration to the south. It must have seemed to the young man that nothing would ever change and that his life would be passed in exile. But this time it was not to be just an ordinary journey—it was to be the beginning of Louis Napoleon's political life : Italy was once again to prove a formative influence in the life of a Bonaparte.

2

Political Beginnings

*"Le rôle des Bonaparte est de se poser en
amis de tout le monde:
ils sont des médiateurs, des conciliateurs."*

Queen Hortense to Louis Napoleon

THE Italy to which Hortense and her son paid regular visits was a strange collection of states—no more a "nation" than a stack of timber is a "ship." To the bulk of the population of the Peninsula this state of affairs was a matter of indifference. Confronted with the problem of survival in a basically poor country, it was easy for ninety per cent of the population to decide its priorities.

However, among the intelligent, educated and wealthier sections of society, there was a great deal of talk about Italy and reform. Partly this was a direct result of the Napoleonic era in Italy, when most parts had felt the benefit of good and central administration. Partly also it was a result of the economic changes in Italian society, which were themselves legacies of the general revitalizing of Europe by Napoleon. Areas of Italy were prosperous, like Lombardy and Venetia, but they were under Austrian rule and so contributed nothing to the general advancement. If their condition excited admiration on other parts of the Peninsula it also aroused envy, since it was foreigners who benefited from these areas.

Elsewhere there were states, like Piedmont, newly enlarged by the 1815 settlement and enriched by the acquisition of the Republic of Genoa, but guided in reactionary politics by their King, who wore an old-fashioned eighteenth-century wig to cover his old-fashioned eighteenth-century mind. So reactionary indeed was Victor Emmanuel that his government had seriously considered whether or not the roads and bridges built during the Napoleonic period should be destroyed; the gas lamps in Turin had been removed as a pledge of good intentions. It did not seem that much would come from an area which was struggling to go backwards.

In the south of the Peninsula lay the Kingdom of Naples, sometimes called the Kingdom of the Two Sicilies. Here the restored Bourbons did their best to maintain a balance between immobility and progress, avoiding political change while building the first railway line in all Italy. The poverty of the Kingdom made it prey to endemic brigandage, and the backwardness of the population made it a breeding ground for secret societies plotting various kinds of political changes.

Of the smaller regions, only Tuscany under an enlightened Austrian Grand Duke, presented a picture of reasonable order and stability. It was perhaps significant that ex-King Louis should have chosen Florence as his place of settlement and that his elder son should have started developing a thriving business in the same region.

Athwart the Peninsula, geographically, lay the Papal States, the visible evidence of Christ's Kingdom on earth, ruled by the Pope and the Papal civil service. In 1815 Papal stock stood higher in Europe than it had done for at least a century, thanks to Napoleon's highly arbitrary dealings with Pius VII—a man of unusual saintliness whose personal qualities had helped to restore sagging Papal prestige. It was Pius who had given the distressed Bonapartes a home in 1815 and who showed himself more charitable to his fallen adversary than any other European ruler. But all this did not make Papal government any better or more palatable and Leo XII, successor to Pius VII, leaned heavily towards the most obscurantist of the Curia. His death and the election of Gregory XVI came at a time when the revolution in France had sparked inflammable situations in other parts of Europe. The same conflagration was not to spare parts of Italy.

Chateaubriand had mercilessly impaled the Papacy on the point of his pen when he was French Ambassador to the Papal Court : "The old men name an old man like themselves as sovereign. This old man, become sovereign, names, in his turn, old men as Cardinals. Turning in this vicious circle, the supreme power, exhausted, is always at the edge of the grave."[1] Nothing could have better illustrated this gibe than the pontificate of Pius VIII who, elected in 1829, died in November, 1830, of simple old age.

During the interregnum, which followed the death of Pius VIII in November, Louis Napoleon arrived in Rome having spent a fortnight in Florence with his father and brother. Attention has already been drawn to the differences existing between the two brothers in terms of upbringing and attitude. Indeed, the two young men had been so little in contact that the nature of their joint entry on the European scene would lead one to speculate that the younger brother was the more persuasive and stronger character as a result of his less conventional upbringing.

This is not to say that Napoleon Louis's life in Florence had been passed in a political vacuum, or that he was totally without interest in politics. He may have been involved with the Italian secret society of the Carbonari, though the evidence is far from conclusive, and, if a later commentator is to be believed, he had evolved a plan for unifying Italy.[2]

If Napoleon Louis was involved in Italian conspiracies for the re-ordering of the country, had he also involved his younger brother? Had the elder led the younger? The question as to whether or not Louis Napoleon was a member of the Carbonari has never been satisfactorily solved, in that a clear verdict for or against his membership cannot be given. Even the most recent investigations leave the question open.[3] Long ago F. A. Simpson concluded that both brothers may have given verbal adherence, but were not sworn members, and that conjecture will serve as well as any other.[4] The important point is that both openly participated in the political events which took place in Italy in 1830-31.

As far as Louis Napoleon was concerned, it would seem that he became involved in an attempt to raise a revolt in the Papal State in late November, 1830. As already indicated the death of Pius VIII produced an interregnum which appeared, to the existing subversive element in Rome, the moment to try and force reforms on the Papal Government. But the time was wrong, and the attempt was a failure, largely because the conspirators had no common aims, no organization, and no real plans for mounting a proper insurrection. At the height of the crisis, on the evening of 10th December, Louis Napoleon tried to urge them to abandon the whole idea which, in his view, because of total popular indifference, could only fail. He was unsuccessful in preventing an attempt on the 11th, which was no more than a police skirmish, and although he had not been involved, he became a victim, in that the Papal Government politely asked him to leave the territory.[5] Louis went back to Florence where he lived with his brother.

In January, 1831, more serious revolts broke out in Italy, in the lesser Duchies of the centre and in the Papal territories of the Legations, Umbria and the Marches. On 25th January Louis Napoleon and his brother left Florence to join the insurgents. Louis gave his mother the reasons in a letter of early February: "Your affection will understand us. We have accepted engagements and we cannot depart from them. The name we bear obliges us to help a suffering people that calls upon us."[6] The letter is a young man's, not least in its calm assumption that a suffering people had called for them, for there is no evidence of this, and the rebel force which they joined at Bologna consisted of at most 15,000 poorly-armed men, officered by men who had formerly served in Napoleon's Italian regiments. This group had, at Bologna, proclaimed the independence of the Legations and set up a provisional government.

Among the Bonapartes in Italy, the shrewdest comment on the revolt came from Hortense, who as early as 25th January had written that: "Italy can do nothing without France . . . a revolt without result would obliterate for a long time the resources of the men of such a group, and one always despises those who fail." This was indeed so; the insurgents had little hope of help from the France of Louis Philippe, who himself was in a shaky position in that interventions by Austria, Prussia and Russia in the affair of the overthrow of the Bourbons in July would have been justified, since it was a breach of the settlement of 1815. The only thing which had prevented intervention was the three powers' preoccupation with revolts in Central Europe and, in the particular case of Russia, with the very serious insurrection in Poland. Metternich made it clear, in January, 1831, that any intervention in Italy would produce a sharp response from Austria and Louis Philippe dared not match his shaky throne against a solid alliance of the three Powers. In fact, all that the French government could do was preach the doctrine of non-intervention—intended as much for its own protection against attack as it was intended to protect others. But in the case of Italy, this would not work, since Austria had treaty relationships which would enable her to move to intervention within the framework of international law.

Furthermore, Metternich was more than a match diplomatically for a group of confused insurgent leaders. He pointed out to the French government that the presence of the two young Bonapartes gave the whole affair the appearance of a serious Bonapartist movement, thereby underlining a fact which would help to discourage Louis Philippe from coming down on the side of intervention. The insurgents, equally aware of this and desperate for French help, requested the brothers to retire. It did not boost their cause, for Louis Philippe still did not lift a finger to help, and it mortally offended the two young men, who refused to believe that their friends could be so callous. Louis wrote: "My dear Mama, the order has just come for us to retire to Ancona. . . . Thus they want us to appear as cowards." On 5th March, from Bologna he wrote: "The intrigues of Uncle Jerome and Papa have been so

successful that we have been obliged to leave the [insurgent] Army. It is
Aramandi [Napoleon Louis's former tutor] who has brought this
about ... for the government at Bologna declared that it would never
have done so." It was hard to be so full of fervour and to be made to
face political realities. It was going to prove even harder in the next few
weeks, for the two brothers passed from being rejected supporters to
being fugitives.

By 12th March Austrian troops were in control and the brothers, in
their flight, had reached Forli. Here disaster struck; with a total lack of
romance Napoleon Louis died of measles on 1th March and was
buried next day in the city. Hortense, unaware of this, but knowing
that a sentence of death passed by the Austrian authorities now stood
against both sons, and in great grief and agony of mind, pressed
forward to Forli only to find one son already dead and the other
seriously ill—for Louis had caught the infection from his brother and
now had measles himself.

The escape of Hortense and her son from Italy is so bizarre and
eventful that even a fiction writer would hesitate to commit it to paper.
It involved disguises and false passports and at one time the young
Prince lay ill for ten days in a room next to that of the Austrian
Commander at Ancona. The flight of mother and son involving
frequent midnight journeys seems like an episode in an historical novel
and, yet it happened. Indeed, this experience may have taken its
physical toll of Louis Napoleon, for he was disguised at one point as his
mother's footman and was compelled to spend one night sleeping,
literally, in the street within days of his having left his sick bed. Little
wonder that in later life Napoleon III was to be a martyr to kidney
complaints.[7]

The destination of the fugitives was France, which was reached in
mid-April, and on 23rd April, after fifteen years of exile, the two were
in Paris in a hotel in the rue de la Paix. Hortense made her presence
known, discreetly, to Louis Philippe and asked for an audience. Temporarily, at least, she and her son were at the centre of French affairs
again.

Louis Philippe cannot have been overjoyed by the arrival of Hortense
and her son, but he owed Hortense some recompense at a personal level
for the kindness which she had shown his mother, the Dowager Duchess
of Orléans, who had received a pension of 400,000 francs from
Napoleon. It was unlikely, therefore, that the King would actually
refuse to see her. A hole-in-the-corner interview took place at the
Tuileries on 26th April, at which the King expressed his regrets at the

necessity for the exile : "The time is not too far distant when there will be no more exiles," he said, but went on to make it clear that the time was certainly not yet. Indeed, given the Bonapartist manifestations which had occurred during the period of the 1830 revolution, and in the first few weeks of the reign, the time could hardly have been more inopportune for the physical presence of Bonapartes on French soil.

What was quite clear to the government of Louis Philippe was that the presence of Hortense and her son in Paris represented a serious threat to the shaky political order which the regime had managed to create. There could be no question of allowing the exiles to remain for fear that Louis Napoleon's contacts with the disaffected sections of French, or more accurately Parisian society, should lead to a real political crisis.

On 5th May, the anniversary of the death of Napoleon I, a demonstration occurred outside the visitors' hotel in the Place Vendôme in which a substantial crowd, socially mixed in composition, cried *"Vive l'Empereur"* until it was dispersed by the National Guard. On 6th May, Hortense and her son were asked to leave France.

For the moment Louis Napoleon had to abandon direct political action and to give up hope of any further direct contact with Bonapartist elements in France. He had, however, been sufficiently stirred by what he had seen in Paris to feel that there existed fertile soil which could be cultivated to bring forth a Bonapartist revival.

Ever since the Restoration there had been a steady increase at all levels of society in the cult of the Emperor's memory. Perhaps the most significant sector of French society to be affected by this was the working population—particularly the urban proletariat. The reasons for their disaffection towards the existing regimes can be stated quite briefly. They were economic. By 1825, a mere decade since Waterloo, the cost of living in the Paris region had risen so alarmingly that the worker could scarcely purchase half the provisions he could buy under the Empire, even if, as in some cases, he had obtained a slight increase in salary.[8] By 1830 the situation had certainly not eased and it was by no means confined to the Paris region.

The main centres of French industrial development lay in the Lille area, the Nord as it is generally called, Normandy, Alsace, and the Lyons/Saint-Étienne area. As in England, in the first period of rapid industrialization, the major development in French manufacturing was in the cotton industry. This rapid expansion of industry was accompanied by great hardships borne by the workers, particularly in Lille, Rouen, Mulhouse and Lyons itself, where living conditions were

atrocious.[9] In any analysis of this type of expansion it must be borne in
mind that an increase in the labour force in any particular industry
produced a real dislocation in that industry. It is not just a question of
long hours, although a sixteen-hour day cannot have been a negligible
factor in contributing to discontent; it was also the problem caused by
the importation of new hands into a "traditional" occcupation. The new
workers, drawn from rural areas, found it hard to adjust to, and to
accept, conditions which were established and accepted by those already
skilled in their trade. Much bad feeling often arose between the new
immigrants and the established workers and this was exacerbated, one
imagines, by increased demands for already inadequate housing. It is
significant that in Lyons, centre of a long-established industry and subjected to just the type of pressures described above, there should have
occurred two very serious outbreaks of rioting in 1831 and 1834. The
revolt of the latter year was so serious as to require strong army contingents to suppress it.

Given these considerations, it will hardly come as a surprise that
there was much political disaffection in these regions. The doctrines of
St. Simon and Fourier spread and there was a ground swell of
republican and radical agitation for change. Secret societies, embryonic
Trades Unions (the *Compagnonnages*) existed, and attempted to maintain a constant propaganda which was repressed by the government as
and when it could uncover such activity.

What had the revolution of 1830 done to satisfy the discontents and
hopes of this class of French society? The simple answer was vitually
nothing. Balzac had seen it :

> Have we not in exchange for a broken-down and laughable feu-
> dalism, acquired a simple aristocracy of money, of power and of
> merit, which, however legitimate it may be, throws no less of an
> immense burden on the masses, imposing on it the patriciate of the
> bank, ministerialism and the fire-power of the press and the orator's
> dais, the springboard of men of merit? Thus, in sanctifying, by its
> return to constitutional monarchy, a deceitful political equality,
> France has only spread the evil; for we are a democracy of the
> rich.[10]

The regime of the bankers and industrialists, that board of directors
which called itself the "July Monarchy" with Louis Philippe as Chairman of the Board, had no thought for those who were not shareholders.
This the French working class were soon to discover. Many had already
done so even before the monarchy was established; there had been more

cries of *"Vive l'Empereur"* and *"Vive Napoléon II"* in the working-class areas of Paris in July, 1830, than there had been shouts for Louis Philippe. As late as December, 1830, this government was still alarmed by disturbances in the working-class faubourgs, openly Bonapartist in form. A working-class pamphlet summed it up: 'Napoleon is in his tomb, but Bonapartism is not dead. It has become Republican."[11]

What were the roots of this working-class Bonapartism which was to be of such importance in the development of French politics at this period? Straightaway it must be admitted that the subject has, as yet, not been sufficiently examined in depth to admit of any hard or fast conclusions on anything but a limited scale.[12]

What seems to be accepted now is the idea that Bonapartism was the rallying point of the *déclassés* in politics, or to put it another way, support for Bonapartism cut across the accepted lines of political division. It had an immediate appeal to all who were excluded from political power by the censitary franchise of the Restoration and the July Monarchy. One could say that Bonapartism stood at the cross roads where liberal democracy and proletarian democracy could meet. Liberal democracy believed in universal suffrage and "the nation." Proletarian democracy also believed in universal suffrage, but included the concept of social justice and "the people." The Republicans clung to the ideas of 1793 with their demands for universal suffrage and the Jacobin constitution, but they carefully excluded any hint of social reform. This explains the later attempts made by Louis Napoleon to fuse masses and classes, for he had perceived that neither the Party of Order, whether Legitimist of Orleanist in form, nor the doctrinaire Republicans could provide a common ground for the two opposed groups in French society. It is doubtful if the prince saw this clearly in the early 1830's, for he was as yet groping towards some kind of political creed. But experience and reflection were to bring about a crystallization of ideas, which were to emerge in his two pamphlets the *Idées Napoléoniennes* of 1839, and the *Extinction du Paupérisme* of 1844.[13]

In 1832, having returned to Arenenberg after a short stay in London, Louis Napoleon wrote a pamphlet entitled *Rêveries Politiques*. He asked Chateaubriand, who happened to be in Switzerland, to read the work. This the great writer did, advising the Prince to substitute the word "nation" for the word "people" on every occasion on which the latter appeared. Significantly, this advice was disregarded and when it was published the pamphlet referred to the "people" and its sovereignty. Indeed, it laid down a simple sketch of a constitution for France based upon the three powers of the state: "The People, the

Legislative Body and the Emperor. The People will have the power of election and sanction. The Legislative Body will have the power of deliberation. The Emperor will have the executive power."[14]

Furthermore, the people may choose their Emperor: "... for, with the accession of each new Emperor, the people's sanction shall be demanded. If it is refused, the two Houses shall propose a new sovereign."[15] It has been suggested that this section represents less an appeal to the people than an open bid by Louis Napoleon for the candidature to the Imperial Throne, since it implies a setting aside of the Duc de Reichstadt and Napoleon I's surviving brothers. But there is no clear evidence that this was so. The Duc de Reichstadt had yet to die, and Napoleon's brothers to prove their indifference to their claims, before Louis Napoleon moved. In any event, when the *Rêveries* were published in May, 1832, there was no knowing that the death of the King of Rome was so imminent, although he was known to be consumptive.

There can be no doubt that, when the death *did* occur, in July, 1832, it immediately changed Louis Napoleon's situation, and it was not only he who sensed this. So shrewd an observer of the European scene as Metternich had, in 1832, written to Count Apponyi, the Austrian Ambassador in Paris "... I beg you to draw King Louis Phillippe's attention to the character who will succeed to the Duc de Reichstadt. I use the word 'succeed' because in the Bonapartist hierarchy there is an acknowledged succession respected by the party. The young Louis Bonaparte is a man tied up with the plots of the societies. He is not formed as in the Duc de Reichstadt under the safeguard of the principles of the Emperor [Francis]. The day of the Duke's death, he will look upon himself as called upon to be head of the French Republic."[16]

Louis Napoleon felt that with the death of the direct heir, the time had now come to put much to the proof : his ideas about Bonapartism, his capacity to become the leading light of the dynasty. Was he really the man Metternich thought him to be? Was he a political reality or only a phantom? It was time to find out.

3

The Official Pretender

*"Les Dieux sont de nos jours les maîtres
souverains.
Mais, Seigneur, notre gloire est dans nos
propres mains."*

Quoted in a letter from Louis Napoleon to
his mother, 13th July, 1834

B ETWEEN 1832 and 1836, with one interruption, Louis Napoleon
lived continuously in Arenenberg. The exception was a visit to
England in the spring of 1833 to meet his uncles Joseph and
Lucien to discuss the affairs of the House of Bonaparte, of which, since
the death of the Duc de Reichstadt, Joseph was officially the head.
What Louis discovered from the meeting was for him extremely
important. Neither of his uncles wanted any disturbances or any upset
in the existing political order in France. As Lucien put it: "I consider
the right of Napoleon as that of yesterday, the right of Louis Philippe
as that of today."[1] The uncles made it clear that they regarded the
nephew as a nuisance and as a possible disturber of the family peace.
Dissatisfied and disappointed, the Prince consoled himself with a tour of
England's northern region, where he was fascinated and impressed by
the new industrial world which he discovered.

For the rest, the meeting had been a disaster and Louis Napoleon
returned to his life in Switzerland disappointed and disillusioned. Again
installed at Arenenberg, his life was a blend of country squire and
military man. In 1833 he produced his *Considérations Politiques et
militaires sur la Suisse,* a reasoned and perceptive analysis of the
problems of his adopted country which earned him the honorary
citizenship of the Swiss Republic. What made the work interesting was
that it was not only about conditions in Switzerland, but also about her
neighbour: "If in speaking of Switzerland I have been unable to
prevent the frequent reoccurrence of my thoughts to France, I trust
that my digression may be pardoned." Since the digressions were
extensive, the apologetic preface was needed.

In 1836 appeared his *Manuel d'Artillerie.* This was a technical work
of some competence, as befitted a Bonaparte, and the Prince saw to it

that the work was disseminated as widely as possible. Military men, not
only in Switzerland, but in France, Britain and Germany received
copies with the author's compliments. Since Louis Napoleon was now a
Captain in the Artillery Regiment of the Canton of Berne, a further
honour from the Swiss, his work could hardly be classed as that of an
amateur. Indeed a five-hundred-page, closely reasoned and highly
technical manual could not be dimissed lightly. Nor was it, for many
military men were impressed, and it served to bring the Prince's name
forward in a new and favourable light among a group whose sympathy
was essential to him.

This literary-political success was the only consolation to be had at
the time. Louis Napoleon's awareness of this was revealed in a letter he
wrote to his friend, Vieillard, former tutor of his brother, in January,
1835:

> I know that I count for much through my name, but as yet nothing
> through myself: aristocrat by birth, I am a democrat by nature and
> by conviction; owing everything to heredity and yet really all to
> election ... charged with personal ambition if I take a step outside
> my normal sphere, charged with apathy and indifference if I stay
> quietly at home. Indeed, inspiring an equal fear because of my name,
> among Liberals and democrats alike. I have no political friends
> except those who, accustomed to fortune's fickleness, think that I may
> among possible future chances, become a useful tool. It is because I
> know the difficulties which will beset my first steps in any career that
> I have chosen as my principle of life to follow only the inspirations of
> my heart, of my reason too and of my conscience ... and to go forward
> always in a straight line ... hoisting myself high enough so that the
> dying rays of St. Helena may still clear my way.[2]

If this letter is indeed a sincere statement of his own position it is of
considerable interest, revealing as it does the Pretender's awareness of
lack of support, except from political chancers who would try to use him.
Yet, at the same time, there is evidence that Louis Napoleon realized that
the time had come for some sort of action: "... to go forward always in
a straight line in the hope of catching the dying rays of St. Helena." The
romantic conception is that of a man of the time, but there is a ring of
determination which lifts it above the mawkish cant of so much
posturing common to the period.

In fact, this apparently desolate year of 1835 was to be a turning
point in the Prince's life, not least because it brought him in contact
with the man who was to be the greatest Bonapartist of them all, the

Vicomte de Persigny.[3] Ironically Persigny, whose surname was Fialin, was really the type of political chancer whom Louis Napoleon had castigated in his letter to Vieillard of January, 1835. He had been in turn Royalist, Republican, and was now a Bonapartist. All that can be said in Persigny's favour in this context is that he had shown more of an aptitude for political change than real political acumen. So far he had consistently backed the wrong horse among all the runners in the field of political possibles in France since 1815. Now he declared, "I wish to be the Loyola of the Empire."

Of his devotion to Louis Napoleon and of his influence on him at this point in his career there can be little doubt. Persigny was just the man required to activate the Prince's none-too-clearly formulated plans and to give them an orientation which they needed. Persigny pressed for the translation of intellectual theory into political practice, and sometime between the meeting in 1835 and the summer of 1836 a plan was made for an attempted *coup d'état* in France. It was decided that the return from Elba would be re-enacted, only this time Strasbourg, and not Fréjus, would be the scene of the landing.

The threads of the conspiracy were drawn by Persigny who, although his own military career, had terminated in 1830 owing to his advanced Republican declarations, had an entrée into French military circles. This was needed, if contact was to be made with the officers of the garrison of Strasbourg, once that town had been selected for the attempted *coup*. Armed with copies of the *Manuel d'Artillerie*, Persigny moved through the military circles of Strasbourg in the summer of 1836. Many of the younger officers responded enthusiastically to his appeal to their sentiment and gallantry. But enthusiasm was not enough and it was essential to have senior men in the plot if the garrison were to be made active. With the help of a singer, Mme Gordon, who was the mistress of Colonel Vaudrey, one of the garrison's commanders, Persigny persuaded this officer to join the conspiracy. This was of importance, for Vaudrey had command of one of the five regiments in the city. But Vaudrey was to be the only mackerel in a shoal of sprats, for Louis Napoleon's imprudent advances to other senior officers, while they did not land him in gaol, brought him no support.

In fact, what *were* the chances of success and why *was* the attempt made at this particular time? It has been suggested by some that the Government of Louis Philippe was seriously alarmed by the attempt of 1836, but there seems little reason for it to have been so. The position of the Monarchy was, if anything, stronger than it had been since 1830. The Government's action in suppressing the Republican and Workers'

movements in Lyons and in Paris in 1834 had curbed the waves of
unrest which had broken immediately after the July Revolution. The
failure of Fieschi's attempt to kill the King by means of an "infernal
machine" in July, 1835, had not only produced a wave of sympathy for
the dynasty, but had also enabled the Government by means of the
press laws and other restrictive legislation seriously to weaken the
opposition movements.

Outside France there was nothing in the European political scene to
suggest a crisis which might be turned to advantage by Louis Napoleon,
as was to be the case in 1840. Indeed, Europe was calm after the
re-affirmation of the solidarity of the Holy Alliance at Münchengratz in
1833, a calm which was not to be broken until the Near Eastern crisis
of 1839-40. So, neither at home nor abroad was there any sign of a
beneficial disturbance, which might lead to an optimistic assessment of
the plot's chance of success.

The choice of Strasbourg as the scene of operations was not without
merit. Apart from the question of its geographical location, close to the
frontier, there were more solid grounds for thinking that its response
might be favourable. The police of Louis Philippe had, in 1831,
uncovered a plot based in Strasbourg involving General Brayer, commander in the region which aimed to raise Strasbourg, Metz, Besançon
and Lunéville in support of Napoleon II. Both Hortense and Louis
Napoleon seemed to have been involved in this affair and, although it
never got off the ground, since the police nipped it in the bud when
they felt the time had come, it had been one of the factors behind the
revival of the exile laws against the Bonapartes on 10th April, 1832.

The fact that Strasbourg had been the centre of this attempt reflected
its own local politics, for, as Granville reported to Palmerston on 4th
November, 1836, after the failure of Louis Napoleon's attempt: "In
that city, perhaps more than any other place in France, a republican
spirit prevails." Certainly the spirit of Strasbourg was radical (indeed
most of Alsace was disaffected towards the Government),[9] partly
because it was *sui generis* among French cities with a strong military
and frontier mentality, and also because it associated the Empire with
its period of great prosperity. The Confederation of the Rhine had
conferred great material benefits on the region, but since 1815 the
Rhine had been a frontier and not a highway. Here, if anywhere in
France, the cross-fertilization between liberal democracy and proletarian
democracy might be expected to produce results, because of the existence of an industrial proletariat in the region, but the attempt to raise
the city for Louis Napoleon, made in the morning of 30th October,

1836, was a failure. By eight o'clock in the morning, the Prince with many of his companions, was under arrest; what he had hoped would be a political epiphany, had turned out to be a political circumcision.[4]

The question now was, what would the Government of Louis Philippe do to punish those who had taken part in this quasi-insurrection? In fact, it did the minimum. In the Strasbourg garrison few were questioned about their activities on the morning of 30th October and the Government did not even question the Prince himself. There was no trial and Louis Napoleon was pardoned and sent off to the United States of America. Louis Philippe was by no means a fool, and the Royal Government, anxious to draw some returns for the pardon, put it about that the young man had agreed not to return to France for a term of years. This, in fact, was untrue, but Louis Napoleon was to find it difficult to have his denials accepted, since an undertaking of this nature appeared to be the logical explanation of such leniency as had been shown him.

The Prince landed in the U.S.A. on 30th March, 1837, and there is an agreeable story that on his first day he wanted to change money and found a shop with a sign: *Ici on change des souverains contre des Napoléons*. "That," as he remarked to his companion, "suits me perfectly."[5] But his stay in the New World was to be short, for whatever he may have intended to do, fate decided for him. On 3rd June, he received a letter informing him that his mother was ill; on the 12th, as befitted one of his rank, he solemnly informed the President of the United States, Andrew Jackson, of his departure from the country and sailed for England. In England he could not obtain a passport from either the French, Austrian, or Prussian Ministers, and he was forced to travel, disguised, on a Swiss passport. In this fashion he reached Arenenberg on 4th August to find that Hortense was, in fact, dying. Although she lingered until 9th October there was never any hope of a recovery. The French Government acceded to her dying request that she be buried at Malmaison, but her son was only permitted to accompany the funeral as far as the frontier between France and Switzerland.

No sooner had Hortense been buried in France, than the Government of Louis Philippe showed great determination in digging out Louis Napoleon from Switzerland. Their pressure produced a diplomatic incident, when France virtually threatened war because the Swiss proved recalcitrant and refused to ask their guest to leave. This provided a fine propaganda plank for the Prince. The case became a *cause célèbre* throughout Europe, and millions previously unaware, were made conscious of the Pretender's existence.[6] The Swiss protested, and the French threatened until, finally, the Prince withdrew himself gracefully. This was a relief to the Swiss, who had not actually wanted to go too far, in defying their neighbour. But it was a humiliation for the French, who appeared as bullies in the eyes of much of Europe, because of their treatment of the Swiss Government, and mean-minded because of their persecution of the young man.

The Prince withdrew to England and set up house in Carlton Terrace, or as Disraeli put it, "Prince Florestan had arrived in town..." But if Louis Napoleon, disguised as Florestan, appeared to gear his life to the *beau monde* of London, there was another side of him. This was soon to be revealed, for the failure at Strasbourg and the death of his mother in 1837 marked a decisive stage in his development. Henceforth he was much more alone, for his relations with his father had been tenuous for some years, and, in any event, he had never at any time been as close to him as to his mother. Her death meant the loss of his one really staunch support, for Hortense might occasionally have scoffed, but she had never wavered in her belief in his destiny. The treatment meted out to him by the Government of Louis Philippe, which had behaved as if the Strasbourg affair was the youthful folly of a not-too-intelligent young man, rankled with the Prince, who felt that it was time for a declaration of faith—perhaps as much to convince himself as others of the rightness of his cause. So, in 1839, appeared *Des Idées Napoléoniennes*, a work which was an assertion of his determination to be taken seriously. It was also a further reminder of the existence of a Bonapartist alternative to the present Government of France. Since the death of Napoleon II, and the Strasbourg affair, heredity and pretention indicated that this must be himself. The work which he now published was, in effect, an appeal to history, vindicating Napoleon I, and a manifesto offering France a new Bonaparte.

"The Emperor is no more...but his soul is not dead. Deprived of the possibility of defending his watchful authority by force of arms, I can at least try to defend his memory by my writings...I am not bound to any party; to any sect; or to any government: my voice is free like my thoughts...and I love liberty."[7]

The main difficulty in dealing with the *Idées* lies in trying to sort out solid political proposals from a heady froth of generalizations about government and society. It was all very well for the Prince to note that government was not: "...*a necessary ulcer* but the beneficent driving force of every social organism"; this most people would admit. The trouble was that in France since the Revolution various driving forces had been used, and the quarrel really arose because no one could agree on which one drove the better. As he himself admitted, the ideas of 1789 were followed by those of 1791, only to be supplanted in their turn by the ideas of 1793. Ruin upon ruin indeed—until the Saviour appeared in the shape of Napoleon I, for "the Emperor must be considered as the Messiah of new ideas."

The main point which early on in his treatise Louis Napoleon was determined to hammer home was that Napoleon I was the heir of the Revolution and the champion of liberty. But it is equally stressed that it was the Revolution purified, and that liberty did not mean licence, such licence as had dragged the original revolutionary movement down into the dirt. Bonapartism was presented as a synthesis, with Napoleon as its living expression, and Louis Napoleon argued that without the existence of the Consulate and the Empire, the whole work of the Revolution would have perished.

The Emperor, he said, knew what was wanted because he was in harmony with his times and understood the needs of France and her people. This latter was the first necessity of any government, and secure in this knowledge he had gone forward triumphantly. This mystical union between ruler and people was, of course, a basic article of Bonapartist faith and one which Louis Napoleon stressed constantly during the whole of his political career. He believed it to be the dominating factor in political development in the nineteenth century and for this reason it is to be found not only at the beginning of the *Idées*, but also in an interesting essay on "1688 and 1830" among the *Fragments Historiques*. Here the theme, virtually Hegelian in content, is set out simply and trenchantly : "Put yourself at the head of the ideas of the century, those ideas will follow and uphold you. Put yourself behind them, they will drag you along. Put yourself in opposition to them, they will overthrow you."[8]

Significantly, even at the end of the Second Empire, in 1870, the new Liberal Constitution retained the plebiscite, for the Emperor refused to break his mystic communion with the people to whom he was, in the phrase of the Constitution, "responsible." He regarded it as part of his duty to keep the direct contact between sovereign and people. Louis Napoleon argued that it was this need to keep in touch with general interests which had necessitated the establishment of the Empire as an "hereditary dynasty which would be the guardian of general interests and whose powers were based solely on the democratic spirit of the nation."[9] To argue on these lines meant that by equating the foundation of a new dynasty with the guarantee of popular expression, there could be no carping criticism of Napoleon I's actions. Not personal ambition, but the desire for public service had made an Emperor of the First Consul; not dynastic considerations, but the need for an heir had made an Empress of the Austrian Arch-Duchess.

In fact, the idea of an hereditary dynasty was basic, because a Bonapartist analysis of society, at least the one proffered by Louis Napoleon, was that society embraced two contrary elements: on the one hand immortality and progress, on the other uneasiness and disorganization. Since the function of government was to see that the people are properly led, in accordance with the spirit of the times, it followed that the charismatic element must not be thrown away, but enshrined in the hereditary family, the living embodiment of the nation who would draw together in himself their opposing forces.

The importance of this attitude was made apparent by Louis Napoleon's analysis of liberty; what it meant, and what it could or could not provide. He himself never abandoned the thesis that liberty is desirable, but he made its appearance conditional on respect for the principles of equality, of legality, of order—and he stressed that this must be a civil and not a military organization.

Because of the complexity of the conditions which must exist if liberty is to emerge, Napoleon I had said that a constitution is the work of time and a large place must be left in it for alterations. This, of course, was an essential tenet of the "death-bed Bonapartism" of Saint Helena which claimed that only time had been lacking to permit the effective liberalization of the Empire. In any event, it could be argued that what was necessary after a revolution was not constiution making, but the creating of a stable system of government which could be adapted and adjusted as circumstances demanded, and as society absorbed the new forces unleashed by the revolutionary movement.

Certainly the history of France between 1789 and 1799 bore out the argument that constitutional solutions were in themselves inadequate as a means of bringing order and stability, and although it was undeniable that Napoleon had been appointed under the Constitution of 1799, he had spent the next fifteen years altering it to suit himself and the institutions which France was acquiring under his guidance. The Emperor's success came from the fact that he had seen and understood what the revolution meant and could canalize and direct it. After all, he had claimed: *Je suis la révolution.*

It must be remembered that, the *Idées*, for all their Hegelian overtones, were not meant to be a work of political science, but a tract for the times. Similarly, it should be remembered that the Constitution of the Year VII had not been designed to be anything other than a vehicle for restoring order in France after the turmoil of the Revolution. It was not what the Constitution had said, it was what Napoleon had done that mattered, for his task had been to: "Reunite the national will against the foreigner, reorganize the country on the principles of equality, order and justice." This task, in fact, had resolved itself into the organization of an administrative system for: "in a democratic state like France the administrative organization had more importance than any other, for it dominates to a certain extent, the political order."[10] To this end, despotic power was not only essential to Napoleon, but also to France and was, therefore, in accord with the needs of the time. Louis Napoleon was not the only one to argue thus, for as one historian has said: "we may call the Government of the Consulate and the Empire a tyranny if we please, but compared with the Government which went before, it was a reign of freedom."[11]

It was this which was the strength of the Bonapartist legend. It existed not only as an intellectual concept, but also it had existed as a political fact. Napoleon *had* ruled, he *had* restored order and, in the context of his time, he had even given liberty. It is important to note that after him France was never again to know a legal terror such as it had known in 1793-94, nor was any law as infamous as the Law of the Suspect ever again enacted. For a state of anarchy tempered by fear Napoleon had substituted a civilized administration and law. The price of this, in administrative terms, had been centralization or, in the political terms of Siéyès: "Confidence from below, power from above." Louis Napoleon, confronted with this fact, postulated the theory that this centralization, indeed as he admitted, the excess of it, had not been a definitive state but a temporary measure. Here Louis Napoleon was wrong, for there is no doubt that whatever his uncle *might* have done he would never have destroyed the centralism on which his whole organization rested, and upon which the whole administration of France depended. No government in France, including that of the Second Empire, has succeeded in breaking out of this particular straitjacket. The *Acte Additionel* of 1815 was only a coat of political gloss paint on the ironwork of the administrative structure. So also, was the sketch of the Constitution for the reign of Napoleon II which the Emperor had dictated to Montholon at Longwood. Napoleon I had not merely been concerned with the immediate effects of his civil service, he had seen it in much larger terms. On one occasion, addressing the Council of State, he had said: "I wish to establish a civil authority in France. Up to the present there have only been two powers in the

world, the military and the ecclesiastical. The Barbarians, who invaded
the Roman Empire, were unable to form a solid state because they
lacked both a body of priests and a civil authority." If the Emperor's
historical judgement on the Barbarian Kingdoms was a little simplified,
there can be no doubt that he was right in pinpointing the necessity for
establishing a civil power in any state to give it durability. The creation
of such a civil administration had been begun in France under Louis
XIV, but it was perhaps Napoleon's greatest achievement to re-establish
such an authority. By 1799 the only coherent force left in the French
state, and the force which carried through the *coup d'état* of Brumaire,
was the Army, yet it accepted a civil organization imposed on it by
Napoleon, whose government was that of a soldier but was not a
military government.

For those who think this was a minor achievement, one can only
recommend a study of countries where the army has refused to be
subordinated to any civil authority. That Napoleon I remained always
determined to avoid such an event is evinced by his remark to
Benjamin Constant in 1815, when Constant proposed a hereditary
Chamber of Peers : "It will soon become either a camp, or a lobby."

In the *Idées*, Louis Napoleon, anxious to refute the charge that the
Emperor's Government had been that of the sabre, underlined the fact
that never had there been an internal organization which was less arbitrary or military in outlook.

> Under the Imperial system no post in the civil administration was
> occupied by soldiers, the man who created civil honours to counter-
> balance military decorations, who, by the instituting of the Legion of
> Honour wished to reward equally the service of the citizen and the
> soldier, who, from his coming to power busied himself with the
> condition of the civil servants, who always gave precedence to the
> latter, who, both at home and even in conquered countries, sent
> Councillors of State armed with a civil authority superior to that of
> the generals, is the man whom the spirit of faction wants to point as
> the partisan of a military regime.

Indeed, as Louis Napoleon went on to point out, the supposed threat of
military rule was largely a posthumous fantasy, for the real danger then,
and now, came from the twin poles of the "terror" and the *ancien régime.*
It was for this reason that the Emperor had taken such care over the formation of a class of administrators who, in education, ability and prestige
could stand among the highest in the land. These were the famous *audi-
teurs* of the Council of State. By 1814 there were 350 of them, who,

whilst reminiscent of the *missi dominici* of Charlemagne and the Intendants of the *ancien régime*, had much that was new, in that they had actually been taught to govern as well as to execute instructions.

Louis Napoleon argued that this stress on governing rather than on politicking was the only answer to the bitter divisions which split France. As he said: "When he [Napoleon I] appointed an administrative head he did not consult the man's political inclinations, but his capacity as a civil servant."[12] It was not, therefore, their political background which he inquired into but their specialized knowledge, and their potential as a government servant.

The emphasis again and again is on the unimportance of politics, and in this context the Prince pointed out, not without reason that only the machinery devised by Napoleon had saved France from collapse over the last twenty-five years. "Under the Empire all the best brains and the talent of France worked to one end, the prosperity of the country. Since then the most intelligent have been busy fighting amongst themselves, arguing about the way to go rather than moving on. Political discipline has been broken so that, instead of marching ahead in a straight line everybody sets up his own line of march and has fallen away from the main body."[13]

Before leaving this analysis of France's internal condition after the Empire, there is a final section in the *Idées* in which the Emperor is made to speak, interrogating his successors on what they have done with his work: "All that I did for the prosperity of France, I had to do between battles, but you, who blame me, what have you done in twenty-four years of peace?"[14] There follow twenty-five rhetorical questions, covering practically every aspect of the country's life from the political and economic organization to its moral and military problems. The answer to most of them, if assessed in the light of what had been done by the restored Bourbons or by Louis Philippe, would be "no." That was, of course, the intention and the moral was plain. The "false copies" of the Napoleonic state to which the Prince referred from time to time in his text, could do nothing good for France—at best they could only maintain, in spite of themselves, the Napoleonic machine. What was needed was an engineer who knew instinctively not only what was required to keep the machine running, but who also knew of what it was capable. The inescapable fact was that Louis Napoleon had pinpointed the basic problem of France since 1815. Either the Napoleonic machine was dismantled, and no one had dared to do this—although Charles X may have been trying—or it had to be kept running. If the latter was the case then the forms of constitutional monarchy which had been tried since 1815 did not seem to be the proper way to make it function and France needed to be put back on her proper course.

Louis Napoleon devoted the last thirty-five pages of his monograph to examining what Bonapartism had meant beyond the frontiers, since it was not merely France which had suffered from Napoleon's fall, but the whole of Europe. Here the ground was more treacherous, and the going rougher, but armed with the maps provided by the cartographer of St. Helena, the Prince set out to justify the Napoleonic system in Europe. There were, he stated, three methods of conducting France's relations with foreign powers:

"There is the blind and inflamed policy which wants to throw the gauntlet in the face of Europe and dethrone all the Kings."

"There is another, entirely the opposite, which consists of maintaining peace by buying the friendship of other sovereigns at the expense of honour and the interest of the nation."

These two systems covered the Revolutionary period and the period from 1815 and both were condemned as being wrong. This cleared the ground for "the third policy" which freely offers "... the alliance of France to all those governments who want to proceed with her in common interests. ... this was the Napoleonic policy." To prove the claim of common interest as a basis for policy the Prince used the argument that the Emperor was supported in his Russian campaign of 1812 by members of most European nations, and that it was not for lack of support that the campaign was a failure— "... it took a combination of calamity and the elements to achieve that."[15]

Obviously Napoleon's foreign policy was the Achilles' heel of Bonapartism, and much of the success of any work of rehabilitation depended on the interpretation of this aspect of the Emperor's career. It was essential for Louis Napoleon to show that his uncle had never been the aggressor in war and also that he had maintained a positive and peaceful aim behind all his military actions. The wars were, therefore, presented as a series of defensive campaigns, necessitated by the endless coalitions which were created against France. These had reached their climax in 1812 when England and Russia had either to be convinced by reason or overcome by force, so that they would accept peace and the Napoleonic structure in Europe. Louis Napoleon admitted that the campaign of 1812 was, of course, a disaster: "... alas, one winter changed everything." But he did not draw the moral from it, namely that the Emperor's Europe was a precarious thing if it toppled in a winter. In fact, he ignored this aspect and moved swiftly to a defence of

Napoleon's refusal to treat with the Allies or to accept a diminished France. The episode of the "Hundred Days" is strangely enough given very slight treatment and in a brief space of time the account reaches Waterloo : "Here every French voice halts and finds only tears, tears to weep for the conquered, and for the conquerors, who will regret, sooner or later, the overthrow of the only man who had become the link between two centuries."[16]

Obviously this last point needed stressing, for it was not enough to prove that the Napoleonic idea was necessary to France, it must also be rendered at least palatable to those Powers of Europe who might be hostile to it. Louis Napoleon was well aware that the settlement of 1815 could not be destroyed easily, though, as he shrewdly pointed out, there had already been one significant breach in Belgium in 1830. He tactfully did not comment on the change of dynasty in France in the same year, though he must have known that this was equally an upset, if not an actual breach, of the same settlement.

What, then, was the Napoleonic scheme which had been wrecked at Waterloo? What *was* the Emperor's European aim? "His genius made him see that the rivalry which divided the different European nations would disappear before a clearly-understood common interest" for, as he himself had said, ". . . as long as we fight in Europe, it is a civil war."[17] Because of his horror of European civil war, the Emperor had set himself the task of making a unity out of the diverse peoples of the Continent; he had intended, in fact, to "make Europe." There would have been for the European people a European code modelled on the *Code Napoléon* of France itself; a European Court of Appeal which would have sat in judgement on the decisions of inferior courts and which would have provided a means of redressing the grievances of any citizen of the European Confederation of States. The tangible manifestations of a common system of justice were to be reinforced by a common system of money, weights and measures, so that at last Europe should have reached the peak of its national progression in history from tribe, to city, to province, to nation, to supra-nation. In such a Europe there would be no conquerors and no conquered; there would be no need for wars, since all would be satisfied.

This construction of "Europe," which bears little resemblance to the actual reconstruction carried out by Napoleon I, was, according to the Prince, the indispensable factor in providing liberty—though here he reasons rather vaguely and it is not clear exactly how this extremely important change was to be brought about. He says simply : "Having once founded the Napoleonic Europe, the Emperor would have proceeded to establish peace. He would have consolidated liberty, he had only to slacken the threads of the system which he had created."[18]

Unfortunately the arguments which Louis Napoleon produced to justify this statement are vague in the extreme. They consist really in a reassertion of the claim that this could have worked because Napoleon had established the prerequisites of liberty in France and he possessed the confidence of the people—which made "everything easy for him." To back up this sweeping assertion, almost moving in its simplicity, the Prince asked rhetorically—what had Napoleon to fear from conceding liberty?

Freedom of discussion in the Chambers would not have been dangerous to the Imperial Government, because everyone was agreed on fundamentals and the opposition would, therefore, have been loyal. But straightaway it should be noted that the Prince overlooked the fact that it was the Napoleonic Senate which offered the Crown to Louis XVIII in 1814 in order to save the social and financial gains it had made under the Empire. He also ignored the situation in 1815 when the Chambers, having under the *Acte Additionel* received power to discuss and query, had shown open hostility to much of the Imperial programme.

For Louis Napoleon, no clash of interests could arise because the Government was firmly based on an identity of purpose between sovereign and people, and this, in his interpretation, was the basis of the whole Imperial regime. The weakness of this interpretation lay in the fact that it was a purely political one, ignoring the social and economic realities, so brutally spelled out by Marshal McDonald who had said in 1815, "Did he [Napoleon] think we would give up all this for him?" By "this" McDonald was referring to the position, and the property, he and his fellow Marshals had acquired under the Empire.

The Prince's argument could not withstand serious examination, for it did not square with the facts of the Empire; the case for the defence which Louis Napoleon presented, was weak. This weakness led to a vagueness in the reasoning in this section of the *Idées*, which is too coincidental to be accidental. It was for this reason, undoubtedly, that the last few pages no longer constitute an attempt to defend Napoleon I, but to prosecute his adversaries. It is argued that they had made their fatal error in overthrowing the only man who had closed the "gulf of revolution" and by their actions had opened it again. "Take care," he apostrophized them, "that this gulf does not swallow you."

History was on the side of Louis Napoleon. It had been said by Metternich himself that the Hundred Days undid fourteen years of anti-revolutionary achievement under Bonapartist rule; for Napoleon, driven into a corner, had again appealed to the Revolution of which he had so often claimed to be the heir. But it is significant that it was only in this moment of deepest crisis that Napoleon had unstoppered the bottle and let out the genie, though he had, from time to time, stressed his title deeds to power. In 1804, when he had ordered the execution of the Duc d'Enghien as an answer to the Royalists, he had said: "At least they will see of what we are capable, and henceforth I hope they will leave us in peace. I am the statesman and I am the French Revolution. I repeat it and I will maintain it." The Emperor was always aware of the strength of the forces on which he balanced so delicately, but his genius lay in convincing the turbulent that equality was better than liberty, and that order was preferable to anarchy and the tyranny of faction. He had controlled the system he created; lesser men since 1815 had been unable to do so.

It was this lesson which Louis Napoleon drove home; the failure of the restored Bourbons, the revolutions of 1830, particularly the movements in Poland, Belgium and Germany, the Swiss Federal Movement, all these owed their inspiration to Napoleon's policy. The Emperor's system, he said, would construct itself because "... everyone sees in it a guarantee of order, of peace and of prosperity." The Napoleonic idea, not one of war but of peace, social, commercial, industrial and humanitarian progress, would triumph because "... free peoples everywhere toil to rebuild your work."

In 1840, the Prince returned to the world of publishing by producing *L'Idée Napoléonienne*. This was a short pamphlet, but by no means an unimportant work because it is a summation of much of the Bonapartist creed and has the directness of an electoral manifesto. In view of subsequent developments in the career of Louis Napoleon in 1840, it may very well have been designed for just this purpose.

The title page bears the comment: "It is not only the Emperor's remains but also his ideas which must be brought back," a reference to the return of the body of Napoleon I to Paris from the island of St. Helena. Through his activities in England, and through the activities of his followers in France, the Prince had done much to stimulate the French Government into asking the English authorities to permit this "return of the ashes." The Government of Louis Philippe hoped that by embracing the Napoleonic legend it could make it official and thereby draw the teeth of the Bonapartist movement. But Louis Napoleon turned it to the advantage of his supporters by pointing out that if the Orleanists had the glory of bringing back the Emperor's body, it was plain to all that that was the extent of their abilities.

The government of France was a disgrace for there was :

Corruption on the one hand, lies on the other, and hatred everywhere, that is our condition! And in the middle of this chaos of
intellect and poverty it would seem that there is no idea strong
enough to rally a majority, and that there is no longer any man
popular enough to become the personification of any significant
group. French Society does not proceed in a forward direction, it
wanders at will.[19]

However, there is an answer to this state of affairs, and here the
voice becomes that of the evangelist who cries : "... the Napoleonic
idea has leapt from the tomb of St. Helena as the authority of the
Gospel rose triumphant in spite of the suffering of Calvary." It may be
doubted if Louis Napoleon was comparing, somewhat blasphemously,
the sufferings of Christ with those of the imprisoned Napoleon, but
there is no doubt that he saw himself as an evangelist who must
propagate the truth and destroy the false prophets who had been active
in France since 1815. The people would recognize the truth when they
saw it, for it had been established in their hearts for a long time—just
as Christianity had been accepted willingly long before its full implications were grasped. So, the Napoleonic idea, standing on the altar of
the fatherland, calls out as Saint Remi did to Siccambrus : "Throw
down your false gods and your clay images; burn what you have
heretofore adored, and adore that which you have burned."[20]

There seems little doubt that the publication of *L'Idée
Napolonienne* was part of a deliberate campaign to draw attention to
Louis Napoleon. It is true that nowhere in the pamphlet does the Prince
draw attention to himself as one of those who were toiling to rebuild the
Emperor's work and to implement the Bonapartist idea. This was left to
Persigny, whose pamphlet *Lettre de Londres, Visite au Prince Louis,* was
published anonymously in Paris in 1840. This was a clear announcement
that France needed the Prince, and that the Prince was ready.

Having prepared the ground by this propaganda campaign, Louis
Napoleon did not wait too long for a specific invitation. In August,
1840, the Prince sailed down the Thames in a paddle steamer, the
Edinburgh Castle, with 56 men, 9 horses, 2 carriages, assorted uniforms
of the French Army, banners, proclamations, food, wine and a tame
vulture in a cage. He was bound for Boulogne as the living manifestation of the *Idée Napoléonienne.*

4

The Manifestation

"J'espère en Dieu et je crois en moi."

Louis Napoleon Bonaparte, 1837

WHAT motives inspired the Prince's descent on Boulogne? The affair has its comic aspects, and because of its failure seemed to be futile. Yet it cannot simply be dismissed as a young man's fancy. It is surely significant that in the year of his success and within a week of his election to the Presidency, Louis Napoleon demanded that de Malleville, the Minister of the Interior, send him the dossiers dealing with his attempts at Strasbourg and Boulogne. These dossiers he destroyed. Louis Napoleon never shirked his responsibilities if he were involved, any more than he refused to accept blame if he were not involved; one can deduce from this that they must have contained information which he did not wish to be disclosed.

Was he protecting himself? Hardly. He was now in a position which made the two events no longer ridiculous. Perhaps he wanted to destroy evidence which might have compromised others. This may show that there had been some sort of conspiracy, with ramifications in France, which involved people whom the Orléans Government did not wish publicly to involve in the trials after Boulogne and whom the Prince decided to protect, in retrospect, from accusations of treachery.

In May, 1839, while living in London, he had been accused by the Orléans Government of being involved in the conspiracy of Barbés and Blanqui which had recently produced an abortive rising in Paris. This he publicly denied, in a letter of 17th May written to *The Times,* in which he said that not only had he been "surprised and afflicted by the bloody events," but also that ". . . had I been the moving spirit in the plot, I would also have been its leader in the hour of danger."[1] There is no reason to doubt the truth of this assertion, for the Prince was personally brave, and it was for this reason that in August, 1840, he had come to lead an uprising of which he was the prime mover and which may very well have had ramifications beyond the neighbourhood of Boulogne.

However, all this must remain speculation. What is clear is that by 1840 Bonapartist sentiment had reached a pitch where it seemed to Louis Napoleon that he had a chance of success. His *Idées* had gone into four editions, selling at fifty centimes a copy. By 1848 the total sales had reached over half a million. This had been a genuine triumph for a work of propaganda, and the potency of the appeal to Bonapartist sentiment was enhanced by the crisis of French affairs caused by the imbroglio in the Near East in 1840. This crisis had arisen because France had attempted to support Mehemet Ali of Egypt in his expansionist aims against the Turkish Empire, and had been forced to yield to a revival of the coalition of Austria, Russia Prussia and Britain. French feeling was expressed by the writer, Edgar Quinet, in the bitter phrase: "Bound by the treaties written with Blood at Waterloo, we are still, in the eyes of the world, the conquered of Waterloo."

The worst of it was that France had not even been consulted by the four powers about the Near Eastern settlement. She had merely been informed three days after the signing of the London Convention (15th July, 1840) that the event had taken place. This Convention not only dissolved the shaky Anglo-French entente, which had existed since 1830, but seemed to indicate that war between France and the rest of Europe was imminent. The humiliation was great, so great that even the timorous Louis Philippe had been on the point of resistance, although he eventually capitulated, and replaced the Ministry of Thiers by the Ministry of Guizot, Guizot who was so anglophile that he was nicknamed "Lord Francis Guizot."

The outcry in French political circles against this "cowardly policy" was extremely sharp. It undoubtedly influenced Louis Napoleon's decision to offer himself as a living representative of the Emperor whose own ashes were in a few months to be returned to Paris from St. Helena. The Bourgeoisie of the July monarchy would accept much in return for a quiet life, but the humiliation of such a diplomatic defeat might stir even them into acceptance of a living Bonaparte as well as the corpse of a dead one. De Tocqueville had noticed that in the year 1840 there had arisen throughout France a wave of discontent and that "for the moment radicalism leans upon wounded national pride." In these circumstances, Louis Napoleon's nomination of Thiers as President of the provisional government at Boulogne was perhaps more than a simple bid for support, for Thiers had assumed a warlike attitude over the crisis and still smarted from being forced to back down and resign from office by Louis Philippe, who had to offer him as a sop to European hostility.

It was against this background that the Bonapartist agents had conducted their activities. So bold had they become that they had dared to appeal directly to the army, whose feelings had also run high during the Near Eastern crisis. This had certainly stimulated a renewed campaign to swing it into support for the Pretender. At the trial of Louis Napoleon, held after the Boulogne affair, the prosecutor alleged that small biographies, the work of Bonapartist propagandists, had been circulating ". . . publicly and in great numbers and, above all, had been cleverly thrown in among garrison towns and barracks in the hope of popularizing his [Louis Napoleon's] name and linking it with that of the Emperor."[2]

Attempts had certainly been made to suborn the army of the North in the spring of 1840. But the Commander, General Magnan, had refused to be implicated, and had informed the Government of Louis Philippe that a Bonapartist plot was being organized. With an appalling lack of tact, Napoleon had sent an army officer to Magnan offering him 100,000 francs in cash and 300,000 to be paid into a bank account in his name if he would join the conspiracy. If there really was this amount of money to hand, it would seem to show that the conspirators did not lack funds, even if they were sometimes deficient in tact.

Others, more reliable than Magnan, must have been contacted by Bonapartist agents, for among the Prince's effects embarked on the *Edinburgh Castle* were maps giving detailed dispositions of all the regiments in the area between the Pas de Calais and Paris. Such information was not gathered from reading newspapers and when the Prince said at his trial that "motives of honour and prudence forbid me to reveal . . . how far-reaching and overwhelming were my reasons for counting on a success,"[3] he may indeed have been telling the literal truth.

The affair was extraordinary: in the early hours of the morning of 6th August the "invasion force" landed at Wimereux near Boulogne, and as at Strasbourg, first efforts were concentrated on winning over the officers and soldiers of the local regiments. Again, as at Strasbourg, the whole thing was a failure, and after some initial success in winning over the men, they abandoned the Pretender as soon as their own officers re-established contact with them. By late evening, Louis Napoleon was under arrest and early on the morning of 7th August, he was transferred to the Fortress of Ham to await trial.[4] Princess Lieven, that indefatigable letter writer, had a comment on it: "This poor fool of a Louis Bonaparte has just been arrested at Boulogne, he and his friends who were going through the streets. It didn't last two hours. I've

just seen the proclamations, nominations, decrees, etc. It's idiotic! The
people did not seem in the least interested. He nominated M. Thiers
President of the Provisional Government. What a laugh like all the rest
of it."[5] One hopes M. Guizot was amused.

The affair had indeed been brought to a swift conclusion; all that
remained as visible traces of the Prince's passage through Boulogne
were copies of the proclamations which had been distributed along with
money to the citizens who were adjured to cry: *"Vive l'Empereur."*[6] It
may safely be assumed that many of those who did cry thus, did it for
the money and not for the proclamations, but to the historian, the
proclamations, for what they reveal of Bonapartism in action, are a far
richer prize than the silver five franc piece which went with them. The
first proclamation was a general one: "To the French people." It
repeated the theme that the Emperor's ashes could only return to a
regenerated France for "It is essential that glory and liberty should
stand by the coffin of Napoleon." The present government had
produced licence and violence and division in society (a direct quotation
from the *Idées*), but: "I wish to restore order and liberty, I wish to give
France true alliances, a solid place, and not to throw her into the risks
of a general war. Frenchmen! I see ahead a brilliant future for the
country. I feel behind me the shadow of the Emperor which pushes me
on."[7] The proclamation was also notable for the fact that it dealt with
economic questions and stressed the social dislocation which existed in
France because of the policies pursued under the Orléans regime.
Frenchmen were asked to remember that the Emperor had sought the
aid of the workers and had chosen ". . . his lieutenants, his marshals, his
princes, and his friends from amongst you."

The second proclamation was addressed to the inhabitants of the Pas
de Calais Department by Prince Napoleon-Louis and signed by
"Napoleon," General Montholon, and Colonels Voisin and Mesonon.
The first sentence attacked the government of Louis Philippe for the
unjust law which prevented the Prince from living on French soil. The
second announced that it was to assure France's future that he was
there, followed by the claim that: "I have powerful friends, both at
home and abroad who have promised to support me." This assertion,
while obviously the common form of this type of proclamation, may, as
already surmised, have had some foundation in fact. Certainly the next
assertion was a lie, for it stated that "soon all France, with Paris first,
will rise to trample underfoot ten years of lies, tyranny, usurpation,
etc." and asserted that the present lamentable state of France would be

transformed by the Napoleonic spirit "which is only concerned with the welfare of the people."

If this were all the proclamation contained, it would be noteworthy only for its manner rather than for its content, which is a repetition of the more general one already quoted. What makes it important is the next paragraph because it deals directly with Anglo-French relations.

> Do not fear that the links which attach you to your neighbour across the sea will be broken. The mortal remains of the Emperor, and the Imperial Eagle are returning from exiles only because of feelings of love and reconciliation. *Two great peoples* [author's italics] are made to understand one another and the glorious Column which proudly stands at the water's edge as a souvenir of war shall become an expiatory monument to past hatred.[8]

This paragraph can hardly have been inserted simply to assuage the fears of the Boulonnais that their Channel situation would leave them exposed to an attack by a British fleet in the event of their accepting Louis Napoleon as their ruler. Surely the proclamation was intended for France, though territorially limited by its actual heading? May not one read in this an affirmation of one of Louis Napoleon's basic ideas, and one from which he never deviated, that England must be a friend? It is a measure of his devotion to this idea that he dared to put it in a proclamation at a time when England was more than usually detested because of the question of Mehemet Ali and the Near Eastern crisis, to which reference has already been made. That the concept of an Anglo-French entente should find a place in a short and, by its nature, highly important Bonapartist document, is a measure of the importance which the Prince attached to this particular aspect of the Napoleonic Idea. Was it a more explicit reference to the "sure alliances" mentioned in the general proclamation, alliances which would avoid the risks of "a general war"?

Whatever its intent, Government action prevented any widespread dissemination of this manifesto. The manifesto was probably little known even in Boulogne itself, and it might well have sunk without trace had not the same Government, by extraordinary ineptitude, given Louis Napoleon an opportunity to reach a far wider audience by giving him a trial. The Strasbourg trial of Louis Napoleon's accomplices had been conducted by jury procedure and had resulted in an acquittal. This time, trial by the Court of Peers was substituted for the former method, an indication that in this way the Government hoped to avoid a repetition of the slap in the face which it had received in 1836. But it would have done better for itself by dispensing with any formal proceedings at all, for *any* sort of trial was bound to arouse public interest and thus provide a platform for the dissemination of Bonapartism. Confronted with an armed invasion of French territory, headed by a man whose second attempt it was to overthrow the Government by force, the Government of Louis Philippe might well have been tempted to act by court martial and in private. One is forced to ask whether it decided to mount a public trial simply in an attempt to show honesty of purpose or because it was caught in a dilemma resulting from Louis Philippe's cultivation of the Napoleonic legend for his own dynastic purposes? Whatever the intention, the result was to give a better platform to Bonapartism than it could ever have dreamed of finding; Louis Napoleon took full advantage of it.

He found as his advocate Maître Berryer, an uncompromising legitimist who, for different reasons, was as hostile as his client to the Orléans regime.[9] Because of this, it meant that the subject of the trial was not Louis Napoleon and his *attentat,* but Louis Philippe and his regime. Berryer used the occasion to examine the whole question of legitimacy and heredity, to the discomfiture of the House of Orléans.

When Louis Napoleon was granted leave to speak, he made no attempt to defend himself, but, to the consternation of the Peers, to attack them. He claimed that the condition of France was such that it was his duty to try and rescue her from her humbled status, and ended with a simple and trenchant statement of the Bonapartist position: "I stand before you the representative of a principle, a cause, a defeat; the principle is the sovereignty of the people; the cause is the cause of the Empire; the defeat, Waterloo. The principle *you* have recognized, that cause *you* have served, that defeat *you* would avenge. No, there is no disagreement between you and me." By calmly taking for granted the fact that only circumstances had made these men his judges and not his accomplices, Louis Napoleon neatly underlined the dilemma in which the Peers really did find themselves. Many were the creation of the first Empire and they were uncomfortably aware that it was prudence and self-interest, rather than loyalty, which had brought them intact through the reigns of Louis XVIII and Charles X to that of Louis Philippe.[10]

Two days later, after various cross-examinations of other witnesses, Berryer himself returned to the attack. Bitterly he accused the Government of hypocrisy in bringing back the dead Emperor with full honours while wanting to do away with the living representative of the Dynasty. Louis Philippe was prepared to honour in death as " ... legi-

timate sovereign of our country" the man whom, in life, he opposed as
the "Corsican usurper."

As to the Peers, Berryer did not even bother with an oblique
reminder of their beginnings, but bluntly told them that had it not been
for Napoleon I, whose heir they now presumed to judge, they would
not be Peers at all. "Who are you then? Counts, Barons, you who were
ministers, generals, senators, marshals, to whom do you owe your titles
and your honours? Undoubtedly because of your capabilities, but it is
no less to the munificence of the Empire itself that you are able today
to sit as judges . . ." If it is held that Berryer should have used his
talents to placate the Peers and thus increase his client's chances of a
limited sentence, then this bitter attack may have been bad legal tactics.
But Berryer was no more there to argue law than Louis Napoleon. They
were both there to argue history, and Berryer was presented with a
superb opportunity to denounce those whom he hated as the destroyers
of legitimate monarchy.

The Peers sentenced Charles Louis Napoleon Bonaparte to perpetual
imprisonment in a fortress within the frontiers of France. One hundred
and fifty-two Peers voted for this, one hundred and sixty abstained. It
was really the latter figure which was important.[11] Not only that; the
trial had been reported and discussed, and the Prince had emerged well.
His steadfast refusal to incriminate anyone, his insistence that he alone
was responsible, and that his friends should be forgiven for following
him, made a good impression. Furthermore, public opinion saw the
incongruity of lifting the dead Napoleon from the tomb while the living
was buried alive.

More subtle observers noted that the Republican Barbès, who was
tried in 1839 for the insurrection he had organized in May that year,
had been sentenced to death and had his sentence commuted to life
imprisonment only because of the activities of the Duchesse d'Orléans.
Louis Napoleon had been guilty of exactly the same crime, an attempt
to overthrow the Government, but the reaction of the Government had
been different. How could it not be?

For some years Louis Philippe had been trying to draw the teeth
from Bonapartism by taking up the symbolic gestures for which its
partisans clamoured. The Arc de Triomphe had been finished. Other
memorials of the Empire had been preserved, restored, or finished and,
as a final gesture, the body of Napoleon was being brought back from
St. Helena to be reburied in Paris. By an ironical twist, it happened
that on 7th October, the day the frigate *Belle Poule* arrived at St. Helena
to bring back the body of Napoleon I to France, Louis Napoleon took

up residence in the fortress of Ham, which had been assigned as the place
of his perpetual imprisonment.

This dull and dreary medieval fortress on the junction of the River
Somme and the St. Quentin canal, a true Bastille, was already familiar
to him, since he had spent several days there immediately after the
attempted *coup* at Boulogne. The thought of incarceration for life in
such a place cannot have been a cheerful prospect for a young man of
thirty-two, even if he did believe in his destiny. In fact, it was only to
hold him for six years—years which he turned to good account and
which he afterwards called "the University Years." On one of the walls
of his "study" in Ham, Louis Napoleon wrote : "The Bonapartist cause
is the cause of the people's interests, it is European, sooner or later it
will triumph."[12] This reaffirmation of his beliefs might seem in the
circumstances to be little more than an historical graffitus which only
subsequent events made meaningful. But to accept this view would be
wrong : contemporary, very contemporary, events were proving the
truth of the assertion even while it was being written.

The decision taken by the government of Louis Philippe to bring
back the Emperor's remains from St. Helena had let loose a renewed
flood of Bonapartist fervour throughout France. As already indicated,
its very strength had been one of the factors conditioning Louis
Napoleon's determination to try his *coup d'état*. Now the government found that, having imprisoned the nephew it could not so easily
dispose of the uncle and it was becoming alarmed at the response which
the *retour de Sainte Hélène* was provoking. Not only was there the
brisk traffic in prints, snuff boxes, statuettes and busts, all depicting
"Him" in one form or another, there was also the recoil from certain
remarks made by members of the Government at the time the decision
was made to bring back the body. It was remembered that on 12th
May, 1840, during the debate on this topic in the Chamber, the
Minister of the Interior, M. de Rémusat, had said of Napoleon : "He
was Emperor and King ... he was the legitimate sovereign of France."
Now in October after the Boulogne affair and the imprisonment of the
Prince, it was Metternich, that authority on legitimism, who pointed
out : "If M. de Rémusat was right, it is clear that Louis Bonaparte is
not wrong."[13] The Government of Louis Philippe was itself uncomfortably aware of the dilemma.

To Louis Napoleon there was no dilemma; the day of the Emperor's
return, 15th December, 1840, he saluted him : "Sire, you come back to
your capital and the multitudes salute your return, but I, from the
depths of my cell can see only the ray of sunlight which illuminates

your funeral.[14] Nevertheless he felt that it was not to the faithless, nor to the heedless, nor to the uncaring that the Emperor spoke, it was to him, for: "From the middle of the procession, ignoring the homage of certain people, you have for an instant turned your eyes to my depressing room and, remembering the affection which you lavished on me in my childhood, you said to me: you suffer for me friend, I am pleased with you."[15]

To Louis Napoleon one fact was clear: until he could escape from captivity he must maintain the Bonapartist cause by proxy. "Publish or perish" became his motto, for this was the only means by which he could animate his supporters and convince the doubting of the inevitability of his success. So, in the spring of 1841, the work began. Significantly he thought first of a *Life of Charlemagne* because, as he said: "It is not just the actions of a great man that one ought to know about, it is above all the effects of those actions on contemporaries and on the era which succeeded him." To help him in his work he found a correspondent, and a "researcher," who was also to become the confidante of many of his views. She was Hortense Lacroix, his goddaughter, who was married to the painter Sebastien Cornu. As the child of Queen Hortense's personal maid, she had grown up with the Prince in the Bonapartist milieux, but in her politics she had become, and remained, a Republican. As such she was to exercise an influence on the Prince which was to have great consequences for the development of Bonapartism.

For the moment, however, Louis Napoleon concentrated on the proposed work on Charlemagne, but it seems to have progressed slowly, if at all. One has the feeeling that, like many another great project, it remained in the planning phase.[16] In any event, the Prince was only preoccupied with the past in so far as it provided ammunition for the battles of the present. For him, the only type of historical work which had any value was the *pièce justificative* as his *Fragments Historiques* proved. These were written less for their historical value than for their political relevance to the situation in France in 1840/41. The ostensible history of England under the Stuarts was really an attack on the government of Louis Philippe and it was hardly the Court and Country parties the Prince had in mind when he wrote, "Governments which are not popular enough to govern by the union of its citizens, nor strong enough to keep them under by oppressing them equally, can only keep themselves in power by fomenting discord between the parties ... the history of such a reign [Charles II's] is sad."

"The Stuarts [read the Orléans dynasty] never looked for a twin principle nor a sound system on which to base the prosperity and ascendancy of their country; instead they sought for tricks and shifts and used hidden intrigue to maintain themselves in power."

This was not meant to be an objective historical judgement on the Stuarts, but it was, and was taken to be, a subjective attack on the monarchy of Louis Philippe.

Less camouflaged by academic parallels were the Prince's open criticisms of the existing regime, which he managed to have published in various newspapers. "Our Correspondent in Ham," signing himself *xx* in an anonymity which deceived no one, became a familiar contributor to the *Progrès du Pas de Calais*. Indeed on 28th October, 1843, the paper admitted that: "For fifteen months, the Prince Napoleon Louis Bonaparte sends articles from his prison in Ham."[17] It can safely be assumed that the newspapers were more widely read by the general public than the *Fragments Historiques*. If the latter could be calculated to annoy the King, Guizot, Thiers and others of the governmental circle, the newspapers provided an opporunity for an *exposé* of the Bonapartist idea designed to impress the average reader.

Among various topics on which he wrote, the Prince attacked the colonial expansion, because the condition of France did not permit such a stretching of resources; he denounced the tendency to lower tariffs indiscriminately, and he deplored the waste of effort "... on the burning sands of Africa and on the Oceanic wastes."[18] At the same time, he produced positive policies, affirming for example that the plebiscite was the proper form of determining public opinion because "... the sovereignty of the people is the fundamental basis of all political organization."[19]

As for Parliamentary government, it was a fraud because it represented factions and interests and not the people. This was certainly true of France in the 1840's, for the narrowness of the franchise and the corruption of the Parliament under Louis Philippe reached such dimensions that ultimately it was to lead to a revolt by the bourgeoisie themselves and the collapse of the regime, The Chamber was, said the Prince, a theatre, because speeches from the Dais were applauded as a display of acting ability rather than assessed on their political content, and he maintained that if the deputy had to speak from his own place, debates would be less dramatic and more productive. Added to this, the constant changes of ministerial posts: "The Minister for Commerce moves to the Interior, the Minister for War to Foreign Affairs," led to confusion and instability, so that policy was maintained by the Civil

Servants and not the Government. France could be thankful that the Civil Service had been created by the Emperor.

The Prince did not confine himself to these political articles, for as *L'Idée Napoléonienne* had revealed, Louis Napoleon had what his uncle had not, that is a sympathy with the popular ideas of his time and an insight into them. It was this which made him take up the social question and it is here that one is led back to Hortense Cornu, for it was she who pushed the Prince to the closer examination of this topic.[20]

Mme Cornu had hopes of reconciling the Prince's Bonapartism to Republicanism, a task which was apparently facilitated by the ease with which Republicans and Bonapartists tended to find pleasure in one another's political company on the basis of opposition to Louis Philipe. The task was one to which the Prince himself was dedicated, and he was convinced it could be successful, provided that one accepted the premise that the Revolution and Napoleon were one and the same quantity.

That Mme Cornu's ideas were not quite in agreement with those of her godfather was proved later when from 1849 to 1860 she refused to see or communicate with him and was only reconciled after the "liberalization" of the Empire in 1860. But all this lay in the future. For the moment it seemed that the Prince was at least accepted as a Republican. The *Journal du Loiret* publicly acknowledged this by saying: "We are only a feeble echo of the national opposition"—it was a Republican newspaper—"but in the name of the ideas of which we are the voice, we publicly announce that our sympathy is with Prince Louis Napoleon. In our eyes he is no longer a pretender, but a member of our party, a soldier of our flag."[21]

It is doubtful if the Government of Louis Philippe was alarmed by the pronouncements of a provincial newspaper, but the issue was not quite so simple as that. The identification of the Prince with Republicanism was more widespread than appeared and, carefully nurtured by him, it was to increase steadily. Already in the *Idées Napoléoniennes*, and even more in *L'Idée Napoléonienne*, the Bonapartist Idea had been presented as one for the people: ". . . it goes into their humble dwellings not with the sterile Declaration of the Rights of Man, but with the means to quench the thirst of the poor and to satisfy their hunger."

Now the Prince went further in his appeal to Republican and working-class sentiment and openly avowed his Saint-Simonian Socialism by producing a summation of his ideas in the famous

pamphlet entitled *L'Extinction du Paupérisme*. The importance of this
pamphlet on the future development of Bonapartism as a political force
cannot be overestimated, for it provided the essential link which was to
connect the original Bonapartist Idea with the society of the 1840's. It
was, in fact, the fusion of Bonapartism and the "Social Question," as it
had come to be called and its appearance firmly identified the
"Republican Prince" with the Republican and Socialist workers. After
its publication it was said that: "He had no admirers, except at
La Villette and in the Faubourg St. Antoine,"[22] and certainly the message
was addressed to the underprivileged of society, for, as the preface said:
"It is natural for those who are unfortunate to think of those who
suffer."[23]

The subsequent analysis of the economic ills of France was on a
parallel with the various political analyses which the Prince had made,
not only in his *Idées,* but also in his various journalistic expositions. The
pamphlet stressed that weak government, factious government and,
above all, selfish Government was responsible for the condition of the
working class:

> It possesses nothing, it must be given property. It has no wealth
> except in its strength, this strength must be given work which will
> benefit everyone. It is like the helots in the midst of the Sybarites. It
> must be given a place in society and its interests attached to those of
> the land. Finally it lacks organization and is without roots, without
> rights and without a future. It must be given rights and a future, and
> it must be given self-respect by partnership (*association*) education
> and discipline.
> Without organization the masses are nothing, disciplined they are
> everything, without organization they can neither speak nor be
> understood, they can neither listen to nor receive a common directive.

It was the masses who must be considered because in the present
condition of society it was they who mattered. "Governing is no longer
a matter of dominating the people by force and violence, it is a question
of leading them towards a better future by appealing to their reason
and their heart."[24†]

It was a fundamental tenet of Louis Napoleon's Bonapartism that in
a healthy society both Government and people should be organized and
the one should interact on the other. In the sphere of social and
economic organization the smooth functioning of this interaction could
be achieved by cushioning so as to avoid a clash of interests between

capital and labour. Louis Napoleon envisaged that this could be achieved by the work of the *Corps des prud'hommes*.[25] These arbitrators would be elected by the workmen of every commune throughout France, in a ratio of one for every ten workers. The only qualification for election was to be a guarantee of upright conduct.[11] These men will fulfil, among the working class, the same role that the non-commissioned officers fulfil in the army."[26] It was perhaps inevitable that a Bonaparte should see the proposed structure in a quasi-military light but it would be wrong to see in this some sort of crypto-fascist attitude. The idea was, of course, not new; Napoleon I had established *Conseils des prud'hommes* in 1803, but these had collapsed by the 1830's largely because the Governments of the Restoration and the Orléans Monarchy had not wished to make them work. The workers were not considered "mature" enough to look after their own interests properly and, in any event, it was felt that even a little power could be dangerous.

The breakdown of this system, plus the total absence of even a primitive trades union organization, were among the main reasons for the bitterness of French workers and their outbreaks of revolutionary violence as, for example, at Lyons in 1831 and 1834. Louis Napoleon, therefore, by a clever stroke linked the future of the workers with the Imperial past and again identified the amelioration of the workers' lot with the re-establishment of Imperial institutions.

The new departure came with his proposals, which owed much to Saint-Simonianism, that the State should found agricultural colonies to use up waste land and surplus labour: "All the poor, all those without work, would find in these places the means of using their strength and their intelligence for the benefit of the entire community."[27] The Prince went on to argue that the colonies would also provide a labour market for private enterprise which could find workers when it needed them from among those living in the colonies. But with this difference from existing conditions, that the worker would not *have* to go unless he wanted to and unless his conditions of work were going to be sufficiently attractive. This would ensure that there would be no longer exploitation based on the surplus of labour and the need to take any work as an alternative to starvation. In the colonies, as elsewhere, conditions of work would be agreed on by using the arbitrators as negotiators again in a proportion of one to ten, and the whole colony would be run by a directorate composed of two-thirds arbitrators to one-third directors.

The colonies were to be run on military lines: " ... for the military organization is the only one which is based on the well-being of all its members and on the strictest economies." At the same time it was stressed that these establishments would not be military, they would only borrow from the army "... its worthwhile order, and that is all."[28]

If the idea strikes the present-day mind as repulsive, this is perhaps because the image of the concentration camp and forced labour are uppermost. If the condition of the working peoples in the middle of the nineteenth century, whether in France or in Britain, is borne in mind the idea of the colony may seem less appalling. It is perhaps worth remarking in this context on the fact that the English solution of the workhouse was mentioned by the Prince as an example of "what was being done for the poor" only to be condemned as inhuman and unjust, both in aim and in practice.

A study of the pamphlet undeniably produces evidence of confused thought—though better economists than Louis Napoleon have been wrapped in greater obscurity, and it is true that it ends on a note of romantic rhetoric: "The triumph of Christianity destroyed slavery, the triumph of the French Revolution destroyed serfdom, the triumph of democratic ideas will destroy poverty."[29] But what mattered was that the whole thing bore the stamp of sincerity and, by its (over simplifi-cation of the problems, was immediately attractive to those for whom it was destined. The Prince did not really hope to move the government by his arguments, but the masses and those who claimed to be their spokesmen. Here his success was immediate, for at the end of 1844 Louis Blanc, one of France's leading socialist thinkers, came to visit the prisoner at Ham and spent three days with him. It would be foolish to make too much of this visit, and yet it is tempting to see in it the germs of the alliance between Republican Socialism and Bonapartism. This is not meant to convey the impression that any formal negotiations marked the visit, nor was it designed to produce any such thing. But the fact was that one of the acknowledged leaders of the Socialist movement had gone to see the Bonapartist pretender; *The Organization of Labour* had spoken to *The Suppression of Poverty*.

There was common ground between the two social critics. Louis Blanc, in his *Organization of Labour*, had posited the right of the workers to employment, arguing that the state must be responsible, for "... what the proletariat lacks is a means of production—it is the government's function to provide them."[30] Louis Blanc's doctrine was by no means violently revolutionary, any more than was that of Louis Napoleon. It was a programme for the reform, not the overthrow, of society. Blanc's state factories were intended to operate in competition with private enterprise and, by implication, because they would be better, overthrow it by reason of their success.

Louis Blanc's plan was as naïve in its way as was Louis Napoleon's Saint-Simonian project including, as it did, a hint of the *Phalanstères* or communes envisaged by Fourier who was of the romantic or "utopian," socialist school of the 1830's. France was a country of agricultural, not industrial workers, and the very facts of the French economy at this stage of the nineteenth century meant that Louis Blanc's appeal was limited. In the immediate future, it did not look as though either project had much chance of realization for in spite of criticism, riot and continued discontent, the government of Louis Philippe seemed strong enough to survive. The Prince was still in prison and began to despair of ever coming out. Observers noted that his health was worse and that he was becoming morbid. Louis Blanc had noticed a tendency to mild persecution mania, and the letters of Hortense Cornu reveal that the Prince was seeking consolation in religion.

It does not seem, however, that religion was his only consolation. Apart from the publication of the manual on *The Past, and the Future of the Artillery* (May, 1846) there were other activities and schemes, but perhaps their very exoticism betrays a state of desperation. Sometime between November, 1844, and January, 1845, Louis Napoleon was approached by a group of "influential men" from Central America with proposals that he seek liberation on the strength of going to South America to set up a Central American state which would produce, in that area, a stable political situation. The Prince seems to have taken it seriously, probably because he really did despair of ever leaving Ham, and the scheme did offer freedom. What is interesting is that even on such a point and in his situation Louis Napoleon was not prepared to move without consulting England, and he took advantage of a visit from his friend, Lord Malmesbury, to consult the British Government as to what its attitude would be to such a move. He sent to the Foreign Office a *Note confidentielle sur l'Amérique Centrale* and received in return an unsigned Foreign Office memorandum to the effect that the British Government could not really support such a move and that, in any event, the Prince had been grossly misled as to the actual conditions prevailing in Central America. The significant point is not only that Louis Napoleon's obsession with English support should have led him into such a correspondence, even if the reply was discouraging, but also, as one commentator says: "His assumption that an European ruler, supported by an European power and European capital could rapidly transform Latin America into an orderly, prosperous area, strong enough to counterbalance the United States, was the same that later led him into disaster in Mexico."[31] In the short run, all that emerged from this was the publication of a pamphlet on *The Advantages of a Nicaraguan Canal*, and subsequent attempts while in exile in London in 1847 to organize a privately-financed company to construct the canal. In the long run, the effects on Imperial attitudes to Latin America were probably much greater.

In the autumn of 1845, the Prince's situation reached crisis point. His father, ex-King Louis, was dying, and wrote asking Louis Philippe to allow his son to come to him in Florence. The King would only permit this if Louis Napoleon would renounce all claim to the throne. This the Prince would not do and wrote to one of his correspondents that : "I shall only leave Ham for the graveyard or the Tuileries." In fact, there was another way. On 25th May, 1846, he walked out of the fortress by the main gate, disguised as one of the workers who were carrying out repairs in the building, and carrying a plank over his shoulder to hide his face from scrutiny. By 26th May he was in London. He had not only escaped, he was convinced of his future : "Since fortune has twice betrayed me, it only makes my destiny more assured. I am waiting." His university years had taught him patience but, in the event, it was not to be stretched too far. He was needed in 1848.

5

1848

THE revolution of February, 1848, which led to the downfall of
Louis Philippe, was accidental. Karl Marx, with lyrical exaggera-
ation, wrote in the *Communist Manifesto* of the spectre haunting
Europe, but this had no relevance to the political situation in France, nor
indeed to the political situation elsewhere in Europe. It was partly a
statement based on fact, namely that there were discontented elements in
most Europan capitals or industrial cities, but it must be remembered that
the real events of 1848 were not precipitated by either "the proletariat"
or "the people." This was a product of Marx's romanticism. They were
the result of a crisis in the ruling class in France brought about by too
much political make-believe combined with economic dislocation arising
from speculation. In both senses it was a crisis of overinvestment aggravated by a too rapid expansion of the major cities.

In France, Louis Philippe had since 1841 worked through and with
Guizot as his First Minister. Thiers and his supporters had formed "the
dynastic opposition," the nearest that French political life could get to
"His Majesty's opposition." The same people were to be found in both
government and opposition, in the sense that they were drawn from,
and represented, a narrow political class. So restricted was the electorate, and so few were the enfranchised bourgeoisie, that even Louis
Philippe's title of Bourgeois Monarch was suspect. No great social or

class cleavage was to be found among the deputies in the Chamber and
indeed its composition was revealed by the attitudes of the Deputies to
the debates on the major topics of the day.[1] About the social problems
of France there was an agreement to take the minimum steps to
ameliorate conditions and the maximum steps to suppress overt discontent. About the constitutional or political problems, which by 1844-
45 had become a question of an extension of the franchise to take in a
wider section of the bourgeoisie, there was measured disagreement.
Only at the last stage, in 1848, did this get out of hand, because Louis
Philippe and Guizot behaved as if their political system was really representative of France. In the condition of French politics it was a
short step from "His Majesty's Opposition" to "Opposition to his
Majesty." Louis Philippe and Guizot forgot that.

Stanislavsky is said to have remarked that when an actor came to
believe he was the part he was playing he should be sacked. *Mutatis
mutandis* this might help to explain the riot against Guizot and Louis
Philippe in February, 1848. In 1830 Louis Philippe had been installed
as Chairman of the Board of Directors of *France* (*Société Anonyme*),
and although the Directors, and even the shareholders, could accept
corruption, and could at a pinch put up with occasional mismanage-
ment, total incompetence proved too much. To put up with a chairman
not open to criticism by the stockholders was impossible. Louis
Philippe's refusal to listen to the complaints of the middle class,
demanding an extension of the franchise, coincided with an economic
crisis through which France passed in 1845-46. This was part of the
general European crisis of the mid forties, and resulted from the fact
that the harvests were poor, trade was slack and there was unrest in the
countryside and in the towns. Too much, however, should not be made
of the factor of social unrest. It may have exacerbated the feelings of
dissident elements in society, but by and large France and indeed most
European countries got off lightly. The real tragedy occurred in Ireland
where one and a half million people died of starvation or in the typhus
epidemic which accompanied the famine. That catastrophe puts, or
should put, much of the events of 1846-48 in the rest of Europe into
perspective. If one is considering the catalytic effects of "social problems" on the revolutionary movement, then in Ireland the entire
country should have been ablaze from end to end. In fact, the only
manifestation of revolution in Ireland in 1848 assumed the form of a
joke in bad taste, perpetrated by romantic clowns in the middle of an
agonized and despairing population too far gone in misery to care
about political rights. There was little room for romanticism in mid

nineteenth-century Ireland. In any event the 1848 revolutions were essentially urban phenomena, as much the product of a breakdown in urban administration in the rapidly expanding capitals like Paris, Berlin and Vienna as they were the product of revolutionary ideas. Cheap lodgings threw students and workers together in physical proximity before revolutionary ideology linked them.

In France a further source of trouble arose. Heavy investment in railways led to the serious rocking of a financial structure which was overextended in credit. The alarm felt by the bourgeoisie at this phenomenon led them to cry out against the government and to demand reform. The fall of Louis Philippe was in part due to a loss of nerve by the old King who saw himself cried down by his erstwhile supporters and in part it was due to the indifference with which the rest of France regarded what went on in Paris. The Paris revolutionaries took up their accustomed stations and re-enacted in a condensed version, and as best they could, the events of 1789-93 with a slightly updated revolutionary vocabulary.

It is arguable that if Louis Philippe had not antagonized the Powers of Europe by the ineptitude of his foreign policy—a policy which had also helped to make him unpopular in French political and army circles —he might have weathered the teapot tempest. To have antagonized England by the affair of the Spanish Marriages without first ingratiating himself with Austria was a blunder. What Lord Palmerston had given, Lord Palmerston could take away, and it was unfortunate for Louis Philippe that Peel and Aberdeen had been replaced by Russell and Palmerston just at the critical moment in his reign. Whatever the *entente cordiale* may or may not have meant, it did mean French subservience in foreign affairs. When Lord Aberdeen talked of "a good understanding" what he meant was that the French King and his Ministers should understand what Britain's interests were and give way to them.

However, it was not Lord Palmerston who cried *à bas Guizot* in the Paris streets on a wet evening in February, 1848. It was the discontented bourgeoisie who, seeking a change of ministry, had abandoned their combination of public eating with political speaking, known as "the banquet campaign," in favour of more direct street action. It should be noted that this was an *ad hoc* decision by those who had turned up to dine and found that the Government, irritated by this mixture of gastronomy and politics, had banned the banquet to be held on 22nd February. Louis Philippe had said: "These banquets are a personal attack on me. We shall see who is the strongest." In fact the events of 22nd and 23rd February, demonstrated the lack of will to revolution on the part of the bourgeoisie, although they revealed that the weaknes of the executive was the greater.

Louis Philippe dismissed Guizot in an attempt to save himself and the regime, but the dismissal only led to exultation by the "Left," while the majority in the Chamber were furious at the King's apparent betrayal of them. All this might have ended in a Parliamentary reconciliation, after much abuse and recrimination, but for the eruption of a new force—the Parisian populace. The Parisians' brush with the troops led to deaths, and ultimately to the fall of the dynasty, though it could be argued that Louis Philippe had already abdicated when he sacrificed Guizot to street clamour. An attempt to save the day by setting up a regency for Louis Philippe's grandson was thwarted by the mob breaking into the assembly and demanding a republic.

So stagnant had French political life become by 1848 that the poet Lamartine now emerged as a key figure. He put himself at the head of the insurgents and set off for the Hôtel de Ville, a traditional home of Parisian insurrections, in order to proclaim the republic decently and in the proper place. The Government which was pronounced at the Hôtel de Ville on 24th February was essentially a compromise between bourgeoisie and radicals, as it had to be, arising from the confusion of aim and interest of those who had been caught up in the unexpected revolution."[2] Basically, it was a government of traditional politicians, whose party labels varied, but whose attitude was a common one, the only exceptions being the socialist thinker and writer Louis Blanc and a worker named Albert. Of the latter personnage little is known except his name.

For the professional politicians the task was clear: Republican reforms but no revolution. For Louis Blanc and Albert there was little to hope for, in the way of real social and economic reforms for the proletariat. They had no support except at street level and any manifestation of that would be severely repressed once the ruling classes recovered their nerve. The more the clamour arose from the Paris streets for a socialist Republic, the closer drew the ranks of the bourgeoisie, whose "Party of Order" represented the end product of the in-fighting which had helped to bring down the Orléans dynasty. Before the abyss of socialism they clung to one another, hoping and working for deliverance, even though for some months their attitude towards the man who offered to save them was more than ambivalent. In fairness, it must be said that Louis Napoleon's own attitude was far from clear even if his initial reaction to the 1848 revolution was swift. He arrived in Paris on 28th February, but left it the next day at the request of the Assembly. He made a dignified protest: "Gentlemen: I thought that after thirty-three years of exile and persecution I had at length the right to find a home in my native land. You think that my presence in Paris at this time would be an embarrassment; I therefore retire for the present. You will see in this sacrifice, the purity of my intentions and my patriotism. . . L. N. Bonaparte".[3]

There were two points of interest in this statement: after thirty-three years it was unlikely that Louis Napoleon would rush things. He also made it plain that he had only retired "for the present." For him, the real victory was that he was thought important enough to be asked to leave. He left behind a representative in Persigny, whose aim it was to organize in Paris a milieu of Bonapartist sympathizers who would as a first step launch a campaign to press for the Prince's right to return to France. The elections for the constituent assembly were to be held on 23rd April and it was essential that the Bonapartist cause be brought forward. The key to the situation was Paris and it is a measure of some sort of success for the propaganda of the Bonapartists that on 16th April a riot took place in the street between veterans of the Imperial Guard, wearing their uniforms, who clashed with the National Guard. The crowd was divided in its reactions, but it was noted that many cried *"Vive l'Empereur."*

Louis Napoleon was not as yet disposed to take up any political attitude. Indeed he refused to stand for the elections. This policy of self-effacement was a masterstroke of tactics for it cannot be doubted that with every fibre of his being he strained towards France and political activity. To pass the time, the Prince soothed himself by walking the London streets in the guise of a Special Constable enrolled to cope with the Chartists from whom the English government expected trouble. Towards the more than Chartist-like disorder of his own supporters in Paris, his attitude was noncommittal. But he was behaving as the Provisional Government had requested, he was staying away until after the elections. The results of the 23rd April election were interesting, not just because they produced a highly conservative Chamber, but because these returns included Prince Napoleon Bonaparte (son of ex-King Jerome), Prince Pierre Bonaparte (son of Lucien), and Prince Lucien Murat. They had all been elected in defiance of the laws of banishment of 1816 and 1832, which had not been repealed. People inevitably asked why they were there and Prince Louis Napoleon was not? The Bonapartist newspapers which now sprang up, thanks to the lifting of the press restrictions, demanded whether his martyrdom was to be endless. The Prince was content to wait. One of his maxims, often used, was "*Il ne faut rien brusquer.*" He had learned the value of patience.

In Paris itself the situation was clearly approaching a crisis. The elections had been a bitter blow to the Left Wing of the Republicans and to the Socialists, who had hoped that the victory from universal suffrage would be theirs. They had mistaken the temper of the country at large, and had confused Paris with France. One correspondent in the provinces had noted in early April that: "The country in general is very calm and very quiet, very cold towards the Republic, colder still for anything else."[4]

The sequence of events between April and June hardened the attitudes on both sides. The peasantry objected to the "Law of the 45 *centimes*," an extra tax levied by the Government to pay for the cost of running the so-called "National Workshop" in Paris, which the peasantry considered to be simply a means of maintaining the *badauds de Paris* in drink and idleness. This is not the place to enter into a detailed discussion of the merits, or lack of them, of the National Workshops, in terms of social engineering or economic policy. Suffice it to say that having been originally established as a political peace-offering, they had now become political dynamite.[5]

They had been set up to provide for the workers in accordance with the declaration of the Provisional Government on the right to work, which stated: "The Provisional Government of the French Republic pledges itself to guarantee work for all citizens. It recognizes that the workers must form associations among themselves in order to enjoy the rights of their work."[6] The whole doctrine of the right to work was itself a concession to the proletarian wing of the Provisional Government which had established itself at the Luxembourg Palace as a commission to survey the setting up of the National Workshops and their direction. The activities of the commission were tolerated by the Provisional Government because it had as yet no mandate from the country to move in any direction, and pending the election of the Constituent Assembly it was disposed to move warily—particularly *vis-à-vis* the Parisian working class. The results of 23rd April produced a hardening of attitude on the part of the Government. Every one of the 2,000 candidates who stood for the 876 seats in the Assembly had stood as a Republican. But that meant nothing, for of those elected 300 were Monarchists, 200 were "Democrats" and the bulk of the rest were conservative "Republicans." In the whole assembly, 34 were workers. It was an ill augury for the social republic and the Paris proletariat showed its awareness of this by the riot of 15th May, the day of the Assembly's opening *séance*, when the workers' clubs held a demonstration which was straightaway suppressed by government forces. Very interestingly, on 15th May the workers demanded not only social reform but even more vehemently demanded that France help to free Italy, Ireland and Poland. Even Auguste Blanqui, the professional revolutionary and the hero of the *faubourgs*, was greeted with cries of *"La Pologne, Blanqui, parlez-nous de la Pologne!"* The new Foreign Minister, Bastide, mounted the rostrum of the packed Assembly to announce that: "These Prussians, and Austrians and Russians will all need to be educated with gunfire. Then perhaps when we are in arms they will stop their martyrdom of the Poles." This was greeted with thunderous applause. As one observer noted, "Only Napoleon was missing."[7] Napoleon would not be missing for long, for on 4th June the country did its second stint of elections. This time Louis Napoleon was a candidate and was elected for Paris and the Departments of Seine, Yonne, and Charente Inférieure. His election was timely, for one of the results of the *farandole* of 15th May had been a movement to set up a Left-Wing Government under Barbès, Blanqui, Louis Blanc, Albert and others, in an attempt to overthrow the bourgeois assembly. But it was no longer the 24th of February and the leaders were arrested and charged with conspiracy. Thus left without a hero the Paris populace soon filled the gap. On 5th June a group of workers from La Villette presented a petition to the Assembly asking that Louis Napoleon be proclaimed Consul. In the districts of the Panthéon, Saint Victor, and Saint Martin (revolutionary in temper and working class in population) the Seventh Legion of the National Guard elected Louis Napoleon as Colonel in place of the imprisoned revolutionary leader, Barbès. Posters appeared, the work of Persigny and his group, which announced: "The people have spoken: they have proclaimed the democratic republic. Louis Napoleon will defend it with us."

The Assembly reacted violently and announced its intention of arresting "Louis Napoleon Bonaparte, 40 years old, 1 metre 66 (height) hair and eyebrows brownish (*châtain*), eyes small, grey, large nose, medium mouth, thick lips, brown beard, fair moustache, pointed chin, oval face, pale complexion. Distinguishing marks: head sunk on the shoulders, back hunched."[8] It was hardly a flattering portrait; police descriptions rarely are. What might well have been added to the list of distinguishing features was "political astuteness." The next few days provided considerable evidence of his ability, for Louis Napoleon was now following events intently.

On 11th June, a deputy named Goudchoux made a speech in the Assembly denouncing the National Workshops and demanding their closure. He called for an end to the workers' demonstrations. On 12th June Lamartine denounced Louis Napoleon as a political threat. The combination of socialism and Bonapartism had proved too much for the Conservatives in the Assembly. An order was issued for the Prince's arrest, but events had gone too far for that. The Order was annulled on the 13th at the same time as the decrees of banishment were repealed.

Knowing that he was virtually master of the situation and, not wishing to be involved in the now inevitable showdown between government and workers in Paris, Louis Napoleon wrote on the 16th resigning his seats. The letter was a masterpiece of moderation and political skill: "*M. le Président*: I was proud of having been elected a representative in Paris and in three departments: it was, in my eyes, an ample reparation for thirty years of exile and six years of prison. But the unjust suspicions to which my election has given rise, the troubles of which it has been the excuse, and the hostility of the executor's power, impose upon me the duty of refusing an honour which I am supposed to have obtained by intrigue. I desire order, and the maintenance of a wise, great and intelligent republic: and since, involuntarily, I am the excuse for disorder, I place, not without deep regret, my resignation in your hands. I hope that calmness will come back soon, and will permit me to go back to France like the simplest of her citizens, but also as one most devoted to the repose and prosperity of my country....Louis Bonaparte."[9]

The government now set itself to try conclusions with the Paris "Reds." On 21st June the Assembly decreed that all workers not of Parisian origin who had come to the capital since February, must return to the provinces, or, if between eighteen and twenty-five, they must join the army. It was declared that the National Workshops would be closed. These measures provoked the long-awaited revolt in Paris which began on 23rd June with the building of barricades in the traditional revolutionary areas of the capital. The Government entrusted the reduction of Paris to General Cavaignac, a staunch Republican and a bitter reactionary, who from the 23rd to the 26th, the "June Days," fought his way along the streets until the insurgents capitulated. *En route* Cavaignac had been given dictatorial powers by the Assembly to facilitate his task of restoring order, and his victory was greeted by the Deputies with great emotion, and with cries and cheers of "*Vive Cavaignac*" and "*Vive la Republique*." Only Tartuffe could have done justice to the scene: the sum total of the victory was five hundred citizens killed on the barricades, over three thousand massacred and nearly five thousand deported. The Republic was indeed saved, in that it was now dead and beyond any further injury. So shrewd an observer as de Tocqueville had seen it was not the Republic which was at issue: "At bottom what France wants is not this or that form of government, it is an orderly and firm government."[10] In these circumstances Louis Napoleon judged that the time had come to accept his destiny. Once again he put himself forward as a candidate for election and in September he was elected for five separate departments with a total of 300,000 votes cast in his favour. He took his seat for the Department of the Yonne and on 24th September, entering the Palais Bourbon quietly by a side door—to avoid the crowd waiting to cheer him—he modestly read his first declaration: "The Republic has happily restored to me my native land and my fellow citizens. May the Republic receive my oath of acknowledgement and of devotion. . . ." It had taken seventeen years to get to the Palais Bourbon, but in the end it had been accomplished quite legally by the method for which the Prince himself had always stated a preference—that of universal suffrage.

He had arrived in time to help the Assembly to produce the final constitution. It had already decided on a single chamber legislature and an executive, in the shape of a President, elected by universal suffrage. The concepts of social change which had been introduced in the halcyon days of February were now discreetly jettisoned. The right to work was merely included among other rights which the Government announced and which harked back to the Constitution of 1791. It was no longer elevated to the first duty of the State, which had been the aim of the Socialist Left in 1848.

The consitution was established by vote on 4th November, 1848. One week earlier the Assembly had decided that the Presidential elections should take place on 10th December. The next few weeks were, therefore, taken up with a furious electoral campaign by the six candidates who had presented themselves: Louis Napoleon, Cavaignac, Ledru-Rollin, Raspail, Lamartine, and General Changarnier.

In fact, the issue can never have been in doubt. Everything conspired, or had been conspired with, to make Louis Napoleon the victor. General Cavaignac himself admitted this in a confidential conversation with Normanby, the British Ambassador in Paris, and added that his only object in standing for election was to *make* the country Republican.[11] But even Cavaignac can hardly have hoped to breathe life into a corpse.

The struggle was really between Cavaignac and Louis Napoleon. The supporters of both were unscrupulous in their attacks on the other side, but the cartoons caricaturing Louis Napoleon were probably the more scurrilous and offensive. The Prince was usually portrayed in full Napoleonic costume, which was always too big for him, engaged in some ridiculous pursuit. Occasionally he was astride a goose, or a balding, nondescript bird which he was vainly trying to turn into an Imperial Eagle. Nothing was left undone to make him comic and shady. But in the long run the attacks rebounded. The links with his uncle could do no harm, for the Great Napoleon could never be funny to any Frenchman, and in any event nothing could remove from Cavaignac the stain of the June Days, which made of him a sinister and threatening figure rather than a comic one. The Prince's election manifesto was moderate and firm, coming down impartially on all sides. It is possible that he could with equal effect have issued the words of "*Au Clair de la Lune*," so long as they were signed by him, for the campaign was not to be decided by electoral manifestos but by history.

The Prince's campaign had been begun for him at St. Helena; he had himself fought it at Strasbourg, Boulogne and Ham. His manifesto was his uncle, his name, his writings and ultimately, based on all these things, his own ability to make himself acceptable to the masses and classes. The real obstacles had been removed by the folly of his opponents in the June Days, and the fact that he had the support of the working classes was as much due to Cavaignac and the *Notables* as it was to his pamphlet on *L'Extinction du Paupérisme*.

At the other end, squirm how they might, it was clear to all that Thiers, Molé, Odilon Barrot and their group were really committed to support Louis Napoleon, either through fear of social revolution or desire for a Bonapartist solution. In the history of the cult of Bonapartism in nineteenth-century France, Thiers had himself played an important part with his *Histoire du Consulat et de l'Empire*. Many of the men of 1848 who made the success of the Prince inevitable were later to denounce Bonapartism as a political whore, but they had nearly all visited the lady in their youth. The notables had accepted a solution from the Right when they had committed themselves to supporting Cavaignac, and there were in fact three Orléanists in Cavaignac's ministry of October, 1848. But, since June, Cavaignac was so unpopular that he was a dangerous cause to support and Louis Napoleon was more attractive from many points of view—not least his electoral popularity with the masses.

De Tocqueville, shrewd as ever, saw the strangeness of the situation :

"The oddest thing, and something which could only be seen in hordes composed of Frenchmen, is that Prince Louis is at one and the same time supported in the provinces by those who want to overthrow the Republic, and at Paris by a large section of the ultra-republicans. If he doesn't get elected by an absolute majority and the Assembly does not choose him, an upheaval in Paris is very probable."[12]

There was no need for an upheaval. Out of 7,327,345 votes cast, the Prince received 5,534,520. Cavaignac had 1,448,107. The remainder did not poll half a million between them, less than six per cent of the suffrage. The fact that Louis Napoleon had won virtually as soon as he presented himself is borne out by an analysis of the results in terms of newspaper and press opposition to his candidature. In areas where virtually the entire press was hostile, the Prince was capable of receiving fifty to sixty per cent of the votes cast. Only in cities like Marseilles, which was a stronghold of legitimism, did the percentage in his favour drop. Here it could be argued that where the press was sufficiently widely read by the electorate it did have an influence, and that the accusation that the Prince owed his election to illiterates is proven. On the other hand, as in the case of Marseilles, there are reasons other than a lack of political awareness, for the fact that people voted for him.[13]

In any event only the blindly obstinate could deny that Louis Napoleon had won a tremendous victory. Victor Hugo later in life reported a conversation he had had with Lamartine some days after the elections:

Hugo : What is happening to us, Lamartine?
Lamartine : We are f...d!

It may be apocryphal, it was certainly as neat a summation of the situation as could be desired. The political romanticism of the *Idées Napoléoniennes* and the *Extinction du Paupérisme* had triumphed over the romanticism of the poets. A fact which the poets never forgave.

The question now to be answered was, "Who was Louis Napoleon?" In political terms, what did the election mean? Daumier's cartoon of 1848 had no doubt; two bourgeois are talking in a Paris street:

"En 1848 nous avions Louis Philippe: si Louis Bonaparte nous arrivait en 1849 ... 1849 serait l'am pire. Hi! Hi! Hi!"

But would it be *l'Empire*? The President took the oath to uphold the Republic and the new ministry he formed could be described as "centre-mediocre," though in political terms its general complexion was Orléanist. Of the leading men of the future Empire the only one to emerge with an office was Baroche who was appointed *Procureur Général* to the Paris Court of Appeal. None of this indicated any hasty design on Louis Napoleon's part to pack the Ministry with his supporters and, indeed, it is hard to see what he could have done immediately. He was virtually a tourist in a foreign country and like others in such circumstances was at the mercy of guides and travel agents. As Persigny said, the Prince "did not know one man of importance who could serve him and had not a friend whom he could suitably make a minister." A further period of waiting was, therefore, indicated until suitable men could be found and the *Notables* could be dispensed with. Hence Ollivier's later designation of this first ministry as *"le ministère de la captivité."* However, after six years in Ham, Louis Napoleon knew all about captivity. He also knew it was possible to escape.

In the long run, the moves which were to lead to the Prince President's assumption of power in the *coup d'état* of December, 1851, were based upon a shrewd assessment of the political circumstances which had led to his election. Louis Napoleon had never any intention of being the dupe of the Party of Order and he had seen the falsity of their position. They had willed the end of order and stability by their actions between February and December, 1848. The logic of this was that they must accept the means; this was what the presidential election of 1848 had really signified. At their worst, the opponents of the Prince could only be factious *frondeurs*. They could not be *real* political opponents, for this would drive them back to the principle of social revolution from which they had recoiled horrified in June, 1848. It was, therefore, only a matter of time before this political group revealed the contradictions inherent in its attitude to "liberty" and "order."

Thiers himself in his letter of congratulation to Baroche, who became Minister of the Interior in the ministry of March, 1849, made the position of the *Notables* quite plain: "My dear colleague, I hasten to tell you that this news causes us all the greatest pleasure. You are a man of intellect and heart whom we will support with all our strength. Count on me in particular. In times like these one must give all one's support to men who know how to be devoted."[14] The point was that Baroche was already very much the President's man, whose only point of agreement with Thiers and the Party of Order (the "us" of the letter of 15th March) was a common dislike of the extreme Republicans.

Here again Louis Napoleon's attitude was one of ambivalence. It was essential to his ultimate design that if the Party of Order was to be revealed as the enemy of the masses, the extreme Republicans must not emerge as their friends. It was not to be Louis Blanc but Louis

Napoleon who would lead them. In his ability to bring this about lay the real test of skill for the President. The *politique de la bascule* was not unknown in France, but in the circumstances of 1848-51 it had to be operated with great care and intelligence. It was one thing to play off the Assembly against "popular rights" and Republican clamour, with the President posing as the unfortunate middleman. It was quite another matter to make sure that the answer came out right—namely that the President finally emerged as *the* man who had the confidence of all, and who was quite clearly the only solution to the clash of irreconcilable claims which tormented France. In moments of exasperation the French frequently exclaim, "*Il faut en finir.*" What Louis Napoleon had to ensure was that it finished with him as the positive ending. It was essential that the Assembly and the "Mountain" should exhaust one another in political struggles while the President should build his stable situation upon the five and a half million who had voted him to power.

The real interest of the two years before the *coup d'état* of 1851 lies not in the manoeuvrings in the National Assembly, which in the long run could only have one end, but in the use which Louis Napoleon made of his name and his position to ensure his success when his time came.[15] The elections of 13th May, 1849, produced an Assembly more Royalist and reactionary than its predecessor, though it had also brought back an increased number of the more extreme Republicans. Inspired by a modest electoral success, the latter, under the leadership of Ledru Rollin attempted an insurrection on 13th June which failed totally and led to Rollin's flight to London. The Republicans were finished, but the Assembly's desire to ram home the point led to a law designed to restrict the franchise—in spite of the President's public opposition to it as an anti-popular and unconstitutional measure. Louis Napoleon's answer to the anti-popular legislation was to increase his appearances in the faubourgs of Paris, and in the provincial cities and towns where he spoke directly to the people. The speeches were all fairly short and to the point; it was only in 1851 within a few months of the ultimate step that they revealed any change of tone, and even then it was guarded.[16]

In June 1851 in a speech at Dijon, marking the opening of a section of the Lyons railway between Tonerre and Dijon, the Prince said: "A new phase of our political era begins. From one end of France to the other petitions are appearing demanding a revision of the Constitution. I await with confidence the evidence of the country and the decisions of the Assembly which can only be inspired by the thought of the public good. If France recognizes that one has not the right to dispose of her without her, France has only to say so : my courage and my energy will not fail her."[17]

The Prince might well have added that he now had at his disposal nearly all the means he required for action if "France" should decide to speak, for it should not be imagined that Louis Napoleon was counting only on his personal popularity. His name was also a programme. A new political force, that of the Bonapartists, had emerged in the provinces. They openly dissociated themselves from the traditional Right where this was electorally possible. Their language was an echo of the Presidential addresses; they concentrated on local issues, canals, roads, railways, and ignored the political vocabulary of the Party of Order with its talk of order, stability and property.[18]

The aim of Bonapartism was to cut across parties and divisions as they had grown up since the fall of the Empire in 1815. This was the real message of the *Idées*. The nephew would resume the work of the uncle and just as Napoleon had reconciled the religious and civil breaches in French society, so his nephew would heal the social and political wounds of the last thirty-five years. It should be remembered in this context that in French political life the whole conception of "party," as such, was held to be intolerable, and a fiction of unity and solidarity in the legislative body had always been maintained—in spite of a great weight of evidence to the contrary. In the parliaments of the Restoration period between 1815 and 1830 there had been frequent assertions that there was neither majority nor minority in the Chamber, but only faithful subjects of the King; the same attitude prevailed under Louis Philippe. Opposition and party were equated with faction in the early part of the nineteenth century in the same way as Robespierre had equated them with faction in the Revolutionary period. In this respect, Louis Napoleon was not new, but he was different and he could hope to rise above, and cut across, the political divisions. It was the same attitude which was to mark off de Gaulle a century later.

The real difficulty, and in the long run it was to prove virtually insoluble, was that Bonapartism could only triumph by putting itself at the head of the new politically active forces in society—as Louis Napoleon himself had already seen. In the France of the 1840's and 1850's this meant the growing industrial proletariat, but it had to be remembered that they were numerically small and politically weak. To give them what they wanted would be to offend the much more strongly entrenched forces of the *Notables* and the Church, while the vast proportion of the population, the peasant masses, would never be reconciled to any hint of a "Jacobin-Social" policy. Hence the Bonapartists stressed local politics and agricultural improvements to allay the fears of the peasantry and to make of them at least passive supporters of the system. They would carry Bonapartism to power with their votes because they trusted Louis Napoleon, who was thus able to collect what working-class votes there were in the towns without losing any voters in the rural areas. This mass electoral basis was essential, for the *Notables* and the Church would only serve Louis Napoleon as long as he served them, and by 1851 they already felt he had overstrayed his welcome when they discovered that his interpreation of Bonapartism was not theirs.

To the authoritarian democracy of the Prince President, based on universal suffrage, the Assembly, representing the *Notables*, opposed a liberal democracy which required a property-based franchise. Hence the Assembly's restriction of the right to vote in the law of 31st May, 1850 —for the three-year residence qualification was expressly designed to disfranchise what Thiers called "the vile rabble." What Thiers and his supporters had hoped to do was to deprive the extreme Republicans of their supporters in the urban constituencies, and this they did. But the advantage went not to them but to the President, who made clear his opposition to the Assembly's action. The Assembly had virtually legi-timized the *coup d'état* in advance—a point neatly taken by a Bonapartist journal *Moniteur du Soir* in an issue of 25th July, 1850. Speaking of the Assembly's attitude to the President over the question of the press laws it said : "In case of conflict the country will support the President. . . . There will not be a *coup d'état,* but a *coup d'opinion.*"[19]

In fact, this was exactly what the Assembly was determined to avoid. If there was to be a *coup d'état*, then it must be made on their terms. It must not be a Jacobin *coup*, in the sense that they lost control of the political scene, and they were determined that the Prince would act in the interest of the classes rather than the masses. This explains their conduct in the period June to December, 1851, when all the man-oeuvres of Thiers and the *Notables* were directed towards driving the President along the way they wanted him to go. They wanted a Prince Consort, not a Prince President, and to this end they rejected in July, 1851, a project to revise the constitution in favour of extending the President's term of office, while in November they refused to restore universal suffrage. It seems almost as though they were resolved to drive Louis Napoleon towards a *coup de main,* from which they would benefit, but from participation in which they could be, at least legally, absolved, even if they remained morally guilty.[20] Louis Napoleon would have preferred a prolongation of his powers, but in the long run he would not draw back from a confrontation.

So, on the night of 1st/2nd December, the long-awaited event took place. The proclamation which appeared announcing the Presidential reasons laid stress on the impossibility of maintaining order and progress under the present conditions. What alternative existed but a *coup d'état*? :

> The Constitution, as you know, had been expressly made to limit in advance the powers which you gave me. Six million votes were a striking protest against it, and yet I observed it faithfully. Provocation, slanders, outrages found me impassive. But today, when the fundamental agreement is no longer respected, even by those who invoke it ceaselessly, and when the men who have already lost two monarchies wish to tie my hands, in order to overthrow the Republic, my duty is to thwart their treacherous schemes, to maintain the Republic and to save the country by invoking the solemn judgement of the only sovereign I recognize in France—the people."[21]

The *coup d'état* of December 1851 has been compared with that of the 18th Brumaire 1799 which set up the Consulate, but on one very important point there was a difference between the new regime and that of the first Napoleon. Universal suffrage was a fact, and to Louis Napoleon a fact which he both accepted and endorsed. Napoleon I had talked at St. Helena about the will of the people as a *principle* of political action. Napoleon III based his actions upon its existence as a *fact* and so the new Constitution, with all that it implied, was to be submitted to a plebscite.

The Constitution proclaimed was modelled on that of the Consulate of 1799; but it also had strong links with the Constitution of the First Empire as it existed in 1807 when Napoleon I had absorbed the Tribunals into the Legislative Body. There was to be a head of state nominated for ten years, ministers appointed by him, and a Council of State and two Assemblies consisting of a Senate and a Legislative Body.

What opposition there was to the *coup d'état* among the professional politicians was so ridiculous as to be almost sad. Only the Legitimists behaved with any show of resolution, led by the indefatigable Maître Berryer (erstwhile defender of Prince Louis at the Strasbourg trial), but there was neither plan nor reason for resistance and no support could be found. Of the events in the Paris streets which took place on 3rd/4th December, much had been made by the opponents of Louis

Napoleon, but most of the barricade building was an affair of a very few diehard fanatics who persuaded younger hotheads to support them, "for the Republic." The real working-class areas of Paris in the East hardly stirred and the only casualties were incurred on the Boulevard Montmartre where it seems some six hundred, including military personnel, died. The figures are atrocious, but they must be seen in the context both of mid nineteenth-century France (compare them with the June Days) and with the results of the plebiscite of 28th December, 1851. Nearly 7,500,000 voted for Louis Napoleon, only 650,000 against. As Simpson put it: "If the *coup d'état* was a crime, France was less its victim than its accomplice."[22]

It was not only France which approved. Austria, Russia, Spain and Naples through their Ambassadors congratulated the Prince. So did England, though it was to cost Lord Palmerston the Foreign Office. Perhaps it was this European recognition which was the Prince's greatest satisfaction. He had been fairly sure of acceptance in France, though he had worked for it; he had not been so sure of Europe, though he had not been idle there either in the period from 1848 to 1851.

6

France and Europe

*"Il ne faut pas que l'Europe se persuade
que la France vote la
guerre en votant pour Louis Bonaparte."*

G. de Beaumont to Alexis de Tocqueville,
11th December, 1848

TOWARDS the end of his reign, Louis Philippe had been trying to redirect the foreign policy of France so that she might be freed from the tutelage of Britain. The Government of France had remained in an invidious position in the field of foreign policy since it had been established in 1830. The support of England at the time of the July Revolution, which breached the Vienna Settlement of 1815, had been bought at the cost of a surrender of initiative by France in the field of foreign affairs as had been swiftly borne out by Palmerston's attitude to Louis Philippe at the time of the Belgian revolution crisis between 1830-32. The crisis of 1841 in the Near East had underlined the fact that British friendship was conditional on French good behaviour. From then on it is clear that not only did Louis Philippe and Guizot pursue a more conservative domestic policy, but that in the field of foreign affairs also there had been an attempt to move France into a conservative alliance with Austria. The affair of the Spanish marriages, and the intervention of France on the side of the Catholic cantons in Switzerland during the *Sonderbund* war, had shown Louis Philippe's desire to achieve greater freedom of manoeuvre in Europe, by ingratiating himself with Austria as a first step to aligning France with the conservative bloc.

It was perhaps unfortunate for France that the climax of her "non-English" policy coincided with the return to power of Lord Palmerston as Foreign Secretary, in Lord John Russell's Cabinet of July, 1846. Palmerston had opined that: "Firm and stout language to the French government and to Frenchmen was the best way of usefully supporting the interests of peace." He expected that French governments would accept this type of treatment without demur and, since Louis Philippe and Guizot seemed not to know their place, it was with indifference, not unmixed with satisfaction, that Palmerston saw the King driven out in February, 1848. He assumed that the new Republic would be as mindful of its manners as Louis Philippe had been in his early days in 1830 when the question of European recognition had been at stake.

Now the mandate to breach the 1815 settlement, given to France by Europe in 1830 would have to be renewed. This time it would have to be in a form even more difficult to swallow, since it was no longer merely a question of a change of dynasty, but of recognizing the existence of a French Republic—with all that this might seem to imply in a European context. It may well have been that had Austria, Prussia and Russia not been occupied with their own affairs, in consequence of the outbreaks in 1848, France would have found herself in a difficult situation. Indeed, inside France, not the least of the factors working for the establishment of a Conservative Republic was the fear of repercussions in Europe. The association of the extreme Republicans with an aggressive foreign policy helped to discredit them. The preposterous declaration of war on Russia and Germany on 15th May, 1849, during Barbès's occupation of the Hôtel de Ville in Paris was a farce; but it was a farce which could have had sinister implications had it been staged by the Government.

The new Republican Government simply had to avoid any entanglement in European affairs which might lead to war and, at the same time, it had to draw as close as possible to England. This latter task was undertaken by Gustave de Beaumont, friend of de Tocqueville and former deputy in the reign of Louis Philippe, who was sent to London in July, 1848, as French Ambassador. Of de Beaumont the *Morning Post* was to say on his departure in December, 1848, after the Presidential election. " . . . the French government . . . having established internal order, recognized how necessary it was to put external affairs in order and resolved to send to the English, with whom a good understanding is so necessary for the peace of the world, a representative who was outstanding both for his worth and his personal character."[1]

De Beaumont could, in reality, do little, since everyone knew that no firm decisions concerning France's foreign policy could be taken until the question of the Presidency was settled in the winter. But, in London, he stressed the policy of co-operation with England, and eschewed any idea that either Power might work without the other one. On 11th November, 1848, speaking in the Mansion House at the Lord Mayor's banquet, he said: "Neither in France nor in England do we any more have the idea that the prosperity of one of the two countries

can exist only at the expense of the other. On the contrary, we think
that the best guarantee of the happiness of one is the happiness of
both."[2]

In point of fact, there was little at the moment which could disrupt
Anglo-French relations, for the simple reason that the major Powers in
Central Europe were preoccupied with suppressing the outcome of the
various revolutionary movements of 1848. The only "national"
question, which became an "international" question, was the problem
of Austria's position in Italy and here Anglo-French policy was one of
joint mediation, as agreed on in August and September of 1848.[3]

The election of Louis Napoleon as President in December, 1848,
meant not only the recall of de Beaumont but also a more decisive turn
in French foreign policy. Some sort of line needed to be established in
order that the new President might emerge on the European stage and
declare himself. In any event, affairs in Italy had now reached a critical
point in a chain of events whose origins had pre-dated the February
revolution in France. In January, 1848, a revolt had begun in Sicily
against the Neapolitan government; the revolt was a curious mixture of
local patriotism, brigandage and mafiosi-type activities, based on the
operations of secret societies such as the Carbonari and the Camorra.
This revolt rapidly acquired the characteristics of a quasi-liberal
national movement, the success of which forced the King of the two
Sicilies, Ferdinand, to grant a constitution. Any hopes Ferdinand may
have entertained of Austrian intervention, as in 1820-21, under the
terms of the Treaty between the two countries, were thwarted by the
outbreak of the Austrian revolutionary movement in March. The uprising
in Vienna resulted in the removal of Metternich from the European
scene as well as from the Chancellorship of Austria, and the removal of
Metternich, unleashing the crisis in Austria, opened up the "Italian
Question."

Meanwhile in Italy it rained constitutions. The Grand-Duke of
Tuscany, the Pope, and the King of Piedmont all granted "liberal"
forms of government in their respective territories to their eager or
indifferent subjects. These events were not in themselves necessarily of
international significance, but the constitutional movement in the north
of Italy, that is in the Austrian-governed provinces of Lombardy and
Venetia, assumed the character of a movement of liberation from
foreign rule. This reached its culmination in March with the proclamation of a Venetian Republic under Daniel Manin. In Milan, the
capital of the Province of Lombardy, the Austrian forces under
Marshal Radetzky were driven out by the citizens, who then appealed

to Piedmont for assistance in driving out the Austrians from the entire province. Charles Albert, King of Piedmont, hesitated for four vital days before deciding to assist the Lombards, but by his decision to act on 23rd March, 1848, no matter how tardily, he immediately provoked an international crisis. Since Austrian possession of Lombardy and Venetia was part of the 1815 settlement, any change of status was of concern to the signatory Powers. Meanwhile the Piedmontese force became virtually a federal army when it was joined by contingents from Tuscany, Naples and the Papal States. As a body, this army was hampered by such divergent aims as the annexationist policy of Piedmont, the luke-warm participation of Tuscany and Naples, neither of whom desired a war against Austria, and the absurdity of the presence of a Papal army. The national movement was, therefore, making a very halting progress when Pope Pius IX, remembering who he was and what he must do, rolled down upon it the Rock of Peter and totally crushed it.

Early in his pontificate, Pius had been a reformer in the Papal States and his somewhat maverick pronouncement on the cause of Italian unity had led many to think that the Pope was not only a liberal, but also a nationalist. This, of course, he was not and could not be; but there was sufficient ambiguity in his attitude to encourage the "patriotic party" into thinking that they had found a champion in the Pope. Not until 29th April did the Holy Ghost enlighten Pius sufficiently to enable him to pronounce on this point, and what he said was fatal to the hopes of those who had looked to him for leadership, or at least a blessing on their endeavours. In a secret allocution, he announced that there could be no question of engaging in a war against the Austrians : "We ... are upon earth the vice-elect of Him that is the Author of Peace and the Lover of Charity and ... we reach to and embrace all kindreds, peoples and nations with equal solicitude of paternal affection." Pius denounced ". . . those who would have the Roman Pontiff to be the head and to preside over the formation of some sort of novel republic of the whole Italian people," and he went on to enjoin the people to "abide in close attachment to their respective sovereigns."[4]

The Pope's defection meant little in military terms, but in moral and political terms it was disastrous for the Italian cause. Without benefit of clergy, a marriage between the Italian states was even more unlikely, and in Lombardy, the rough wooing of the Piedmontese Party led to reaction among the partisans of unity who were not prepared to accept annexation of Italian territory by the House of Savoy. In any event, the long-term decisions in Italy would be made by Austria, unless she herself succumbed to revolution, and in that event there were the other Powers to reckon with. By July, 1848, Austria's collapse in Italy seemed unlikely, for the Piedmontese army was defeated at Cutozza and for the moment, the situation in Northern Italy was saved for Austria by the Armistice of Salasco.

Through all this period, French policy was that of mediation in conjunction with England, and in any event the view was that Charles Albert, as head of a sovereign state with an army at his command, had to abide by the consequences of his actions. Much more serious was the situation of the Pope, whose popularity in the Peninsula had now reached zero and whose own city was rapidly falling into anarchy.

In military terms the Pope was in no position to rescue himself from a real political crisis involving the use of force. It was, therefore, not surprising that on 14th August he appealed to France for help. Cavaignac, then head of the state, refused to intervene directly, not least because the Papal position was of keen interest to various political groupings in France, whose votes would be needed at election time. In this situation, the Pope had to shift for himself. His appointment of a Prime Minister, Count Rossi, in September, 1848, was an attempt to come to terms with the forces of turbulence in Rome. But it failed, for Rossi was assassinated and the Pope, besieged in his palace, was forced to accept a ministry composed of the Roman political group.

This situation made some sort of move by France inevitable. In November Pius fled to Gaeta and in view of this, Cavaignac, in spite of the impending presidential election, dared not avoid action to help the Pontiff. It was proposed to send three ships and three thousand men to the port of Civita Vecchia to protect Pius IX. In the vote on this in the French Chamber, Louis Napoleon abstained and, when attacked for his abstention, defended it on the grounds that: "Although resolved to support all measures really calculated to guarantee the liberty and authority of the Sovereign Pontiff, I could not give the approval of my vote to a military demonstration which seemed to me a danger even to the sacred interests it was intended to defend, as well as a menace to the peace of Europe."[5]

Although speaking of Europe in general, Louis Napoleon had undoubtedly noted the distaste felt by England in particular for the intervention of French troops—though it had no objection to French ships. The British Ambassador in Paris, Lord Normanby, pointed out that such action might lead to a general extension of the conflict and that Austria might respond as to a challenge. Lord Palmerston said the same thing to the French Ambassador in London.[6] It was clear that the situation might, therefore, lead to an estrangement between France and Britain. Whoever else was prepared to risk that, Louis Napoleon was not.

In effect, it was only after his election to the presidency that the two moves in January and March, 1849, were made which affected France's foreign relations. Significantly, they involved direct proposals to England. Firstly, Louis Napoleon suggested a limitation of naval armaments between Britain and France, and secondly a congress of the major Powers to settle outstanding questions which might disturb the general peace of Europe. In making this latter proposal Louis Napoleon, while putting forward a scheme which was a fundamental part and parcel of his political baggage, may well have been trying to solve the question of the Papacy multilaterally. Presumably the French scheme envisaged a reconsideration of the 1815 settlement. The answer cannot be given to this speculation, since Lord Palmerston refused to entertain either proposal. Mindful of how useful the "Waterloo coalition" had been in 1840-41, Palmerston was not inclined to throw away a diplomatic advantage.[7] So, Louis Napoleon had to soldier on —and it was evident that soon this would be more than a figure of speech.

In February, 1849, the Pope had appealed to the Catholic powers to restore him to his territories. Could France remain inactive if, as seemed likely, Austria were to join Spain and Naples in their expedition to save the Pope? There were two reasons why she should not. Firstly, it would be an affront to the national dignity if France remained aloof. Secondly, a restoration by an alliance of Austria, Spain and Naples could only be politically reactionary, not only in the sense that it was a reaffirmation of the 1815 order, but also in the sense that there would be no Liberal party left in the Papal States if Pius were beholden to this group for his restoration. Could France accept such a situation?

The answer was that some in France could. The Legitimists upheld the Hapsburg-Bourbon intervention and so did many of the "Republicans". Because of what it implied, they were no more for Liberalism in the Papal States than they were for it in France. In these circumstances, Louis Napoleon might have got away with non-intervention without damaging himself. But the whole situation was altered in March, 1849, by the folly of Charles Albert of Piedmont, who broke the Armistice of Salasco and attacked Austria. Having been unable to defeat Austria when she was weakened in 1848, it was highly unlikely

that Piedmont, could defeat her in 1849 when she was in a much
stronger position. So it fell out. In four days it was all over, and the
Piedmontese had been routed at the battle of Novara.

Now the position in the Peninsula had been entirely altered, for
Austria was mistress of the situation. It was clear that she would exact a
high price for all her troubles, and not just in the matter of the Papal
restoration but in Italy as a whole. Austrian control of Italian affairs,
implicit since 1815, would now be made explicit: the Hapsburg
Empire would hardly allow any renewal of the revolutionary situation
which might encourage the annexationist aims of Piedmont in Northern
Italy.

As for the Piedmontese Kingdom, its very survival appeared to be
threatened, though it was unlikely that Austria would actually dismember a state which owed its present frontiers to the 1815 treaties. Any
attempt so to do would have involved Britain and, in the present
circumstances, must also involve France. It was precisely this point
which forced Louis Napoleon's hand. He had previously warned
Charles Albert that if he renewed the war he must not count on French
support. The totality of the Piedmontese defeat did, however, alarm
Louis Napoleon to such an extent that, if Thiers is to be believed, he
was prepared to go to war. Thiers, never one for underplaying his role
in international affairs, claimed to have averted this as a result of a
conversation between himself and the Austrian Ambassador in Paris,
Baron Hübner.[8]

In fact, Piedmont herself was taking steps to avoid any further
conflict and, in the final reckoning, little was owed to France or to any
other powers in the settlement which emerged. Since Charles Albert
had abdicated after the defeat at Novara, the agreement was a simple
arrangement between the new King, Victor Emmanuel, and the
Austrians. Austrian moderation towards Piedmont, based undoubtedly
on the fact of that state's international position, led her to agree to the
maintenance of her territory and even to the existence of the famous
Statuto, the Constitution granted by Charles Albert. In return, Victor
Emmanuel agreed to crush the Republican and Annexationist majority
in the Piedmontese parliament. Since these revolutionary groups were
inclined to be anti-dynastic, the King was only too willing to suppress
them, but it was put about that he had saved his country's independence and its constitution in the teeth of Austrian pressure, and thus he
acquired, quite fallaciously, the reputation of a "liberal" sovereign.[9] So
successful was this reputation that it influenced the whole course of
future development in Italy after 1850 when Piedmont was held to be a

liberal and progressive state and an example to the rest of the Peninsula. This myth was also propagated by pro-unificationist historians who justified much of the subsequent highly dubious practice of Piedmont in achieving her aims, by pointing out that she was a constitutional kingdom, and by implication, enlightened.[10]

Whatever the case of Piedmont, the facts of Austria's advance in the rest of Italy were plain to see. By April the Grand-Duke Leopold was reinstated in Florence. In the same month, Ferdinand of Naples had subdued Sicily and turned his attention to the mainland. Here, Austrian forces were now advancing south towards the Papal States, and had already reached Ancona and Bologna. In these circumstances, Louis Napoleon acted. On 21st April, 1849, a French force of some 7,000 under Marshal Oudinot landed at Civita Vecchia, the outpost for Rome. Oudinot was a man totally lacking in political sense, and he now demonstrated that he was also without military talent. On 30th April, without waiting for instructions and, even worse, without reckoning the forces opposed to him, he attacked and was defeated outside Rome by Garibaldi's volunteer forces.[11]

Oudinot's appointment had been made by the French cabinet rather than the French President, but in defeat no one should have chopped logic about who had or had not sent Oudinot. Unfortunately, that was precisely what happened, for Oudinot had been foolish enough to proclaim his intention of restoring the Pope, without any mention of terms or conditions. Now the opposition in the French Chamber clamoured that he had been sent to keep out the Austrians and not restore Pius. At that moment, it was a singularly unfruitful point to debate, but this was not the view of those with an eye on the May elections in France.

Louis Napoleon, mindful of Europe, kept his eye on the Austrians and their advance towards Naples. The French defeat could only encourage them to move faster in order to achieve a solution of the Papal problem before the arrival of the reinforcements promised to Oudinot by the President in his letter of 9th May. Reinforced, the French army did attack again in July, and this time took Rome.

The Pope was now determined to reassert his authority in his dominions and hot on the heels of the French army arrived, not the Pontiff himself, but three Cardinals, "The Red Triumvirates," as they were mockingly called. Their reactionary attitude was such that Louis Napoleon felt constrained publicly to put forward France's aims in intervening.

The French Republic did not send an army to Rome to stifle Italian liberty there, but, on the contrary, to regulate it by preserving it against its own excesses and to give it a valid foundation by restoring to the Pontifical Throne the prince who was the first to place himself boldly at the head of every useful reform ... I understand, by the temporal power of the Pope the following : a general amnesty, the secularization of the administration, and liberal government ... when our armies made the tour of Europe, they left everywhere, as a mark of their passing, the destruction of feudal abuses and the seeds of liberty. It shall not be said that in 1849 a French army could act in any other way and with other results.[12]

On 4th September Pius IX, who was not to return to Rome until 1850, issued a *motu proprio* announcing an amnesty. Although the document was hedged about by qualifications, which probably reflected the advice of Cardinal Antonelli, there was nevertheless a substance of reform contained within it. Such anyhow, was the opinion of de Beaumont, now French Ambassador at Vienna. To him it "contained three principal points about which one would be wrong, in my opinion, to dispute their liberal worth." He instanced the municipal organizations, the provincial organizations, and the consultative body which were established by the decree. But, at the same time, de Beaumont echoed Louis Napoleon by deploring the absence of a general amnesty and the lack of secularization in the administration.[13]

The real thorn in the flesh was that the Papal attitude reflected the triumph of the pro-Austrian faction at Rome. Louis Napoleon had saved the Pope, the Pope had said "thank you" to Franz-Josef. At Vienna, Schwarzenburg the Austrian Chancellor assured the French Ambassador that the failings of the Papal government were as well known in Austria as in France. But the Prince pointed out that it was the continued presence of the French army which prevented the Pope returning to his city and thus precluded the putting in hand of any changes or reforms.

The point was neatly put, but for Louis Napoleon the position in Rome was complicated because he could not find an ally with whom he could work. England would not move to support France in that area. Educated English opinion found the Papacy distasteful, while the bulk of the country associated it with Guy Fawkes; and there was just at that time, an outburst of "no-popery" sentiments culminating in the Ecclesiastical Titles Bill of the following year. It was clear that if this aspect of his Italian policy was essentially an expression of Louis

Napoleon's personal will inside France, it was unfortunately no less so in a European context. Only in Piedmont could Louis Napoleon count on England's support and that was limited to continued mediation *vis-à-vis* Austria. For example, both France and Britain protested about Austria's treatment of the political prisoners who had been taken during the Italian uprising. The same subject brought the two Powers together in a common grouse against Tsar Nicholas of Russia who threatened the Sultan of Turkey because he would not hand over Kossuth and other Hungarian revolutionaries who had taken refuge in the Ottoman Empire.

Since this firm line of opposition to Austria and Russia is usually attributed to Lord Palmerston's initiative, the dispatches of the French Ambassador in Vienna are worth noting. De Beaumont wrote to his Foreign Minister on several occasions that, although the two Powers were in agreement, the English Ambassador, Ponsonby, was seen in Vienna as following the policy of France. He reported Schwarzenberg as saying that if any concessions were to be made by Russia and Austria "... it is to France they must be made."[14] As de Tocqueville had warned de Beaumont that Palmerston was Schwarzenberg's *bête noire,* it perhaps is not surprising that this was so. Louis Napoleon now made a further bid for a diplomatic arrangement favourable to France. Relying on Austro-Prussian rivalry in Germany, where King Frederick William was attempting to form a confederation allied to Prussia, the President dispatched Persigny with a view to procuring a Franco-Prussian-English agreement. In the long run, this type of diplomatic reshuffle was unlikely to succeed because Prussian possession of her part of Poland, a possession reinforced by the Pan-German sentiments revealed in the debates at Frankfurt in 1848, depended on strict co-operation with Russia. Prussia would not, therefore, risk a quarrel with Nicholas I by making some will-o'-the-wisp agreement with France and Britain. It was true that joint Anglo-French pressure had caused Nicholas to withdraw his forces from the principalities of Moldavia and Wallachia, and that the Tsar was vexed by this. But the estrangement was likely to be only momentary and Prussia would have been foolish to base any important policy moves on such a situation.

Since these were early days in France's new diplomatic offensive, the failure of this particular hare to start was not in itself very serious. Much more serious from Louis Napoleon's point of view was the *malentendu* with England which came about over the Don Pacifico affair in the spring and summer of 1850. In this instance, Palmerstonian bellicosity had led Britain to take up the claims for damages against the Greek government made by Don Pacifico, a Portuguese Jew born in Gibraltar and technically, therefore, a British subject. In face of Greek hostility to the British demands, a crisis arose which led to Louis Napoleon offering mediation with Greece on the grounds of the Convention of London of 1832, made by Britain, France and Russia. This might have gone well had not Admiral Parker, Commander of the English naval squadron blockading Piraeus, decided to pursue a little gun boat diplomacy of his own and refuse to accept the word of the local French agent about the acceptance of mediation by both governments.

Parker's hostile action led to the President's withdrawing the French Ambassador from London, thus showing his own countrymen that there were limits to his desire for co-operation with England, and that his second name was Napoleon and not Philippe. The action had some effect on Palmerston who, in spite of his exculpatory *civis Romanus sum* speech in the House of Commons, did accept mediation; Don Pacifico's extravagant claim for damages was much reduced in size. In consequence, France's ambassador was restored to London and in November, 1850, Louis Napoleon had the satisfaction of seeing England accept his offer to mount a joint Anglo-French naval force to be sent to Cuba in support of Spanish influence there, against freeboot-ing attacks from the United States.

Thus, at the end of two years of power as President, Louis Napoleon could derive some satisfaction from his conduct of foreign affairs for France was now a power to be reckoned with in the affairs of Europe. Two further things had emerged. Firstly, it was clear from the number of foreign ministers who flitted in and out of the Quai d'Orsay (eight in two years) that the foreign policy was the President's. Most of these foreign ministers, with the exception of de Tocqueville and Drouyn de Lhuys, had been of no substance, and all of them had been quite clearly informed by the President of his intentions and wishes in the conduct of foreign affairs. Secondly, although the English alliance was clearly the cornerstone of French foreign policy, it had been made plain that there were limits to Louis Napoleon's desire to please, as the Don Pacifico affair had shown.

It is true that much of France's activity had been made possible partly by the disarray of Austria and Prussia, both preoccupied by German, or Italian and Hungarian affairs. But it had been made possible, too, by the attitude of Nicholas I. The Tsar had reputedly reacted to the proclamation of the Republic in February, 1848, by interrupting a Court ball in St. Petersburg with the words: "Saddle your horses, gentlemen, the Republic is proclaimed in Paris", but he showed no hostility to Louis Napoleon. In effect, Nicholas regarded the election of the Prince as merely an underlining of the fact that France had taken a conservative turn—"*il n'y a de république que le nom*" —and made it clear that he regarded the continuance of the Republic with a benevolent eye. This attitude was extended even to the *coup d'état* of 1851 when he wrote: "As a soldier I am personally proud to see established in France a stable regime, the enemy of revolutionary movements which have brought so much disturbance to Europe."[15] But, at the same time, he had warned the French Ambassador, "*Gardez-vous de l'Empire*," an indication that Nicholas would consider such a re-establishment as a breach of the 1815 settlement whereas the setting up of a Republican regime, especially since it was conservative in outlook, was for him a purely domestic matter.

When the *coup d'état* came in December, it was accepted by all of Europe with alacrity, a fact which says a great deal for the success of Louis Napoleon's foreign policy. By a bizarre twist, the one country in which it had serious repercussions was Britain, for Palmerston's swift recognition of the new order brought about his dismissal from the ministry of Lord John Russell. It was unfortunate that Palmerston had left himself open to condemnation at a time when Russell was being subjected to considerable pressure by the Court and the press to remove him. Both groups had been clamouring against his "pro-revolutionary" policies since 1848, such as the reception of Kossuth in 1849, and the comments made about the Austrian General Haynau in 1850 when he was mobbed while visiting a London brewery. Perhaps in the short run Palmerston's removal did Louis Napoleon a service, for England's foreign policy fell for a time into the care of Lord Malmesbury, who was a personal friend of the Prince and with whom he maintained close relations. At a time when much of English political opinion was hostile to France, Malmesbury's tenure of office, though only one year in terms of time, may have helped the President's European position by showing at least at governmental level an England which was friendly.

As France in 1852 moved inexorably towards the restoration of the Empire, Louis Napoleon was careful to keep an eye on possible European reactions. The famous Bordeaux speech from which it was clear that proclamation of the Empire was virtually inevitable was made for Europe, since by the winter of 1852, virtually all of France had already accepted the Empire *sans conditions*. When the President announced, "*L'Empire, c'est la paix*," it was to reassure those European nations who saw in the resumption of the Imperial title a possible resumption of the Imperial aims. The sharpest reaction to the Bordeaux speech came from Nicholas I, whose words about the restoration of the Empire had not been spoken lightly. When, in spite of his warnings, the Empire was proclaimed, Nicholas immediately tried to revive the coalition of Austria, Prussia and Russia. When this failed he manifested his own displeasure by refusing recognition of the new sovereign until 1853. Even then the normal diplomatic exchanges were avoided, for the Tsar refused to treat Napoleon III as "brother" but only as "good friend." The Letters of Credence were addressed to "*Très sérénissime, très excellent et très puissant Prince, notre cher ami, Napoleon, Empereur des Français.*" By a skilful piece of chancery drafting, the new Emperor had no numeral after his name for the Tsar wanted to avoid any impression of continuity or legitimacy in the Bonapartist dynasty. In St. Petersburg the reign of Napoleon II had passed unnoticed, though the Tsar could well have argued that its brevity was an excuse for the omission. Napoleon III is reported to have said, on receiving the Letters of Credence, that ' one chooses one's friends, one accept one's brothers."

Elsewhere the Empire was accepted with better grace. Short of launching a general European war against France it is hard to see how it could have been prevented, and it would have been difficult to find a cause for attacking a new Emperor whose avowed policy was one of peace. It remained to be seen, of course, what exactly Napoleon III had meant by his words, and how "peace" would be defined in the political as opposed to the etymological sense.

7

Political Order and Political Liberty

*"Je ne ferais pas comme les gouvernements
qui m'ont précédé, et je ne vous dirai pas:
Marchez, je vous suis; mas je vous dirai: Je
marche, suivez moi!"*

Louis Napoleon Bonaparte,
9th November, 1851

"**M**ORE than seven million votes have just absolved me by justifying an act which had no other aim than to spare our country, and perhaps Europe from years of trouble and misfortune." In these words Louis Napoleon addressed the Consultative Commission which had been established to organize the plebiscite of December, 1851, in which the people had been asked to show their acceptance, or rejection, of the Prince President's *coup d'état*. Fortified by the results on this the last day of the year, the Prince gave further indications of his hopes: "... to assure the destiny of France by founding institutions which will simultaneously fulfil the needs of the nation; its democratic instincts and its desire, universally expressed, to have from henceforth an Authority strong and respected."[1] At this point the Prince felt shriven and free from political sin, for the prophesies had been fulfilled, and baptism by universal suffrage had given him the result which he had expected. Now that the dreams of the *Rêveries Politiques* and the *Idées Napoléoniennes* had come true, they must be given practical expression. Bonapartism was no longer to be an affair of sentiment, of pictures and busts sold in the shops, or of histories of the "Great Man." The time had come to make of it the mainspring of the institutional machinery of France.

This was not difficult, for much of France, legally and administratively, was as Napoleon I had left it. The new constitution issued on January 14th, 1852, was virtually that of the Consulate in the Year VIII. Only at the centre were structural changes needed. The administration remained as it had been, involving merely a replacement of the personnel, and that only in cases where the incumbents would not accept the *coup d'état*. The Civil Code was again styled the *Code Napoléon* and it continued to function as it had before and after 1815.

Louis Napoleon never sought to make a mystery of the constitution which was promulgated in 1852 :

> I have taken as a model the political institutions which have, since the beginning of the century, and in similar circumstances, consolidated a society which had been upset (*ébranlée*) and which raised France to a high degree of prosperity and greatness. I have taken as a model those institutions which, instead of disappearing with the first breath of popular unrest, had only been overthrown by a coalition of the whole of Europe against us. In a word, I said to myself : since, for fifty years, France has only gone on because of the administrative, judicial, religious and financial organization of the Consulate and the Empire, why should we not also adopt the political institutions of the period?

At the centre, the new governmental structure revolved around the President, who was now to hold office for ten years. His powers were extensive, ranging from the right to declare war and make peace and treaties, to the right to clemency. The ministries were dependent on him for their office and the laws depended on him for their maintenance, their initiation, their sanction, and their promulgation. The only limit to his authority lay in Article 5 of the Constitution which declared : "The President of the Republic is responsible for the French people." In this way, the fact of universal suffrage was integrated into the constitutional structure.

The legislature was divided into two houses, the Senate and the *Corps Législatif*. The latter, although chosen by universal suffrage, was totally dependent on the President : he could call, prorogue and dissolve it at will. Its official term was six years, and its members, who numbered 261, were elected by direct suffrage—35,000 electors to one representative. To make certain that the representatives built up no local vested interest which might clash with the intentions of the central administration, the government had the right to alter electoral boundaries as and when it thought fit, ostensibly to keep in step with population changes.

The *Corps Législatif* to which the deputies came was not an exciting parliamentary arena, but neither was it a mere processing plant for governmental artefacts. It did have the right of voting the budget and it could suggest amendments to the laws proposed for its consideration.

There was more work than glamour attached to membership, for there were no newspaper reports of breathtaking parliamentary exchanges or brilliant verbal duels, but then these are not necessarily the attributes of an efficient legislative body.

As to the Senate, it was limited to 150, selected by the President on a basis of "... men who, either by reason of their name or their position, their talent, or the brilliance of their services, recommended themselves [to the President]." Apart from this group, Cardinals, Marshals of France, and Admirals sat as of right. The Senate was not meant to be a refuge for the privileged, but a repository of skill and intelligence. Initially its members were unpaid, but eventually it carried a sum of thirty thousand francs as reward for nomination. Interestingly enough, the Senate was the only *constitutional* check on the President, for it could neither be dissolved nor suppressed—though it could be prorogued. Its existence was more than a mere symbol of an upper house, for it could even put forward bases for legislation "in the national interest." It was, furthermore, a body possessing constituent powers, since it could make decisions as well as laws and could modify the constitutional laws by issuing *Senatus consulta*.

In this type of institution much, of course, depended upon the character of its personnel, and neither by inclination nor by age were the senators a revolutionary cohort. On the other hand, they were not a collection of reactionary dead-heads and their record over the twenty years until 1870 was to be a reasonable, if not outstanding, one. However, both the *Corps Législatif* and the Senate were essentially consultative bodies, for the real power house of government lay in the *Conseil d'État*, where the work was done. The President was himself the President of the *Conseil*, thereby linking it directly to the Executive Power, and at the same time ensuring his personal supervision of what was done in his name. After the proclamation of the Empire in November, 1852, when it became no longer possible for Louis Napoleon to be President of the Council, he continued, as Emperor, to work with it as the main organ of government.

Since the *Conseil d'État* was responsible for preparing all legislative measures, for "the rules concerning public administration, and the resolving of difficulties which may arise in administrative matters," it was a day to day affair, and its control of the budget and financial measures gave it charge of the economic policy and commercial development. The *Conseil* had forty members, mixed in political origin, and ranging from liberal monarchists to "hard liners" of the Party of Order who had rallied to the Prince. One of the latter kind was

Baroche, who had accepted the office of *Procureur Général* in Paris in
1849 and who now became first Vice-President, and then President, of
the Council from 1852-63. Under him, the various committees of which
the Council was composed, for it was divided into sections correspond-
ing to the major departments of government, had a varied and
politically wide-ranging membership. As one member put it : "Although
all the Councillors accepted the Imperial regime without reservations,
the number of men blindly devoted to the sovereign, or convinced of his
infallibility . . . was few."[2] This said, it should be noted that each
section head was a man of proven fidelity, for the Government never
took too much on trust. Considering that much of the personnel of
administration, particularly in the judicature, remained Orleanist, it is
not surprising that most key positions went to convinced supporters of
the new regime, even though, as in the case of Baroche, they supported
Louis Napoleon as a guarantor of social order rather than from
devotion to Bonapartism.

This problem of selecting personnel presented itself in a much more
difficult form when it came to the question of election to the new
Corps Législatif. Who would be found suitable as a candidate? To
what sections of society would the regime address itself? The answer to
both questions was clearly indicated by Louis Napoleon's determination
to reward those who had elected him (for him this meant "the people")
by demonstrating his care for their necessities. This was the motive
which lay behind the decrees of 22nd January, 1852, confiscating part
of the domains of the former Royal House. Louis Philippe had, by a
shady financial transaction in 1830, managed to avoid surrendering his
private property to the State as French law required of a new sovereign.
Louis Napoleon now sequestrated this portion of the Orleanist fortune
amounting to some 300,000,000 francs.

The wits punned on *Le Premier vol de l'aigle*—but what was
interesting was the direction of the eagle's flight, or the disposal of the
stolen goods, whichever way one wished to look at it. Of the money
10,000,000 francs went to mutual benefit societies, 10,000,000 for the
construction of workers dwellings in industrial towns, and 5,000,00
towards a new pension fund for the most needy of France's aged. In
case the effect on the forthcoming elections should not be widespread
enough, 1,000,000 was to be given to any Department which wished
to set up a branch of the *Crédit Foncier*. The decrees did not send the
Orléans princes to beg in the streets; they still had 100,000,000 francs'
worth of property, and both the Duchess of Orléans and Louis

Philippe's widow continued to draw 300,000 francs per year from the French government.

The sharpest reaction to the decree came from *notables* who wondered if their new gamekeeper had turned poacher. Louis Napoleon had certainly sent the birds up from cover, for in the ensuing battle over the decrees it was clear who was, and who was not, hoping to use the new regime as a continuation of the Orléans system in a modified form. Four of the ministers resigned : Fould, Rouher, Magne and Morny, the President's half-brother. It is true that two, Magne and Rouher, did subsequently accept posts in the *Conseil d'État,* and significant that neither of these two had been highlights of the Orleanist regime. But advantage was taken of the four ministerial vacancies which were filled by men who formed the hard core of the Prince's supporters. Persigny and Maupas, two of the prime figures in the *coup d'état,* plus Abbatuci and Casabianca, two Corsicans whose devotion to Louis Napoleon was unshakeable, were now elevated to first rank ministerial positions. It was thought to be important that while the elections were being held the men who controlled them at the centre should be absolutely reliable. However, this was not enough in itself : the problem of finding candidates for the *Corps Législatif* still remained. Even if the "official candidates" could be sure of the votes of those who had waited for their revenge on "the great ones" who were now being humbled, or at least brought to heel, by the President, this did not guarantee total success. The peasantry remained always the most loyal and stable group until 1870, for to them, a vote for the official candidate was less a sign of dependence on the Imperial regime than of independence from the local squirearchy or the priest. The element of radicalism in this type of voting should not be underestimated, but the government's problem was to find candidates as radical as their electors.[3]

It was all very well for Persigny, as Minister of the Interior, to launch encouraging instructions to the Prefects adjuring them to : "Appeal to the sentiments of the people. It is the masses who make elections today and not the old influences." The Prefects might well reply that the masses were not candidates. Persigny himself was frequently compelled to accept second best for lack of alternative.

There was no Bonapartist organization as such in the Departments. The "Societies of 10th December" had been dissolved, and so an *ad hoc* party organization had to be created in a hurry. For reasons already indicated, no party organization was set up on a permanent basis, and in 1871, after twenty years of the regime, it was as conspicuous by its absence as it had been at the beginning.[4] The

President would not permit party, for it was the antithesis of what Bonapartism meant to him. It would only lead back to the discredited parliamentarianism of 1815 to 1848, which was in any event incompatible with universal suffrage. It was accepted that at election time each *Préfecture* should become a "committee room" for the official candidate. But it was as firmly rejected that there should exist a permanent party caucus or clique continually working over the electorate and creating their own vested interests at a local level. In these circumstances the Prefects became the key figures. Much had to be left to their discretion and the government, even if reluctantly, had to accept this situation.[5]

By doing this the government hoped to steer a middle course between the Orleanists and Legitimist *Notables*, and the petit-bourgeois flotsam who made up the 10th December Societies.[6] In theory this middle course was possible but in fact, the government had to rely fairly heavily on the *Notables*, since they had the education and the capacity for the work of administration. Since the Deputies were not paid, and since no civil servants were eligible for election, it needed a rich man to take up the burden of legislator.[7] The meek would need training and discipline if they were to inherit the earth, or, as one Prefect put it in 1852, "to be able to go into society."

Twenty-ninth March saw the opening session of the first *Corps Législatif*, which, it has been too often and too easily assumed, was a collection of mediocrities who had wriggled through the net of the Prefects. To think this way is to neglect the possibilities which were open to candidates to present themselves to the electorate in opposition to the regime. The presence of the "official candidates" with government backing did not preclude anyone else from standing in that electoral district. In these circumstances it is not surprising that the members elected to the *Corps Législatif* showed considerable diversity. Although 70 of the 261 deputies were Bonapartists, less than half of these were the "mamelukes," as the opposition christened the die-hard supporters of the new régime. An equal number of emmbers were "oppositionists" in the sense that they came from Orleanist or Legitimist backgrounds.[8] Of the five Republicans elected three of these, Cavaignac, Carnot and Héron, refused the oath and were unseated. The bulk of the *Corps Législatif* were "situationists"; they were the sort of men who were found under any representational system. Their presence in the first Assembly of Louis Napoleon is no more or no less a slur on the nature of that body than is the presence of a substantial group of passengers in the English House of Commons today. It has been said of this first

Corps Législatif, which lasted until 1857, that its members were "At bottom very easy to manoeuvre, on condition that one respected and flattered them, that above all one had the art of persuading every one of them that they were the object of particular attention . . . it [the Chamber] was a docile instrument—very docile even, on condition one led it with skill and did not over-abuse it."[9]

In fact, in the first five years of its existence the *Corps Législatif* avoided a violent conflict with the executive, though frequently it demanded to be taken seriously. The real problem was what *was* it to do? It was required merely to sanction the "Projects of Law" which emanated from the Council of State and although discussion was permitted, it was rather in the form of a medieval disputation than an open-ended debate. As the Constitution put it: "Since the ministers do not participate in the Chambers, and since the Projects of Law are upheld by speakers in the Council of State, time is not wasted in silly questions, frivolous accusations and inflamed struggles whose only end is to throw down the ministers in order to replace them."[10] The short answer, therefore, to the question "what did the Legislative body do?" was that it legislated, no more, no less.[11] But it was never reconciled to the role of a mere rubber stamp and its very existence presupposed development of some kind as it acquired experience and grew in capacity.

The first President of the Chamber was Billault, a man who like Baroche, had moved from the Orleanist opposition to the conservative Bonapartist ranks. The Duc de Morny, his successor in 1854, who was to continue in the office until his death, was an unrepentant but pragmatic Orleanist whose world revolved round the Bourse and the Jockey Club. Neither man was liable to run foul of the *Corps Législatif,* for neither was liable to push views abhorrent to the mass of the Deputies. Both were liable to maintain an equilibrium in the House, largely due to the fact that little change occurred in its composition even after the elections in 1857, and also because Morny, with great skill, always identified himself as "a man of the *Corps Législatif,*" not just its President.

In the most important Constitutional event of 1852, the official re-establishment of the Empire on 1st December, both the request to Louis Napoleon to assume the title and the decree establishing the Empire were the work of the Senate alone. The *Corps Législatif* was not involved until all was over and it was a question of counting the votes which had been cast in the plebiscite. The answer to the questions put by Louis Napoleon's *voyage d'interrogation* of the autumn of 1852 was clear: 7,824,000 voted "yes," 253,000 voted "no." It is true that two million answered not at all, but in spite of the number of abstentions the result was a triumph. Even more so if one considers that most of the abstentions came from the Royalist Departments where the diehard monarchists could not accept the Empire though they were glad to accept the political stability and social order Louis Napoleon had brought. The new Emperor, in his address to the Chambers and the State Councillors on the evening of 1st December at Saint Cloud, made his dynastic position clear: "My reign does not date from 1815, it dates from the moment when you made known to me the nation's wishes. . . . Help me, gentlemen, to found a stable government which has for its basis religion, honest dealing, justice, and the love of the suffering classes."[12]

In fact, the re-establishment of the Empire was marked by several significant moves on the part of Napoleon III which involved him in difficulties with the legislative power. The question of the succession caused problems because Prince Napoleon, the Emperor's cousin and heir-apparent, was intensely disliked not only for his radical anti-clericalism but for his personal bad manners and lack of common-sense. The Senate Committee objected strongly to his nomination as heir to the Emperor and so the succession was simply to be: "in the Bonaparte family," but at the Emperor's discretion. If this formula was merely evolved in a desire to save the face of the Senate, since everyone knew it must still mean Prince Napoleon, it served also as a means of slapping the faces of the legitimist Catholics, who had hoped to avoid the anti-clerical heir altogether, believing that Napoleon III was fundamentally as Catholic as themselves and would dance to their tune. And there was yet another aspect to the succession settlement, for like Charles II and his brother James, who would pull down Napoleon III to make Prince Napoleon Emperor in his place?

Yet another conservative group received a knock when articles of the Constitution expressly reserved to the Emperor the right to make commercial treaties and the right to authorize public works without reference to the Chambers. Combined with the decree which laid down that the budget be voted by Ministries and not by items, the supreme control of finance and trade was now in Imperial hands. Significantly, these decrees were drawn up by three of the "new men" of the reign: Rouher, Baroche and Delangle, whose plans for the future of French industry and commerce were not shared by the conservative agricultural and protectionist groups.[13]

What was clear to all was that for the first time since 1815, with the exception perhaps of the Ministry of Villèle in the period of the

Restoration, there was power at the centre of French affairs and the will to use it. That this *was* recognized by contemporaries (even if latter-day historians have often been reluctant to concede it) is evidenced by the reaction of the Senate and the *Corps Législatif* to the new decrees. The Senate demanded a share in controlling commercial treaties: "The Senate would not wish to intervene to protect this or that industry, but property in general," and as far as the budgetary decrees were concerned there were objections to the government's "blanket-budget" proposals. But the protests were of no avail. The Emperor's attitude was revealed in the appointment of Baroche, as President of the *Conseil d'État* where he was to remain until 1860, precisely because he had defended the Government's proposals. Other key posts were held by Rouher, Delangle, Fould the banker and, as Minister of Public Works, Michel Chevalier, one of the leading Saint-Simonians. None of these men were easily intimidated by the criticisms of the Senate nor were the restless movements of the *Corps Législatif* likely to throw them off course.

It is true that time and experience led first to *a modus vivendi* and then to changes. But there was no hint of this in the first years of the *Empire Autoritaire*. Indeed, the Senate's only triumph in affairs of state in 1852 was to persuade the Emperor to marry on the grounds that: "Since the Empire was established with regard to the future it should carry with it all the legitimate effects which will preserve this future from uncertainties and shocks."[14]

Even here the sovereign's independence was demonstrated, for the choice of wife was his own. On 22nd January, 1853, the Emperor announced his decision to marry Eugénie de Montijo, of non-royal though of noble blood: "I have," he said, "preferred a woman whom I love and respect to an unknown woman with whom an alliance would have had advantages mingled with sacrifices." The logic was a little muddled in that Eugénie could just as well demand sacrifices as any other woman, but at least it was a marriage and not a dynastic alliance. It has been said more than once that Eugénie was only a "second-best," the result of Napoleon III's failure to win a royal princess. It has equally been said that only the *parvenue* was fit for the *parvenu*. As for the first point, Napoleon's courtship of Eugénie had begun when he was still President and was well advanced at the time his ministers were tentatively sounding out royal courts. An acceptance from one of them would not at all have suited the Emperor.[15] As to the second criticism, it may be said that this type of vulgar snobbery usually misses the point.

To *parvenir* is no disgrace at any time; during the Second Empire it was a distinction, as it should be in any democratic society.

The celebrations for the marriage were lavish. The real *fêtes Impériales* had begun, and included balls for the Emperor and Empress given first by the Senate and then by the *Corps Législatif*. Cynics noted that the Speaker's rostrum in the Chamber, removed since 1851, was on that occasion replaced by an orchestra and the Parisian wags made great sport of it. The joke was understandable, but it was based on a misconception, for the simple reason that the Chambers were never a nullity between 1852 and 1860, the period usually known as the "Authoritarian Empire." It is true that the sparkle had gone out of debates, but as Baroche told Hübner, the Austrian Ambassador, in 1857: "...it may be less brilliant than the Chamber of Deputies (1830-48), but it has done more and better for the affairs of the country than that body did."[16]

It should not be imagined that the Chamber considered its work was done by nodding its head at the request of the *Conseil d'État* or the Emperor. During the period when Billault was President, the discussion of the budget in the session of 1853 gave an opportunity for the opposition deputies to attack the government and manifest their displeasure at the extent to which they were restricted in the free expression of their opinion. As it was, the budget of that year was subjected to eighty-two amendments and at the request of the Chamber, a reduction in the projected expenses for that year had to be agreed by the Council of State. Again in 1854, despite an agreement by the *Corps Législatif* to accept the floating of a loan for 250 million francs, necessitated by the Near Eastern crisis, the budget proper again produced a clash between Deputies and the Ministers.

Had all this been of no importance, the government would not have taken the trouble to appoint as President of the *Corps Législatif* the Duc de Morny. Morny, half-brother of the Emperor, and descended through several quarterings of bastardy from both Louis XV and Talleyrand, was one of the ablest men the Second Empire produced.[17] That he held the office of President of the Chamber from 1854 to 1856, and again from 1857 to 1861, is an indication of the importance which the Emperor attached to the post. Morny's qualifications for office were, like those of his sovereign, unorthodox, but were based on a greater experience of French political life. His Orleanist background, plus his financial and political connections, linked him not merely to the public life of the legislature, but also to the backstairs intrigues of the Bourse and the boardroom. He combined knowledge of the world with a quick grasp of men and their motives and this, allied to a judgement which was singularly unclouded by any application of principle, made him well suited to political manoeuvre. In the case of those whose actions were clearly motivated by self-interest, he was shrewd enough always to attribute their designs to the strength of their convictions. Added to this, Morny was also capable of playing the part of *grand seigneur,* and often in the day-to-day business of the *Corps Législatif* his mocking half-smile from the Presidential Chair in the Chamber reduced many would-be impassioned speakers to a faltering silence.

Frequently his talents were needed, for as has been pointed out, the *Corps Législatif* gave battle when it could. Not only were the budgets of 1853, 1854 and 1855 the subjects of sharp debates as to the manner of their presentation, but in 1856 the Chamber actually acquired some measure of control over the question of supplementary budgetary claims. It was generally over monetary and tariff questions that the government experienced the most difficulty and was subjected to the sharpest attacks. In 1856, a year notable also for the temporary absence of Morny as Ambassador-Extraordinary to St. Petersburg, the *Conseil d'État* suffered a virtual defeat over one of its major projects. Various tariffs had already been lowered by Imperial Decree, under the powers given to the Emperor in 1852, but in 1856 it was a question of extending the principle of free trade more widely. This time the revolt of the protectionists both in the Legislative Body and among the industrialists was so sharp that the government, although not yielding to the pressure of the Legislative Body alone, inserted a notice in the *Moniteur* of 17th October promising to maintain the existing tariffs until 1st July, 1861. At the same time it saved its face by announcing that the delay was to give French industry time to prepare itself for the new commercial regime, making it plain that there would be a stay of execution and not a reprieve.

The same year saw an attempt at interpellation of the Ministers by the Deputies in the Chamber, a thing which was expressly forbidden by the Constitution and should therefore not have been permitted. But it is a measure of the Chamber's progress that Baroche, as President of the Council, while reminding his audience of the existence of constitutional prohibition did give them an answer.

Thus, although the government had hoped that 1856, which saw the triumph of the Peace of Paris (marking the end of the Crimean War) and the birth of an heir on 17th March, would have made the Chamber more docile, this had not been so; and in 1857, with the knowledge that it was no longer dealing with a simple rubber stamp, the government entered an election year in which it would submit the first five years of the Empire to popular judgement.

It is the view of one authority that: "In many ways the year 1857 ought to be regarded as a prominent landmark in the development of the Second Empire."[18] This is so if one accepts the thesis that the shifts in the voting pattern of 1857, in so far as they differed from those of 1852, were primary motives behind the subsequent changes in Imperial policy. But in fact the election results were virtually a foregone conclusion and the level of abstention (thirty-five per cent of the electorate) showed how quiet the country was politically.

Numerically the count was virtually the same as it had been five years earlier, though the arithmetic of an increasing population raised the actual number of deputies from 261 to 267, and the opposition collected only 665,000 votes as against 5,471,000 for the Ministerial candidates. With the Republican opposition increased by one, there was really little to cause grave apprehension among the ruling group. Yet there is little doubt that the more conservative section of the government was rattled by the results. Baroche lamented the effects of universal suffrage: "A deplorable principle, full of dangers for the future,"[19] and the conservative Bonapartists felt that, " . . . if the Emperor is convinced that a strong and respected authority is the salvation of the country, one must get back to it to stifle the germs of agitation."[20]

In fact, the Republicans had made a great deal of noise, but it was as much against one another as against the Empire. Their electoral results had been meagre, as the Emperor himself noted and he did not share the disquiet of his Ministers at the election of five Republican Deputies. To him, as he wrote to Billault, "the difference between 1852 and 1857 is very good and ought to be pointed out." Although he was aware of "the evil dispositions of the great towns" there is no indication that he shared the general alarm of the Ministers. Indeed, Rouland's comment (echoed by Fould, Magne, Billault and other conservatives), *"if the Emperor is convinced . . ."* (author's italics), would seem to indicate that Napoleon was not convinced by the results in themselves. Even if one considered the election of five Republicans as sinister, it should perhaps be noted that this time unlike the three in 1852, they all agreed to take the oath and bow the knee in the house of Rimmon. One of them, Emile Ollivier, had begun a journey which was to lead him to office in 1869.

One historian has said of the new Chamber on its opening day, 28th November, 1857, " . . . nothing had changed, there were the same faces; the same places showed on the same benches, there were the same Councillors of State, and, if appearances were anything to go by, would be the same for a long time : there would also be the same state of being in the shade, the same slightly monotonous existence, the same docility, tempered from time to time by fleeting moments of independence."[21]

Yet there were to be changes, and why not? "A constitution is the work of time"—so Napoleon III had said, quoting the Great Emperor. There was room for modifications and it cannot be doubted that the Emperor himself welcomed them. The fact that they were also the product of various pressures does not make the changes less virtuous, though it may have hastened their coming.

For some time the exclusion of Ministers from the Chamber had been seen as a weakness, just as it had been in the Constitution of 1791. It was impossible to have a legislative body, no matter how docile, without some form of direction so that the government could get its business transacted. This was the opinion of Morny, based on his experience as President of the *Corps Législatif*. It was also the view of Thiers. Thiers had the honesty to admit that in reforming the structure :

> ... the Emperor followed partly his own inclinations and partly the way things pointed. His personal inclination has always been to think (he often used to tell me so) that repression was by nature temporary; he realized that sooner or later he would have to yield a little to the re-awakening independence of opinion, and he found it gave him an appearance of great wisdom to forestall the day when concessions would no longer be voluntary. I think also his very strong affection for his son played its part in deciding him. Obviously he wanted to prepare the future for this child.[22]

Thiers meant that Napoleon III was sincere in his desire to "crown the edifice with liberty." Apart from these considerations, and perhaps more important than any feelings or intentions on the part of either the Emperor or the *Corps Législatif*, were the cold financial facts which weighed more heavily than electoral results as forces working for change. Now, as always, finance proved the key which opened the door to liberty of discussion in parliament. This was the opinion of the Republican Deputy Darimon who noted that " . . . it was the budgetary commissions which began the concealed work of rebuilding the constitutional regime after 1852."[23] This was particularly true of the occasions when the conservative sections felt that the government's tendency to lurch towards free trade, threatened their protectionist principles. Such attacks, even if for a limited objective, could not but assume wider implications, and in any event, intelligent criticisms needed intelligent, well-informed, ministerial answers if the government was to make a good case. Baroche himself had virtually admitted this in 1856 when, having first pointed out that the constitution did not permit it, he *had* replied to a question. That it was better to be there to answer unconstitutionally than not at all, was made plain by the report on 1st July, 1856, of a debate which erupted on the question of railway concessions. The Prefect of Police in a report to the Emperor qualified this session as: "Scandalous and deplorable ... the most vulgar inter-ruptions and the most wounding questions led one to think of a return to the worst days of parliamentarianism."[24] What is significant about the outburst is that Baroche was absent from the Chamber on that day and no one else on the government side was of sufficient stature to cope with the situation. Clearly, some form of ministerial representation was essential to prevent repetitions of this type of scene which were harmful to the government's prestige.

The financial crisis of 1857-58, which was general in Europe, hit France as elsewhere, and the government's financial necessities, parti-cularly the need for state loans, were immediately exploited by the Chamber. The Empire was heavily involved in a programme of public works, and the scarcity of private capital threatened its continuance at a time when the financial condition of the *Crédit Mobilier* was weak, and when it was being attacked by the Rothschild group of banks.

In these circumstances, the pretensions of the Chamber could not but increase, and the effects of the Orsini bomb plot to assassinate the Emperor and Empress on 14th January, 1858, although it gave rise to the repressive "Law of General Security" could only produce a tempor-ary reassertion of the completely authoritarian Empire, no matter how much the "mameluke" Bonapartists might wish otherwise.

Certainly the outrage led to a clamour which produced the "Law of General Security." But even in the teeth of ministerial pressure the *Corps Législatif* obtained important modifications of the law, an occasion which provided Ollivier with his first opportunity to make a speech in which he displayed not merely a spirit of criticism but also constructive moderation.

In any event, nothing could obscure the fact that the governmental system as it existed was unsatisfactory, even if a dozen laws of general security were passed. Prince Napoleon pointed this out to the Emperor in his letter in which he announced his resignation from the government (over a question of foreign policy) on 5th March, 1859. "I have against me not only my colleagues, but also the *Corps Législatif,* inspired by its President, where a campaign is being prepared against me *which can only be overborne by the President of the Conseil d'État* [my italics] himself hostile for the most part, to the measures which I have submitted to the Emperor."[25] Given the character and attitude of Prince Napoleon, the Emperor may well have thought it no bad thing he was debarred from defending himself in the Chamber. Nevertheless, the implications were important and bore out what was now well known, that modifications to the constitutional position of the *Corps Législatif* must come.

The year 1859 opened with Napoleon III's cryptic comment on Franco-Austrian relations to the Austrian Ambassador on the New Year's day reception. When the Emperor commented to Baron Hübner "I regret that our relations with your government should not be so good as in the past," no one knew what he had meant to convey by his remarks. The announcement that the Emperor would himself open the new legislative session with a speech from the throne increased speculation as to what was afoot. The Imperial speech of 7th February was so enigmatic that most of the audience could have been forgiven for thinking that they were listening to the oracle at Delphi.[26] At the end, they were still unclear as to what the Emperor wanted, but when they returned to the Palais Bourbon they were given a clear lead by their President, Morny. Because of Morny's strong exposition of France's need for peace, without any of his half-brother's equivocations, the *Corps Législatif* found itself in the position virtually of debating the speech from the throne. To the survivors of 1830-48 it must have seemed a heady moment of return to the good old days and another step in the direction of parliamentary liberty. Furthermore, if the expression of a desire for peace was an attack on Imperial policy, it was also a means of preventing a financial crisis which a war might cause, and most of the deputies, not least Morny himself, had more than a passing interest in the state of the *Bourse.*

However, the session ended without any further decision on the question of war. Not until the Easter recess were the deputies recalled to be told officially of the declaration of war against Austria and to be asked to vote for the army credits. Morny, while expressing the firm hope for a short war, appealed to the Assembly for unanimity in the face of the enemy in particular and foreign opposition in general. The Chamber obliged with cries of *"Vive l'Empereur!"*—aware that any other course would have been fruitless, for the Emperor made it plain to them that he had not given them control over foreign policy or any share in his right to make peace or war. This was not given even to his ministers, and, in a sense, as in 1856, the episode sharply reminded the Legislative Body where the making of policy took place. However, a substantial consolation prize was on the way, for at the end of the Italian war, at the height of his popularity and in the fullness of his personal power and prestige, Napoleon III decided to concede the first measures of parliamentary liberty.

Before the decrees of 1860 and 1861, which liberalized the regime, Napoleon III had already indicated the direction in which his mind was moving by granting a general amnesty to all political criminals who had been condemned either in 1851–52, or during the short-lived period in 1858-59 when the Law of General Security had been in operation. This amnesty was not simply an appeal to the Republicans to let bygones be bygones. It was a reminder to them that basically the Emperor was no conservative and he was only too willing to seize the opportunity, which popular support for the Italian war provided, to extend a hand of friendship to the radical elements. The applause from the crowds in the working-class Faubourg St. Antoine on the day the Italian army had passed in review was a tremendous boost for Napoleon III's morale and it must have seemed as if his desire to be the people's Emperor could yet be fulfilled.

To argue, therefore, that the decrees of 1860 and 1861 were extracted from Napoleon III because the consequences of the Italian war had alienated the Catholic party and the Church, thus forcing the régime to lean on more liberal and radical elements, is to vastly oversimplify the factors at work in the Emperor's mind. Likewise, considering the argument that the free-trade treaty with England of January, 1860, had antagonized the protectionists and the conservative capitalists, who had also moved into opposition, it should be remembered that these political figures had never been whole-heartedly for the Empire except when it appeared to suit them. Their opposition was no new threat in that it had always existed. Furthermore, the pressure for change came as much from the need to make the constitution work effectively, as from the attitude of either the Church or the protectionists. Both these groups might grumble, but not all French Catholics were ultra-montanists and not all French industrialists were protectionists. Neither would work to overthrow the regime which still stood for order and security, even if it was freer in its trade and its parliamentary practice than many of them wished.

Therefore, while it is true that these factors existed, and form a background to the changes, it must be stressed that the decrees had their roots in the Emperor's own thinking and writings which few of his contemporaries (and fewer historians) have bothered to read. Emile Ollivier, one of the few who tried to understand the workings of the Imperial mind, saw this clearly. "The treaty of Commerce and my readings of his work on William III,"[27] he wrote in his diary of 17th June, 1860, "make me think he will grant liberty if he is pressed."[28]

In fact, the Emperor needed no pressing. His advice to his protesting ministers when the reforms were discussed at the *Conseil d'État* had been to "go way and think it over." But he had already decided and their thinking it over could at best only modify his plans. He had no intention of deviating from them in any major fashion.

The decrees which brought about a more "liberal" or "parliamentary" situation were issued at various times. On 24th November, 1860, a decree emanating from the Emperor, was followed by further decrees, which, since they involved constitutional changes, were issued as *Senatus Consulta,* on 2nd and 3rd February, 1861, and 31st December, 1861. The total effect of these decrees was to restore liberty of debate to the *Corps Législatif* and virtually to accord it the right of interpellation. This was not specifically granted, but since the debate on the speech from the throne was to take place ". . . in the presence of the ministers who had authority to give the Chamber all the necessary explanations on both the internal and external policy of the Empire," the right of questioning government policy had been established. There was, of course, no question of ministerial responsibility to the Chamber and in fact the government's spokesmen in the Chamber were partly composed of ministers without portfolio, such as Billault and Magne. These two were men of experience, and Billault had for a time been President of the *Corps Législatif*; the Government had no intention of putting mere passengers into the Chamber.

As well as the right to debate, the right to have the debates published in full was restored. The Deputies could feel they had once more established contact with public opinion, instead of functioning in a vacuum in the Palais Bourbon. This right of publication was a renewal of the practice common under the Restoration and the July Monarchy. An even more important reversion to previous practice was the granting of the Chamber's right to vote the budget in ministerial sections and not *en bloc,* thus giving some control over departmental expenditure. At the same time, it was decreed that any supplementary budgetary votes must have the sanction of the Legislative Body.

It may have been slightly humiliating for the *Corps Législatif* to have concessions given as a present from the Emperor rather than to feel they had been won as a result of struggles in which the Imperial authority had been worsted, but they were still concessions. What is more they were meaningful concessions which had altered the nature of the Empire and not merely its constitutional structure. There could be no question of going back on these reforms which had ended the authoritarian phase of the Empire.

It was Ollivier who saw the true meaning of what was happening and who, totally rejecting the sterile and rancorous reception of the reforms by his fellow Republicans like Jules Favre, said: "I do not think that this measure or any others of the same type that may follow it weakens the Empire; far from it, it will consolidate it if the Emperor perseveres in this wise habit of making more and more liberal concessions."[29] Perhaps the greatest justification for Napoleon III's first ten years of rule was that the most favourable speech in the *Corps Législatif* had been made by the most intelligent member of the opposition. Ollivier said in his speech of 14th March, dwelling on the importance of the reforms: ". . . as for me who am a Republican, I shall admire, I shall approve, and my support will be all the more efficacious because it will be completely disinterested."[30] Was not this a fulfilment of the basic dream of the Emperor—a real unanimity, based on the Bonapartist consensus in its widest form but giving a chance for variety in its expression?

When Morny asked Ollivier if he was satisfied with the reforms, the latter replied, "if it is an end, you are lost; if it is a beginning, you are established."[31] In fact, there could be neither an end nor a going back. To imagine either possibility was totally to misunderstand Napoleon III's reasons for seeking power. The real problem was whether an extension of parliamentarianism could be equated with an extension of democracy, in the sense in which the Emperor understood the word, for no one could be sure in whose interests the parliamentary liberty would be used. Would it benefit the masses or the classes? The answer to this would depend on how far the Emperor could keep the traditional and conservative forces in check by calling in the masses to balance the classes, so that an extention of parliamentary liberty did not lead to a restoration of Orleanism.

8

Masses and Classes

"The fact is that public opinion is much
more felt and more loudly expressed in this
country [France] than anyone in England at
all imagines."

The Duke of Cambridge to Queen Victoria
(1851)

"I shall always govern in the interests of the
masses."

Napoleon III

WHEN the Emperor had said, "I shall always govern in the
interests of the masses," what did he mean? Did public opinion
guide and influence the policies of the Second Empire, or was it
conditioned and controlled and *then* followed? In any attempt to
answer this question, it should be remembered that in France, since
1848, universal suffrage had given public opinion a chance to express
itself to a degree unknown elsewhere in Europe. Universal suffrage had
to be made to work if government was to be workable—not only
because it existed, but because the Emperor believed in it. It was not
just that he had said so; his action in quashing the disfranchising decree
of the Assembly after his presidential *coup* had proved his determination to keep universal suffrage as a political fact.

Accusations against the Imperial régime charge it with manipulating
public opinion so that the Emperor could rule as an autocrat, surrounded by the trappings of democracy. One historian has called him
"a Mountebank Dictator"; another, more kindly, has called him "a
Democratic Despot." Either way there is an inference of dictatorial
control—but is this a true judgement? What was the government of the
Second Empire to do but to direct a mass electorate which was not
politically experienced? That "political order must precede political
liberty" was the maxim of the sovereign himself. If it summed up an
attitude of paternalism, one should remember that there was consultation, not just by election but also by the plebiscite on all major issues.

It could be argued that no government in Europe at that time took so much care to inform and to listen to public opinion. It is the opinion of a recent French commentator that the two chief legacies of Bonapartism to the political growth of France are a tradition of political thinking and the progressive education towards democracy which it provided.[1] In any event, arguments about "totalitarian" and "democratic" states have in the last decade lost a deal of the surety of definition which was formerly common to such disputations. A cynical modern definition of the difference between a totalitarian and a democratic state could be that in democracies people discuss and the government does what it wants, while in totalitarian states the government does what it wants. Furthermore, in an age increasingly aware of the skilled techniques of manipulation employed by all governments, a cooler appraisal of the attitude of Napoleon III's government is more possible.

The Bonapartist movement, from the Prince downwards, had always been "popular" in the sense that it had directly appealed to the people. It could not be imagined that once in power the Imperial regime would in any way lessen its activities in this direction. On the contrary, and it would have been political madness to act otherwise, it increased them. But there was a difference. Once power had been achieved the Imperial Government, just as so many others since, had to modify its propagandist proposals for change in France as soon as it was confronted with what the professional politicians always call "the realities of power." The cry of "soak the rich" which had echoed in Bonapartist press and pamphlet between 1848 and 1850 had to be muted in face of the continuing power of the *Notables* at so many levels of government and administration.

Yet to see the Second Empire as a confidence trick played on the workers and peasants by a man who posed as their champion but who was, in fact, a reactionary intriguer is not enough. To Karl Marx, Napoleon III was always "Crapulinski," the willing tool of greedy financial sharks who, having paid his debts to make him their debtor, used his regime to suit their capitalist aims. To others, not least to these very financial sharks, the Emperor was a social revolutionary who went to ridiculous and dangerous lengths in the pursuit of utopian schemes. Marx complained that Napoleon III was not like his uncle. Many of those close to Napoleon III complained that he was too like Marx.

Napoleon III's social policy began with his accession, for as he had said : "I often think of the duties society owes to the disinherited and the more I reflect on them the more I am convinced that there is still much to do in this respect. If I should one day attain power, I will not fail to use it to right these wrongs." This was the thinking which had lain behind the confiscation of the Orléans families' property, of which mention has already been made. A further Presidential decree ordered that no work should be permitted in public enterprises on Sundays and holidays; while yet another established the famous "chaplains of the last rites" for the poor which meant that no one need go to the grave without benefit of clergy for lack of the necessary funds. If it is argued that it would have been better to succour the living, rather than console the dying, then one can point to further legislation designed to do just that.

It would be wrong to overestimate the effect of much of the "social" legislation in the early part of the reign, but it is worth noting that changes were made in the methods of apprenticeship and an easing of the regulations concerning the workers' pass books (the *livrets*) was decreed. At the same time legal aid was granted for those unable to pay if they became involved in lawsuits. A much more important indication of social policy was the decree of 8th March, 1855, setting up the National Hospital at Vincennes, which was to take care of the victims of industry. It was to be for the worker what the *Invalides* was to the wounded soldier. Since provision had to be made for convalescence, envisaging a fairly lengthy period of residence in the hospital, the Emperor himself decreed that "each patient was to have a room to himself, there was to be space, air, light and places for walking. An atmosphere of bleakness, gloom and monotony was to be avoided." Perhaps Napoleon III remembered the workhouses he had seen while living in England.

At the same time, the workers were, during their stay in hospital, to be offered mental sustenance in the shape of lectures from distinguished people and were encouraged to discuss the lectures. Since an average of ten thousand workers a year passed through Vincennes, one must not underestimate either the size of the institution or its effectiveness as a "set piece" of Imperial propaganda in the battle to win the proletariat for Bonapartism. Many of the lectures were printed and published which considerably enhanced their value both as *pièces éducatives* for the workers and as evidence of the government's interest in the masses.

How successful this type of workers' educational programme was remains a matter for debate, but it is doubtful whether it can be dismissed as a total failure, as many of the critics of the Second Empire have maintained.[2] The government certainly needed to take this type of education seriously, for the continuing growth of an urban proletariat during the Second Empire meant that sooner, rather than later, a working-class movement would emerge. Napoleon III was determined, if possible, to canalize the workers' movement so that it ran in directions which were beneficial rather than injurious to the state. At the same time he hoped to bring the workers to a point where they would cease to regard the government as being hostile to them, leaving them no alternative but to be hostile in their turn. Here, the most important factor was the Emperor himself, for many French workers displayed an ambivalent attitude in which personal affection for, and loyalty to, the person of Napoleon III, was frequently combined with a hatred of the *patronat* and the rich. The phenomenon resulted in a paradox, for the elections frequently produced results which were disagreeable to the government, in that they returned "opposition" candidates, while the plebiscites produced a resounding "Yes," as an endorsement of what was felt to be the Emperor's own policy.[3]

In a sense, the workers' instinct was correct. *Moustachu*, as they called the Emperor, was their man, the tragedy was that he could not be so exclusively. Neither political theory nor practice made this possible in nineteenth-century France, and the Second Empire had too little time to resolve the dilemma of pleasing masses and classes, even supposing such a thing had ever really been a practical possibility.

Had Napoleon III really been the dictator his enemies accuse him of being, he might have been able to achieve more than he did. That attempts were made is evident, not only from the legislation, but from the actions taken in an attempt to mitigate the rigours of a system which operated against the workers. In many instances, the Emperor was thwarted in his aims because the social and economic structure of nineteenth-century France was too strong to be dismantled. The example of this was the question of the *livret* or "pass book" which by a law of 1803 the French worker was forced to carry. Since all changes of employment had to be noted, and the reasons for the change also inscribed, this meant that a worker who had taken part in strikes, or who had been difficult with his employer could easily be identified as a trouble-maker. Not only that, a worker frequently borrowed from his employer, using the *livret* as a pledge, and this had the effect of preventing the worker either from leaving his employment, or complaining about his conditions. Not surprisingly, the workers hated the *livret*. Napoleon III was well aware of this, and a decree of 22nd June, 1854, while it re-enacted the legislation about carrying the *livret*, forbade any entries, other than comments on the workers' capabilities. The existence of the decree of 1851, which prohibited the employers from keeping the *livret* against an advance of salary, was again stressed. The law did make the *livret* less of a force for blackmail against the worker, but it did not abolish it.

This question provides a very good illustration both of Napoleon III's attitude to the workers' problems and of the difficulties which arose when changes to this type of legislation were proposed. Those who saw in the workers a threat to the established order could not accept with indifference any alteration in the laws which had been set up to control this class of society. The dilemma which faced the Emperor was one of trying to please both the masses and classes but in such a situation it was the influential and important who carried the greater weight, even though Napoleon III may have disliked this reality.

In 1869 when the Emperor made it plain that he intended to abolish the system, the announcement was again greeted with cries of hostility from the employers, and not until twenty years after the fall of the Empire was the *livret* finally abolished. By that time the existence of universal military service enabled the government to keep tabs on all its citizens. In an attempt to produce that reconciliation between workers and employers which Prince Louis Napoleon had stated as one of his aims in *L'Extinction du Pauperisme*, the Imperial regime retained the *conseils de prud'hommes* which had been set up by the Republic.[4]

These organizations, based on their respective industries, did establish a meeting place between the workers and their employers so that they could deliberate together and act as social peacemakers, and as a formal channel for airing grievances their value was recognized by both employers and workers. Each group elected their representatives to the *Conseil* on a basis of equal representation, but the Emperor nominated the president and vice-president. Here at least the sovereign could try to get as close as possible to the actual problems of industrial relations through contact with the key men. The *Conseils* were active, for it is reckoned that the average number of meetings, in the Paris region for example, was fifteen to twenty per month, which would seem to indicate that the machinery was used but like any other organization its real effectiveness is hard to assess without a detailed analysis of cases and as yet this has not been attempted.

However, the government was in an ambiguous situation, for if there was the *Conseil*, there was also Article 1781 of the Civil Code. This article laid down that in case of a dispute over wages between a worker and his employer, the court was obliged, in default of evidence to the contrary, to take the employer's word. Such a law pressed heavily on the worker, particularly because for most of the period of the Empire the judiciary remained in the hands of Orleanists who were socially and economically more sympathetic to the ideas of the *Notables* than to the utopian schemes of the Emperor. The French worker was to find early on, just as the English worker was to discover in the 1900's, that the law is not necessarily an ass when it comes to deciding what is what in labour disputes. In this context, the Decree of 1851 which increased legal aid facilities to those who needed, but could not afford them, appears as more than just a meaningless gesture.

Whenever and wherever he could, the Emperor pressed for amelioration. As one authority on the question of working-class conditions has put it : "The Emperor wanted the worker to be well fed, well housed, with regular work, and shelter for his old age. But Imperial goodwill often wandered in the clouds and was not always translated into precise actions."[5] The Emperor's dream of a sort of state socialism, or welfare state, was frequently dispersed by those in his entourage who were Bonapartist with strong Orleanist overtones. In particular, their attitude was that in a modern state, whatever its political structure, the key figure was the manufacturer and they held that the State's duty was one of non-intervention except, of course, in the interests of the manufacturers.

The Emperor was not at all inclined to accept this attitude and, where possible, the administration was encouraged to intervene on the side of the workers. There is evidence to show that in various regions of France the Prefects and the Mayors intervened on more than one occasion in disputes between employer and worker, thus neatly bypassing the legal system, and their intervention was generally to the benefit of the workers.[6]

Perhaps the most famous and direct intervention was that of the Emperor himself in 1861 when it came to the question of sending delegates to the International Exhibition of 1862 in London. Not only did the Emperor overrule objections of his Prefect of Police in Paris to the attendance of the French delegation, which had been elected by the direct votes of the workers in Paris and the major towns, he contributed 200,000 francs towards making it physically possible for them to attend and named three of the delegation *Chevaliers* of the Legion of Honour. It is true that this type of action may be dismissed as a crude attempt to win over the urban proletariat to the support of the Empire, but whatever the motives, there is nothing comparable to it elsewhere in the Europe of the 1860's.

As further evidence of the Emperor's attitude, it is noteworthy that when the International Workingman's Association, the First

International, was founded in 1864, the French section was enabled to set up an office in Paris, although it was hardly within its legal rights to exist at all. This open evidence of Imperial favour, not only scandalized the conservatives, it also, ironically, made the workers suspect that the members of the International were simply stooges of the Imperial government which had bought and paid for them.

The ambivalent attitude of the Imperial government towards the working-class movement was, however, based on one very real fear, namely that the workers might forget the June days of 1848, and all that they implied, and turn once again to the Parliamentary democrats. While it is true that such an alliance would be a danger to the whole Imperial regime, it was not just a negative attitude which inspired Napoleon III's attempt to placate the various working-class movements. There was also the positive factor arising from his belief, not unfounded, that he had proved, and would prove, a better friend to the workers than any liberal parliamentary regime and in this context it would be wrong to underestimate the political perspicacity of many sections of the French working class itself. The pamphleteers of the 1860's whether partly inspired by Prince Napoleon's *Palais Royal* group of Bonapartist workers or not, showed that the workers were aware of how hollow the pretensions of the liberal-democrats were. Intellectual liberty was all very well for those who were comfortably off, but to the worker, physical necessities overrode finer points of constitutional procedure. While admitting that there still remained much to be done, many of the working-class pamphleteers were like Chabaud, the tin-worker, or Bazin and Coutant the typographers, who concluded that the hope for the masses lay not in systematic opposition to the regime, but in the hope that "... the elected of the Nation [the Emperor] will at last listen to our demands."

Chabaud, in an article which appeared, among others, in a brochure entitled *Le Peuple, l'Empereur, et les anciens partis*, called upon the workers not to be fooled any longer (*ne soyons plus dupes!*) by the blandishments of Legitimists and Orleanists who had no interest in social reform. The people should not allow themselves to be fooled into supporting agitation against the dynasty and the Emperor by those who only wished to use them to overthrow a regime which they no longer found to their tastes.[7]

From the various pamphlets which appeared, one other fact emerges clearly and that is a demand that the masses reject any attempt to restore political parties : "For the people, like the Emperor, desire that the government be the government of all and not of a party." Here was

an affirmation of a fundamental Bonapartist tenet, namely, that party
was noxious and factious, and a negation of the idea of universal
suffrage. That this theme should have been developed at a time when
the Imperial regime was faced with a resurgence of the party spirit may
reveal either guidance from above or the result of clear thinking by the
workers who could see the same phenomenon of party resurgence and
who liked it as little as did the Imperial regime. Whether inspired or
spontaneous, the working-class opposition to an 'Orleanist' resurgence
cannot have been fortuitous. And it should not be forgotten that for a
decade and more after the fall of the Empire in 1870 there was a
substantial element of Bonapartism among the French urban working-
class—and there was then no governmental propaganda machine to
direct it.

It is fairly clear then that if Napoleon III strove for order and
stability, it was with the determination that they should not be achieved
at the expense of depriving the working peoples of reforms which he
considered just and necessary. He was not a Jacobin Emperor out to
spread the doctrine of revolution, but he was a reforming Emperor who
believed that elementary social justice could be achieved without a class
war and that only by social justice could class war and the cycle of
revolution-reaction be avoided. In a sense, his foreign policy also
reflected this attitude, in that he believed it was possible to achieve
international justice without national wars. The fact that he was partly
in error in both assumptions does not invalidate the worth of the intent.
Nor can either aspiration be dismissed as utopian, except by those who
believe that most change is damaging and progress unlikely.

As far as the internal aim of reform and social change was concerned, two things conspired to thwart the Imperial plans. The first was
the numerical weakness of the French urban working class and their
concentration in relatively small areas. As late as 1870 the industrial
workers numbered only two-and-a-half million out of a population of
thirty-eight million, and agriculture was still France's major industry. It
is against this background that one should consider a point, frequently
made by writers on the Second Empire, that the regime never managed
to "capture the towns" when it came to elections, and that this fact
implies its rejection by the urban proletariat. This is, however, an
oversimplification.

To begin with not all the towns which rejected the Empire were
necessarily working-class in composition, and local interest, rather than
class consciousness, may well have played its part in influencing voters.
To what extent Marseilles was anti-Imperialist because of the attitude

of the regime towards Algeria, which the Emperor was not anxious to hand over to commercial exploitation, is one problem among many which need investigation.

Again, the point about the scattered nature of the working class is of importance because in many regions, not necessarily urban agglomerations, Legitimism was frequently a feature of the local scene. The local *seigneurs* in parts of south and south-west France still exercised considerable influence and many of the Legitimist quasi-secret societies numbered workers among their supporters and even among their organizers.

The picture of an organized and united Republican opposition, based upon discontented workers dedicated to overthrowing the Empire will not stand up to hard scrutiny. It was largely an invention of the Third Republic which, when it tossed uneasily on its own bed, blamed the previous regime for putting the lumps in the mattress.

Yet it would be wrong to see the Second Empire as a period of either great working-class prosperity or contentment. There was a great deal of misery and wretchedness and the novels of Emile Zola, although they exaggerate for political reasons, do give a picture which, when modified, does bear some resemblance to the actual state of affairs. With the working day at a twelve-hour norm, there can have been little pleasure in being a factory hand and, in spite of government pressure, conditions of work in the factories and workshops remained poor. There were individual instances of employers who tried to help their workers and to ameloriate the harsh effect of boom and slump. But these efforts were sporadic and the bulk of the factory owners regarded their workers as a source of revenue rather than an object of philanthropy.

The period between 1850 and 1870 was, in any event, marked by several severe crises, that of 1857 to 1858 and again during the American Civil War in the 1860's, and these economic crises affected the workers. It has in fact been calculated that only in the mid and late 1860's were wages actually higher than prices. There can be no doubt that the worker was better off both in terms of wages and conditions than he had been in the 1840's and early 1850's and the regime could, therefore, claim credit for a considerable amelioration. But the weight of opposition to drastic social reforms as well as the actual economic structure of France worked against dramatic improvements.

There were probably fewer paupers in France in 1870 than there had been in 1850, but the social and economic position of the workers *vis-à-vis* the rest of French society was only relatively better. The rich were undoubtedly richer, but the poor were only marginally less poor.

It was the realization of this which led, towards the end of the Empire, to an increase in class consciousness, and it was the emergence of this class consciousness which made the bourgeoisie become more restive and fearful of the consequences of Imperial policy. Under Louis Philippe the masses had been virtually inert until 1848 had unstoppered the bottle and let the genie out. But now there was less a spontaneous revolutionary movement than the growth of an organized and persistent working-class movement. This, the government tried to shape and direct so that working-class aspirations were linked to the belief that the Emperor would satisfy them. To some extent, this policy of Napoleon III was successful, in that he drew the teeth of the revolutionary movements, but he replaced them by a growing *étatisme* which, if it encouraged the workers to look to the state for the necessary reforms, also encouraged them to blame the government if they did not get them.

Unfortunately, the logic of capitalism implies that those who contribute most to industrial growth—that is the investors—should be those who profit most from this growth. In the France of the Second Empire, many of the enterprises were to a much greater extent than in England, family concerns. To the bourgeoisie who controlled them, any interference by the State must be in their interests, since their prosperity meant the prosperity of the State. By the 1860's they felt they were being compelled to pay a high price for the political security which the Empire gave them. On the one hand, it was pleasant to have greater profits than in the 1840's, but on the other, to have less assurance over their control because of the actual, or threatened, extent of state intervention was an irritating worry. This goes far to explain the increasing determination of the bourgoisie to reassert their own type of political organization which, in this context could only mean some form of Orleanism with its "parliamentary" bias. The genesis of the Third Republic was already there, and it is interesting to speculate as to what type of showdown might have come between this group and Napoleon III had not Bismarck intervened and destroyed the Empire from outside. In this respect Ollivier's ministry of January, 1870, gives clear indications of what policies were intended by the conservative-Orleanist group.

When one talks of "bourgeoisie" in this context it should perhaps be made plain that it is the industrial-banking complex which is under discussion. This was the group which provided the investment in the private sector of industry, as opposed to the extensive programme of governmentally-inspired public works.[8] It was this group which viewed with alarm the Saint-Simonian tendencies of the Emperor and in particular worried about the threat of free-trade—which became a reality with the Anglo-French treaty of 1860, a treaty carried through in the teeth of substantial opposition from a sizeable section of industrialists. Though in the long run the treaty did prove a stimulus to French industry, there can be no doubt of its unpopularity and of its immediate effects, for a decree of 1st August, 1860, offered governmental assistance to industries needing help with re-equipment or modernization. Like most capitalists, the French industrialists failed to denounce this type of State intervention.

Yet a large section of the financial interests had remained hostile to much of the economic activities of the government and the Rothschilds never ceased to work against the operation of the *Crédit Mobilier*, from its foundation in 1852, which made possible the accumulation of capital for the use of the State. The activities of the Péreire brothers, which did so much to advance the economic prosperity of France both by their operations at home and broad, were never liked by the orthodox bankers who saw the system, rightly, as a threat to their monopoly. Not only that; a new type of financial entrepreneur was emerging which, though rooted in the bourgeoisie, was drawn from the ranks of the petty rather than the great of that particular class.

It was this new group which produced, through its feverish and constant financial activity, the atmosphere of *affairisme* which dominated the financial world of the Second Empire. The success of the *Crédit Mobilier*, with its funds drawn from the small investor and saver, seemed to presage a democratization of credit and an end to the aristocratic closed-shop traditions of the Bank of France and its offshoots. It was this new financial class or group which benefited most directly from the economic growth during the period, for the investment pattern was linked to the railway building, not only in France but in Europe, and also was actively engaged in the vast programme of public works. Haussmann's rebuilding of Paris was a rich field for the up-and-coming speculator.

The circumstances in which many of these transactions were carried out often led to shady deals, and their exposé, as in the scandal of the *Affaire Mirès* in 1860-62.[9] With such a welter of speculation, carried out against a background of bitter warfare between the Péreires and the Rothschilds, scandals were inevitable. The amazing thing is that there were not more, rather than that some existed, or at least came to light. It should be remembered that the Second Empire was, in the long run, neither more nor less scandal-ridden than either the July Monarchy or the Third Republic. Public scandals, particularly financial ones involving politicians, have been a feature of French political life and it would be well to avoid a moralistic approach.

As with every regime, scandal was useful to the opposition. The interesting thing about the financial scandals of the Empire is that they linked together very diverse elements ranging from the orthodox bankers (Baron Rothschild said "L'Empire, c'est la baisse") to the Republican radicals, and the Legitimist Berryer, who denounced the *Crédit Mobilier* as the "greatest gambling house in the world." Not the least of the reasons why denunciation of the financial system was popular was the fact that everyone interested in "orthodox" finance knew quite well that the whole edifice of the *Crédit Mobilier* rested upon government backing. Without such support the system of the *Crédit* was impossible to maintain and also to attack the Péreires and their organization was to attack the regime. Hence Henri Rochefort's gibe: "Her Majesty, the Empress, presided at a meeting of the Council of State. Madame Péreire presided at a meeting of the *Crédit Mobilier*."

The fact that the government and the *Crédit* were so closely linked was, of course, a double-edged weapon. It was not merely government *support* which annoyed the Rotheschilds and their group, it was government *initiative* which was even more disliked. The whole financial policy, linked to the free-trade policy, was odious to the conservative section of industry and finance, but it was not easy to prevent the success of either. The Emperor's own inclinations and the structure of the regime until the 1860's precluded any control of financial or economic policy and this meant that it was difficult for critics to pin the government down in financial matters. By 1865 nine major commercial treaties, all with a free-trade bias, had been signed between France and other European states.

Quite apart from any governmental support, and direction, the success of the new financial organization was a guarantee of its continued growth, and this growth was facilitated by the fact that a vast influx of specie took place during the period, thus increasing the circulation of money and capital inside France. Most of the industrial nations of Western Europe benefited from the discovery of the goldfields of California and Australia, as did the U.S.A., but France benefited more than most. It is reckoned that forty-four per cent of the gold found its way there and by 1865 gold, although it had not ousted silver as the norm of metal currency, as the Emperor would have liked, had led to the formation of the Latin Monetary Union and an agreed policy of bimetallism.

But if the influx of capital benefited the "unorthodox" policies of the *Crédit Mobilier*, it also benefited the traditional banking institution, not least the formidable Bank of France itself, whose reserves by 1870 stood at one million francs in gold. Against the Fort Knox of French capital, the Péreires beat in vain, and in 1863 they overreached themselves by attempting to turn the society into a bank of issue. This drew down upon them the full fury of the Bank and its supporters. Even more alarming, in view of their relationship, the government would not support the *Crédit* and agreed with the Bank that it was an infringement of its privileges. This was a considerable triumph for orthodox finance and revealed to what extent orthodox politics had also come to power.

One of the drawbacks of the Péreires' system had been that so much of the capital involved became tied up with land purchase, railways or property investment and this, inevitably, weakened the credit upon which the whole organization depended for its continuance. The nadir of the Society's fortunes came in 1867 when it had to go cap in hand to the Bank of France to ask for a loan in order to prevent total collapse, and only the intervention of the government led to the Regent's even considering to help. As it was the terms of the loan were harsh and the Bank had its revenge in that the Péreire brothers were forced to sever all connection with the Society.[10]

In a sense, the end of the *Crédit Mobilier* came in 1867, though the funeral was postponed until 1871. Its demise had resulted from the strength of more traditional financial methods, re-asserting their control by stages. A decree of 1863 had created the limited liability company. Now, in 1867, a second instalment of corporate independence for financial institutions was granted. Under the new law, free incorporation with limited liability, the creation of the *société anonyme*, marked a retrogression in the "democratization of finance" which had been the aim of the *Crédit Mobilier*. To a degree, the Government protected itself *vis-à-vis* the type of new companies in that it expressed the hope that there would be investment in state enterprises, but this was an affair of boards of directors and chairmen as opposed to the halcyon days of the fifties and early sixties when the public had been approached directly and when the great enterprises had been affairs of state in which capitalists participated. Now it was the other way round.

It must already be clear that a reversion to orthodox finance was both reflected in, and assisted by, a reversion to more orthodox politics.

The effect of the *Affaire Mirès*, to be followed by the financial scandals attending the Mexican expedition, led to a feeling that too many in governmental circles were touching pitch, and that much of it was sticking. Significantly, Morny and Fould, both old July Monarchists and basically Orleanist in temperament, began to detach themselves from the Empire in the mid-sixties.

Fould, speaking for a whole clique, denounced the use of the Emperor's fiat, which had enabled the free-trade treaty with Britain to be railroaded through, and labelled it a *coup d'état douanier*. In his view "It was indispensable . . . that some intermediary be created between the sovereign and the Nation so that the destinies of the latter are fixed on a more stable basis than the will of one man."[11] Here was the authentic voice of the Party of Order: the man who denounced Persigny as a purveyor of "political bric-à-brac," the man who detested the financial unorthodoxy of the Péreires and the jugglings of Haussmann, had finally formulated the complaints of those who had put their money on the Empire in 1850 thinking it to be a sound business proposition, and who had seen it run for a decade like a bucket-shop.

By the mid-sixties it was clear to both masses and classes that a crisis point in the development of the Empire was being reached. Both sides began to draw up their forces and to seek a means of asserting their claims. On the workers' side, new organizations, like the International were competing with Imperial policy for the proletariat's allegiance. The French working class, though still basically nurtured on the doctrines of Louis Blanc and Proudhon, with a strong tincture of *L'Extinction du Paupérisme*, were beginning to find a new and more coherent orientation. This made the government's attempts to capture and keep working-class support much more difficult, though it never ceased to try and it never, as will be seen, totally failed.

As far as the employers were concerned, the increasing weaknesses of the Imperial regime and the growing possibility of re-asserting some form of parliamentary control over policy, led to the formation of parties pledged to work for "liberalization" of the Empire. What they meant by liberalization was in fact a return to a conservative and class-based parliamentary democracy, such as was established under the Third Republic.

The clash between these opposing forces in society meant that the Empire was faced with an internal crisis at the same time as it was passing through a period of external difficulties, for the foreign policy had reached and passed its zenith by the sixties. Even more important, the Emperor himself had passed his zenith, just at a time when both his tactical sense and political skill were needed to keep the nation together and to keep France ahead in Europe. The mandate of heaven was running out, or as one historian has put it, "the Emperor was becoming a nuisance."[12]

9

The Power Game

"The Policy of France in the Crimean War
defies accurate interpretation, historians of
the Second Empire admitting their inability
to unravel the mystery through silence or
indefiniteness."

Puryear, *England, Russia and the Straits
Question*

"L'Empire, c'est la paix."

Napoleon III

IN a more leisurely age, this chapter might well have been entitled
"In which our hero receives an inheritance and wanders from his
purpose through a misapprehension of its value." That is to say,
Napoleon III did not foment the Crimean War, as the nineteenth-
century historian Vinglake avowed (and others have since maintained)
in order to give himself or his dynasty prestige. The Emperor did not
invent French policy in the Near East any more than he chose the site
of Constantinople. France's interests in the Mediterranean were long-
standing and the later eighteenth and nineteenth centuries had merely
given them greater impetus and definition. The more France was
precluded from manoeuvre in vital areas in Europe, as she was after
1815, the more she turned to peripheral and safer ventures. Spain and
Algeria were better fields to roam in than Belgium, the Rhine or
Northern Italy and were less likely to involve her with the signatories of
the Vienna settlement.

It should never be thought, however, that France ever regarded these
marginal manoeuvres as a substitute for the real thing—any more than
Tonkin or the Sahara was a substitute for Alsace and Lorraine after
1870. They were fringe benefits, which were only of real value if they
could be linked to the central plan of recovering a primary position on
the international scene. This was a constant aim, irrespective of the
political regime, a fact which was made plain as early as 1829 when
France had envisaged a total redrawing of the map of Europe based

upon an agreement between Russia and herself. Charles X's Minister, Polignac, had produced a scheme in the September of that year which offered to Tsar Nicholas I areas in the Balkans and in Asia, including, as first steps, the annexation of Moldavia and Wallachia and the acquisition of Constantinople. In return for this, France would achieve her aim of annexing Belgium and the Rhine frontier. At the same time, to facilitate Russia's Balkan take-over, the Austrian Empire would be demolished and in its place would emerge an independent Italy and a Germany consolidated in a federal form with its capital in Berlin.

As a further point, Russia would be expected to look benevolently in France's expansion into North Africa and Egypt. Whatever chance this grandiose fantasy ever had of emerging from the offices of the Quai d'Orsay was thwarted by the Treaty of Adrianople of 14th September, 1829, and the decision of Nicholas I, taken at the famous conference on the future of Turkey, held two days later in St. Petersburg, that Russian policy would in future be to uphold Ottoman integrity. If that had not been sufficient, the revolution of 1830 in France which overthrew the dynasty and removed Polignac from the scene would have been equally effective in preventing any implementation of this particular "Grand Design."[1]

The Revolution of 1830 changed the dynasty, but did not end France's interest in the Near East. Louis Philippe, aware of the need for caution in foreign policy, moved slowly and discreetly until French support for Mehemet Ali, the Pasha of Egypt, whose desire to extend his dominion further into the crumbling Ottoman Empire led to the crisis of 1840-41, when France was flushed from her cover. An irate Palmerston made it plain just how much France had a real need for a cautious approach, for he revived the Waterloo Coalition against her which, as Palmerston himself remarked, put her in her place.[2]

The fear of a more active French policy facilitated the subsequent Anglo-Russian *rapprochement* in 1844. Inspired by Tsar Nicholas's attempt to find a solution to the Eastern question which would be in consonance with Russian policy, this involved breaking the very shaky English entente with France, and it severely circumscribed further French moves in the area.

The unpopularity of the foreign policy of the July Monarchy, which contributed to the revolution of 1848 not only removed Louis Philippe from the French domestic scene. In the sphere of foreign affairs it led to an open declaration by Lamartine, the Foreign Minister of the new Republic, that "The Treaties of 1815 have no longer any lawful existence in the eyes of the French Republic...," at least verbally striking a firmer note than had been played since 1850, and thereby making the basic aim of French policy clear. It is true that Lamartine took care to add that the treaties were a basis for France's relations with other nations and that ". . . the good sense, the moderation, the conscience, the prudence of the Republic exist." But in spite of the very diplomatic language in which the declaration was couched, it was evident that France had announced her intention of returning to the international scene.[3]

The internal condition of the country and the fact that a "forward" foreign policy was associated with the lunatic fringe of the "1848'ers" prevented any overt manifestation of France's new course. Although much of Lamartine's "Manifesto of the Peoples" was directed to the cafés of Paris rather than the foreign offices of Europe, recent research has shown that Lamartine would, given a chance, have intervened in Italy along the lines of the policy which Napoleon III followed in 1849 had he not been held back by the Executive Committee of the Republic in May, 1848.[4] It was left to Louis Napoleon to put his balancing capacity to the test on the tightrope of the Roman question in 1849-50 after his election to the Presidency.

To the new regime and to the new President even more than to any preceding French government, the treaties of 1815 were an affront, not just to national, but to personal dignity. Article 2 of the Second Treaty of Paris of 1815 declared that "Napoleon Bonaparte and his family . . . have been forever excluded from Supreme Power in France, which exclusion the Contracting Powers bind themselves by the present act to maintain in full vigour and, should it be necessary, with the whole of their forces."[5] Quite clearly, by 1850 the Powers were unlikely to resort to force to remove Louis Napoleon, but it was no empty gesture that Louis Napoleon should announce "L'Empire, c'est la paix." Nor, as will be seen, was it without point that Nicholas I should fret over the numeral III in the new Imperial title and refuse the address of "brother" to a man whose family his own brother had sworn to prevent ever assuming supreme power in France.

The great question for Europe once the Empire was established was what Napoleon III's foreign policy would be. The Empire might mean peace—but peace for whom, and in what form? Those who had taken the trouble to read the *Idées Napoléoniennes* could claim to have found in it a blueprint for the new Emperor's redesigning of Europe along the lines which his uncle had sketched out. Briefly: the latter had wished to use his conquests for the establishment of a European confederation—based upon "a Holy Alliance of people and not of

Kings."[6] If the successor was intent on fulfilling this aim, how would it be achieved? Perhaps aware of the Chinese proverb—"A journey of a thousand miles begins with one step"—Louis Napoleon in 1850 had begun by trying to get his foot in the door of the Holy Places at Jerusalem, thus involving himself in the Eastern question. By the time he had done so, Nicholas I had read the *Idées Napoléoniennes*.[7]

It is important to remember that the Russian Court's attitude to Napoleon III's title was not just an example of a stuffy insistence on a point of etiquette. The dispute which had arisen betweeen the Greek and the Latin monks over the custody of certain of the Holy Places in Jerusalem marched contemporanously with the move towards the throne by Louis Napoleon. Indeed the timing seems too coincidental to be accidental for it was early December, 1852, that the keys of the Holy Sepulchre were handed over by the Orthodox to the Latin Patriarch at virtually the same time as the Senate was handing Louis Napoleon the Imperial crown. Rarely had God and Caesar been rendered to in such an harmonious fashion. In fact the affair of the Holy Places was an easy victory for Napoleon III and it was in his tradition, already set out, of guarding France's interests and prestige where he felt it was necessary so to do. This had been his view on the Roman question and during the Don Pacifico affair.

The trouble was that this time the incident would not be so easily closed; the main protagonist in the area of the Ottoman Empire was Russia, and Nicholas I was not the man to accept any alteration in the *status quo* without considerable protest.

As far as Russian policy was concerned, Nicholas took the Straits Convention of 1841, followed by his *rapprochement* with England, as the more immediate basis of his position. Further back lay Unkiar Skelessi (1833), Adrianople (1829) and Kutchuk Kainardje (1774), all treaties or agreements which testified to Russia's "special relationship" with the Ottoman Empire.

By and large, until 1844, Russian policy had adhered to the decision taken in 1829 to maintain the integrity of the Turkish Empire, although this had not precluded Nicholas from manoeuvring for advantages as and when the occasions had presented themselves. Anxious, therefore, to maintain the good relations with England which had arisen from the obstreperousness of France between 1839 and 1841, Nicholas had, in 1844, reached a secret accord with the English Government, in which both Powers had agreed either to maintain the *status quo* in the Ottoman Empire or to act in concert if there were to be changes. The agreement was based on the view, which Nicholas now

firmly held, that the Turkish Empire was either dying or dead and that
the twitches associated with a stage of *rigor mortis* should not be
confused with the movements of a living body. Nicholas felt that the
time had come for testamentary dispositions, but agreed that it was
better to pretend for as long as possible that the Ottoman Empire was
alive, rather than to announce a death which would only provoke a
dangerous dispute about inheritance.

Now, with the advent of Napoleon III, and with, as Nicholas
thought, evidence of his intent to press France's claims in this area,
Russian policy altered decisively. The time had come to announce the
loss of an old friend. France's victory in what Napoleon III called the
"foolish affair of the Holy Places" had in itself nothing to justify panic
measures at St. Petersburg, but Nicholas linked it with the appearance
at Constantinople of a French man o'war, the *Charlemagne* and also
the rise to power of the pro-French Reshid Pasha as Grand Vizier to
the Sultan.

In Russian eyes, the first action was a flagrant breach of the 1841
Convention forbidding armed warships to pass the Straits, while the
second implied a threat to Russian influence at Constantinople.

The Tsar decided to act, feeling that he could rely on the support of
the English government in defying France. After all, one of the two
major points of agreement had been that in any eventual partition of
the Ottoman Empire, France should be excluded.[8] Nicholas likewise
expected support from Austria, where Russian intervention in 1849 had
saved the Empire from possible collapse, and where at the moment the
Vienna Government was engaged in a minor war with Turkey along
the Montenegrin frontier.

Perhaps it was the autocrat in Nicholas which made him believe that
things would be as he wanted them to, simply because he wished it.
Unfortunately, circumstances had changed beyond recognition and
what had been valid in 1844 was far from being so in 1853. It was a
refusal to recognize this which helped to produce the crisis and then the
war in 1854.

To begin with, Nicholas was right in assuming that France's policy in
the Eastern Mediterranean was "aggressive." The France of Napoleon III
was not that of Louis Philippe—particularly in that the expansion
of French industry and trade was now a more important factor than it
had been in 1840-41. The influence of the Saint-Simonians and
Napoleon III was of considerable significance in forming the Emperor's
attitude to the Mediterranean, a sea which he had already described in
1852 as "a French lake." Michel Chevalier, the leading Saint-Simonian

thinker, member of the *Conseil d'État* and Professor at the *Collège de France*, proposed a "Mediterranean System" which would comprise rail and steamship links, including the Suez Canal project, and which would emerge, *bien entendu,* under French political and financial direction.[9] Even more important from Russia's point of view was the fact that England was no longer sure if her policy in the Near East coincided with the Tsars for the development of British India had led to a growing fear of a Russian threat in that area. The England of the 1850's was expansionist and thrusting, a state of affairs which was reflected in Palmerston's truculent attitude in foreign policy. Nicholas may have thought he was safe with Lord Aberdeen, but Aberdeen did not represent the real trend of English political feeling, which was better incarnated by his Home Secretary.[10]

Any expectations which Nicholas entertained of Austrian support were equally illusory, partly because the Empire was going through a severe internal crisis arising from the aftermath of 1848-50 and partly because Austrian and Russian aims were far from coincidental in the Near East. When Nicholas began hinting to Franz-Josef of his intention to move in the Near East, the Austrian Emperor did his best to restrain his fellow-monarch.[11]

Nesselrode had already warned the Tsar that he was likely to be unsupported, but Nicholas was resolved to find out for himself. In January, 1853, at a reception at St. Petersburg, he informed the British Ambassador, Seymour, that "the bear dies . . . I repeat to you that the bear is dying . . . and we can never allow such an event to take us by surprise." (By the bear Nicholas meant Turkey.) This in itself might not have been alarming, given Nicholas's view of Turkey's condition since 1844, but greater point was added by the dispatch of Prince Menschikov on a personal mission to the Sultan at Constantinople. Menschikov was to demand the repeal of the privileges granted to the Latins in 1852 and at the same time to obtain a reassurance that the Porte regarded Russia as having the right to protect the Orthodox Christians in the Ottoman Empire. This latter point could have been obtained by straining an interpretation of the Treaty of Kutchuk Kainardji of 1774, but Menschikov was instructed to ask for a new and more specific treaty on this particular question of protection of the Christian subjects.

At this stage it might be claimed that Nicholas was doing no more than Napoleon III had done in Jerusalem, that is, asserting a prestigious right rather than a territorial claim. This could not be, however, for the implications were different. Russia was too much *en place*, and Menschikov's demands alarmed both Britain and France, particularly as a Turkish refusal to meet the demands led to a rupture of Russian-Turkish diplomatic relations and the withdrawal of Menschikov in May, 1851.

There can be little doubt that it was English pressure which caused the Sultan to reject the Russian demands. Whether this was or was not simply the result of the personal attitude of the British Ambassador, Stratford Canning (Lord Stratford de Redcliffe) rather than that of the English Cabinet is beside the point.[12] The effect was the same and it forged the Anglo-French alliance, for on 13th-14th June a strong combined naval force appeared in Besika Bay. On 1st July, Russian forces occupied Moldavia and Wallachia, but far from obtaining approval for his action from the Eastern bloc, Nicholas found himself confronted with a protest by Prussia and Austria against the occupation of the Principalities.

Since such a state of tension could not be left unresolved, there were now only two courses open to the Powers: war or intensive diplomacy. It was at this stage that the mainspring of Napoleon III's policy was revealed, for it was he who took the lead in diplomacy and who drew up the Vienna Note of July, 1853, which was sent to Nicholas as a basis for discussion as representing the views of France, Austria, Britain and Russia. The terms of this Note made plain Napoleon III's intention to avoid war, since not only were they favourable to Russia, but they also attempted to take the steam out of the situation by avoiding any reference to territorial changes. In the matter of religious changes the Note said: "The Sublime Porte, moreover, officially promises that the existing state of things shall in no wise be modified without previous understanding with the Governments of France and Russia."[13] What Napoleon III was seeking was Franco-Russian co-operation, but against a background of European consent. The Vienna Note had been approved in both London and Vienna and this represented an international approach which Napoleon hoped to crystallize in a European Congress.

Nicholas accepted the Note but the Sultan rejected it, moved partly by the counsels of Stratford, and partly by the fact that in the Ottoman Empire there was a rising clamour for a Holy War against the infidel occupation of Turkish territory. This had already led to the sending of a strong Egyptian force to Constantinople. The Tsar still remained conciliatory, for the simple reason that if his diplomatic position was strong, since his acceptance of the Note, his military situation was weak for he was without allies. His visit to Franz-Josef at Olmutz in

September, 1853, produced, through the medium of the Austrian minister Buol, a further conciliatory plan in which the Tsar virtually agreed to a very restricted watching brief over the Orthodox Christians in line with the concessions of Kutchuk Kainardji. Napoleon III was willing to accept this as a basis for further negotiations, but it was England which foiled this by determining to send up the fleet. France could not but follow or Napoleon III would forfeit his cherished entente. For the same reason, he could not avoid the actual outbreak of hostilities between the Powers and Russia once the Russo-Turkish war had begun in October. As he said to Morny: "I cannot separate myself from England merely because the northern courts desire it. Without England I will be isolated in Europe. Moreover, in the eyes of the continental courts I am a revolutionary, they do not care for me."[14]

There could be no localization then, unless England would agree, and any chance that this might happen was wrecked by the famous "Massacre" of Sinope on 30th November, in which a Turkish squadron was sent to the bottom by Russian warships. Since Turkey had declared war on Russia, she could hardly complain if she became involved in hostilities, but the effect in England was equivalent to that of a "massacre" of innocent victims. *The Times* assumed that " . . . peace is no longer compatible with the honour of the country," and the *Globe* decided that Russia was not " . . . accessible to the ordinary motives of the rest of the human family." This nonsense merely revealed the bellicosity and Russophobic ignorance of large sections of the populace. That it should have been pandered to by Palmerston, who resigned from the cabinet in December and then rejoined it, having made his point, was disgraceful.

Even then the situation was retrievable had anyone had either the wit or the will to talk sense. In his letter of 29th January, 1854, to the Tsar Nicholas, Napoleon III tried to prevent war by proposing that:

> If Your Majesty desires a peaceful solution as much as I do, what could be simpler than to declare that an Armistice will be signed this day, that things will be taken up again diplomatically and that all hostilities will close and that the belligerents will retire from places to which the necessities of war have called them?
>
> Thus, Russian troops would abandon the Principalities, and our squadrons the Black Sea. Or, if your Majesty should prefer to treat directly with Turkey, he should name an Ambassador to negotiate with a plenipotentiary of the Sultan, a convention which could be submitted to a Four-Power Conference.

5—N III * *

Napoleon went on to say that the Queen of England was in accord and that if Nicholas could not accept this proposal then war was inevitable.[15] Nicholas's rejection led to the war becoming an accomplished fact in April, 1854.

Napoleon III continued to press for a United European front. The treaty of alliance between England and France had invited all European states to join a coalition, and officially the war was the result of an agreement between four Powers, France, England, Austria and Prussia, although the last two were non-belligerents. The basis for this was the declaration of 9th April, 1854, in which all four had proclaimed the integrity of the Ottoman Empire and demanded the evacuation of the Principalities. It was likewise a quadripartite declaration in August, 1854, which was proclaimed as a basis for peace negotiations.

The real issues were now emerging. They resulted from an attempt to find, half-consciously and half-unconsciously, a new balance in Europe. Napoleon III had said as much in the speech to the French Chambers on 2nd March, 1854. While announcing that the time for conquests had passed, the Emperor went on to point out that the results of an open and disinterested policy on the part of France were already to be seen: England was an ally, Germany had recovered freedom of action after forty years of subservience "to the policies of the Cabinet of St. Petersburg." Austria would soon join the Alliance.[16] This was the reckoning which had been produced as a result of the Tsar's demands at Constantinople. It seemed that in effect, the Holy Alliance was doomed and that an era of international lockjaw was ended. The foundations which had held up the 1815 settlement had been steadily eroded, and the Crimean War appeared to reveal just how worn they had become. Much of the confusion and hesitation surrounding the diplomatic preliminaries between 1852 and 1854 can be ascribed to the fact that many of the traditional patterns which had been visible since 1815 had disappeared. It is sometimes remarked that had Metternich, or even Schwarzenberg, been in charge of Austrian policy, rather than Buol then diplomacy might have been better handled and war avoided. In the case of Metternich, this seems unlikely, for he had been already out of touch by 1848. In the case of Schwarzenberg it seems improbable, even though he had shown signs during his tenure of office of being aware of the necessity for change in Austrian foreign policy. The tragedy for Austria was that neither Franz-Josef nor Buol were capable of coping with the changed circumstances in a resolute fashion and so the policy of the Empire was one of vacillation and ineptitude, though it should be noted that a recent authority is of the opinion that farsightedness and resolve would have availed Austria little.[17] The rivalries between Austria and Russia in the Balkans had been present ever since 1827 through Russian control of the Danube mouth. They had been still further exacerbated by the Montenegrin clash of 1852. A revengeful Prussia was already resolved to wrest from Austria her predominance in the German confederation and Cavour was equally resolved to challenge the Empire in Italy.

Apart from that there was the perennial problem of Poland. If the Austrian Empire entered the war, the Allies could attack Russia in Poland. This could mean that the whole Eastern European situation would crumble and that Austria would derive little benefit from such an event, particularly in view of Napoleon III's attitude to a restoration of a Polish state. Austria would have been mad to facilitate such a proceeding and that is why she dare not break with Russia unless driven to the last extremity by Britain and France. Here was the real weakness of Austria; not her vacillation in her approach to the Crimean War question, but her inability to maintain herself without Russian military support, as 1849-50 had revealed.

In December, 1854, when Austria finally committed herself, with reservations, to aiding the Western Alliance, she did so not only in order to obtain the Principalities which she had occupied after Russia's withdrawal, but also because of a very real fear that Napoleon III might activate the Polish question by more revolutionary methods than diplomacy.

Napoleon III was irked that Austria would not actually go to war, although Article V of the Treaty of December had envisaged this step unless Russia should have agreed to peace on the basis of the Four Points of August 1854. But the existence of the agreement was in itself, he thought, another blow to the Holy Alliance and a tribute to the potency of the Polish Question as a blackmailer's weapon.

Buol, the Austrian Chancellor, justified his country's attitude by saying:

What more can the Allies expect? What is the urgent motive and justification for a declaration of war against Russia at this time? Our task was to obtain, by force if necessary, the evacuation of the Principalities. Russia preferred to yield this region. It is permissible to state that our attitude has contributed to the result for the Allies which would have cost them an immense amount of effort and a bitter struggle to obtain.[18]

His special pleading was not just an excuse. The simple fact was that unless the army was demobilized the Austrian state faced bankruptcy.

An equally agonizing problem, apart from financial weakness, was made clear by Buol's saying to Drouyn de Lhuys "that a declaration of war by Austria would only serve to strengthen Russian influence in Prussia and the German states."[19] He might have added that it was unlikely that this time Russian policy would be deflected by a gambit like the Carlsbad Decrees of 1819, which Metternich had used to make a Russian presence in Germany superfluous. He certainly had the sense to point out to Franz-Josef that only wishful thinking could make anyone believe in the immediate possibility of the re-establishment of the Holy Alliance. As if to prove his point Nicholas I, one of its main defenders, died on 2nd March, 1855.

With Nicholas's death, the end of the war moved perceptibly nearer. For a time the Russians thought that if they held Sebastopol until a second winter began, the Allies might be forced to come to terms more favourable to Russia. But the fall of the fortress in September, 1855, put an end to any illusions on this score, although the new Tsar, Alexander II, continued to talk of a "Holy War."[20] The condition of Russian finances and the Russian army meant that peace must not only come, but come as quickly as possible so long, as Nesselrode said, the terms "shall be compatible with our honour." It was not only the Russians who wanted peace. Napoleon III had shown more vigour than anyone in his desire to prosecute the war and indeed had shown more sense in his attitudes to it than anyone else involved, but by the autumn of 1855 he too was ready for peace.

It was true that the war had done much to cement the entente with England. The visit of Prince Albert to Boulogne in November, 1854, had been followed by a visit of the Emperor and Empress to England in April, 1855. This had been a personal triumph for Napoleon III who had succeeded in captivating Queen Victoria in a way in which he had not been quite so successful with Prince Albert. Albert had found the Emperor quiet but humorous and at his ease: "The Emperor smoking cigarettes and not being able to understand my not giving in to it. He is very chilly, complains of rheumatism, and goes early to bed." Albert also noted that Napoleon was: "more like an 'Amateur Politician' mixing very sound and many crude notions together."[21]

The Queen, obviously less demanding, wrote: "He is evidently possessed of *indomitable courage, unflinching firmness of purpose, self-reliance* and *great secrecy* ... and at the same time he is endowed

with wonderful *self-control*, great *calmness*, even *gentleness* and with
a *power of fascination*, the effect of which upon all those become
more intimately acquainted with him is most *sensibly* felt." The
highest compliment perhaps was that: ". . . the Emperor is as unlike
a Frenchman as possible, being much more German than French in
character." Coming from one whose knowledge of Germans was
extensive and whose knowledge of Frenchmen limited, the Queen's
compliment must be put in perspective. But it was the intent behind
it which was most revealing and it is the extent of the royal italics
which make this clear. Henceforth the Queen had another man in
her life—probably some way between Lord Melbourne and Prince
Albert. That the Emperor was aware of the value of his charm as
of the alliance itself was revealed when a return match brought
Victoria and Albert to Paris in the August of 1855. Here, forty years
after Waterloo, the Queen, leaning on the arm of the Emperor, and
gazing at the tomb of Napoleon I, was thrilled to see ". . . the old
enmities wiped out over the tomb of Napoleon I, before whose coffin
I stood (by torchlight) at the arm of Napoleon III, now my nearest
and dearest ally." This was not the only apotheosis of the *Rêveries
Politiques*, it was the apotheosis of the Romantic movement.

It was as well that Napoleon could draw personal comfort from his
fellow sovereign at a time when he could draw little from his own
family, for the exploits of Prince Napoleon at the Crimea had
brought nothing but contempt on the Imperial House. Prince
Napoleon prided himself on his physical resemblance to his uncle. He
certainly had nothing else of him and most particularly was he
deficient in warlike qualities. Having first of all filled the air with
lamentation as to the probable duration and difficulty of the war the
Prince had come home from the Crimea because of a weakness in his
bowels. The Parisian wits immediately changed his nickname from
"Plon-Plon" to "Craint-Plomb" (the bullet-fearer") and it was unfortunate that he had already been awarded the *Médaille Militaire* for
bravery before this inglorious return.

The Emperor was furious at this conduct from the man who was
still heir to the throne and it was undoubtedly the seeming cowardice
of his cousin which, as much as anything else, lay behind his decision
to go to the Crimea to restore the family honour. It was this
determination which had led to the pressing invitation to visit
England in 1854. As Lord Malmesbury put it: "The English and the
French governments have prevailed upon Louis Napoleon to pay a

visit to England, the main object being to prevent his going to the Crimea which he was bent upon."[22]

The Emperor could perhaps feel that his visits to England, and the Queen and her Consort's visit to Paris, had bolstered any sagging of Imperial prestige caused by Prince Napoleon's conduct, but the Prince was not the only worry. There were signs that the war was unpopular in France and there were threats of both a bad harvest and a financial crisis. If grain was scarce, so was gold and silver. Now that Sebastopol had fallen the Emperor was under pressure to make peace, not least from Morny and others with considerable financial interests in the stability of the Bourse. Morny was deeply involved in the affair of financing the new railways to be built in Spain where he had obtained concessions for those companies in which he was interested. This was a risky operation, not merely because of the instability of Spanish governments, but also because it involved both the rival banking groups of Rothschild and Péreires. In these circumstances, peace was essential to produce calm on the Bourse.[23]

Public opinion throughout France, which had never been more than lukewarm in its support for the war, was likewise a factor in pushing the Emperor towards decisive peace moves. The man who had said in 1849 "I shall constantly govern in the interests of the masses" had meant it, and he continued to mean it for the rest of his reign.[24]

In this particular instance, the problem was how to please his ally while pleasing public opinion in France. Napoleon III knew that Palmerston's bellicosity and Russophobia inclined him to a continuation of the war. Anxious not to break the entente, Napoleon faced the delicate task of persuading his ally to become more pacific.

In November, 1855, after Palmerston had made a bellicose speech at the Lord Mayor's banquet, Persigny, the French Ambassador in London, informed him that France needed peace because of her financial situation. He pointed out to Palmerston that if peace did not come by the spring of 1856, there would be a severe financial crisis, and the crisis would not be limited to France.[25] In fact, although contemporaries did not perceive its full implications, the great financial crisis of the mid-fifties was beginning and Persigny's prognostication was truer than he could possibly have known.

Napoleon III did not himself try to influence his ally by stressing the economic factors. Instead he decided to cut through the diplomatic triangle, almost stupefying in its complexity, which had been created by the months of negotiations in Vienna' between Austria,

France, Russia and Britain.[26] Weary of endless talking over details with no apparent result, Napoleon III had, in September, 1855, thrown the whole discussion wide open by introducing the question of Poland. The British Government had immediately jibbed at this, as the Emperor very well knew they would, although in the extremity of a wartime alliance they agreed that the reconstitution of a Polish Kingdom could be accepted in principle.

Napoleon now had the diplomatic initiative and in November, with the signing of an alliance between Sweden and the Allies, the prospect of activating the Polish question was brought a step nearer. As far as Russia was concerned, Sweden's adherence to the Allies raised the whole problem of Finland which was quite ready to exchange Russian for Swedish rule in defiance of the 1815 settlement. The Emperor was, therefore, able to use a strong stick with which to belabour the Tsar Alexander, for he let it be known indirectly at St. Petersburg that: "If in the spring [of 1856] no understanding has been reached I shall appeal to the nationalities and in particular to the nation of Poland."[27]

The prospect of a real upset in Europe caused general alarm. The King of Prussia wrote to the Tsar urging him to make peace pointing out the dangers which would arise if war were prolonged: ". . . for the real interest of Russia, Prussia herself, and for the whole of Europe . . . Once subversive passions are unleashed, who can estimate the consequences of a universal upset?"[28]

Harassed on all sides, for Russia's internal condition gave cause for great alarm, Alexander finally agreed to come to the conference table, armed with an assurance that Napoleon III would seek an entente with him as soon as possible.

Was Napoleon III serious in his threats to drag the Polish question on to the European stage? There is no doubt that the Polish cause was a popular one in France, particularly among Republican and "advanced" political circles. Had the Emperor needed to continue the war and been anxious for public support, he could hardly have chosen better than to take up the cause of Poland. But the financial situation of France precluded an adventurous policy at that moment, even had the Emperor really been inclined to pursue it and, in fact, it would seem that Napoleon was merely using a diplomatic *coup d'état* in order to bring his ally to her senses and at the same time to bring the war to an end. Apart from that, if one bears in mind the Emperor's genuine devotion to peace, it was possible that the Congress which was now to assemble at Paris to settle definite peace terms could produce the desired results of changes in Europe without further necessity for war. In a sense, it would be fair to say that the whole Crimean War had been an error which could have been avoided by skilled diplomacy. If, as seems probable, the Emperor's original aim had been for a Congress without war, then it might be said that in 1856 he had achieved his aim in spite of the war. Since there were representatives of all the leading Powers at Paris, the Congress was less a congress of victors than a meeting of the European states, and Napoleon III's attempt to mollify Alexander II began, as had been noted, even before the Congress met. They were to be increased during the time the Congress was sitting.

There can be no doubt of the pre-eminent position of Napoleon III in 1856. The war may not have been desired by him, but he could draw dividends from it, for if France's military performance had been merely less lamentable than England's, her diplomatic performance had been spectacular. That was the Emperor's personal triumph. He had ended the war by outmanoeuvring both his ally and his enemy. He had avoided the conservative entanglements of an Austrian alliance which would have tied his hands in any proposed redrawing of the European map. He had thrown the King of Prussia into a fright by threatening to bring up the question of Poland and, furthermore, he had left Austria and Prussia isolated, not merely one from the other in Germany, but both in Europe. The Emperor had also been angered by the selfishness displayed by the Austrian government during the diplomatic haggling of 1855. It was this which had led to the jettisoning of the pro-Austrian Foreign Minister, Drouyn de Lhuys, in the summer of 1855. As the Empress Eugénie had put it to Hübner, the Austrian Ambassador in Paris, "You did not conciliate Russia. You did not regain your influence on Germany, and you cannot count upon the gratitude of France and England."[29]

Even more ominous for Austria was the fact that Piedmont, her enemy in Italy, had been an ally in war and was to be a counsellor in peace. The question of the nationalities had been brought into the open and in a legitimate form. The question now was, how would Napoleon III implement his ideas on nationality and what form would the implementation take? What was certain was that nothing could go on as before. Metternich, living in retirement and isolation in Vienna, put it neatly. "It is peace," he said, "but it is not the peace of order."

Frontiers and Nationalities

*"L'Empereur Napoléon I a cru devoir
conquérir les peuples pour les affranchir;
Napoléon III veut les affranchir sans les
conquérir."*

Anon. Pamphlet: *L'Empereur Napoléon III
et l'Italie*, Paris, 1859

*"Dans ce probleme des frontières le souci de
la sécurité nationale emportait sur la justice
à l'égard des peuples."*

Paul Henry

WHEN Prince Metternich commented on the Treaty of Paris that "it was not the peace of order" he meant, of course, a diplomatic, settled, European order as opposed to an unstable and revolutionary situation. The former Austrian Chancellor had fought all his political life to maintain such an order or equilibrium in international affairs, not just because the existence of the Hapsburg Empire depended upon it, but because he had lived through a period of great disorder. He had seen that the internal stability of states was affected by international disturbance and that if revolution bred war, war was a breeder of revolution.

It was fear of this type of cycle that had lain behind the European attitude to France's revolution of 1848, and, although Louis Napoleon had mastered the "reds" with their lunatic foreign policy, it seemed as if there was still reality behind the original fear. Out of 1848 had come Louis Napoleon, and within a few years had come the first international war since 1815. It remained to be seen whether Napoleon III was a disturber of order because he was a revolutionary figure or whether he was simply a French sovereign pursuing the eternal aims of the French Monarchy which, in their latest phase, had taken the form of breaking the bonds of 1815. One contemporary dissented from the latter view, for Marx was convinced that the Crimean War was fought not to break but to extend the "Vienna System." This, however, was an idiosyncratic approach.

To most statesmen of the time it was clear that Napoleon III was a revisionist. The question was, what motivated his revisionism? And did revisionism imply revolution? Any consideration of the answers to these questions leads to an examination of the famous *Politique des Nationalités*, an aspect of foreign policy of Napoleon III which has been much discussed and which is still a matter for debate. The Emperor himself must bear a great deal of the responsibility for the fact that so much controversy has arisen, for he was, from the outset of his political career, prone to talk in terms which seemed to give substance to the idea of a "policy of nationalities." The *Idées Napoléoniennes* contain passages on the concept of a Europe of nations, the ultimate aim, according to Louis Napoleon, of his uncle. In subsequent pronouncements once he was himself Emperor, Napoleon III appeared to be invoking a "national principle" as a reason for re-ordering the European states system.

It might be said that the principle of nationalities had as much to do with French foreign policy between 1850 and 1870 as communism had to do with the foreign policy of the U.S.S.R. a century later. That leaves the question ideologically open, but it does not, in either case, preclude an examination of the facts and events which have taken place. In the case of Napoleon III's foreign policy, some interesting points emerge which lead toward the conclusion that the policy of nationalities was more myth than reality.

What appears to have produced the confusion of Napoleon III's foreign policy with emergent nationalities in Europe is simply a co-incidence in time. Everyone in Europe was aware as early as the 1820's and 1830's that changes were occurring and that these were bound to increase in both scope and nature. The extension of industrial and economic growth, and the rise of a new type of Western European preponderance based upon that growth, predicated some alteration in the European states system. This in itself was neither new nor threatening; periods of equilibrium and immobility had been rare in Europe since the heyday of the Roman Empire. What was new was the form in which the changes presented themselves, and this in turn conditioned the way in which they were used by the European states to increase their power.

All this took place behind a verbal smoke screen; "pan-Slavism," "manifest destiny," "nationalities," even "the white man's burden" were expansively invoked, in an age of expansion, to justify the foreign policies of the Powers involved.

As far as Napoleon III was concerned, his main aim was to restore France's position in Europe, but he was sufficiently perceptive to realize that the best way to do this was to draw sustenance from the situation as it existed. Napoleon III did not "make" or "ferment" problems in Europe in the period in which he ruled France. He used them, turning them where possible to the advantage of his own country. Until he was challenged by Bismarck, who was more adroit and more realistic than himself, he had a measure of success. But it would be wrong to dismiss Napoleon III as an impractical dreamer who was overcome by a hardheaded realist. It would be safer to indict him for hesitancy at a time when decisiveness was the cardinal quality which was needed and to accuse him of an attempt to achieve by pacific means what only war could have won. It is, perhaps, the latter factor which makes his failure honourable and it may be true to say that: "[the policy] . . . had not only generosity, but grandeur. Carried to its conclusions, the plan would have gained for France an increase in power and an extension of territory."[1] That said, the fact remains that it failed and the Empire fell, but it fell not through the pursuit of chimeras, but because it was diplomatically outmanoeuvred and then militarily outgunned.

The high point of Imperial policy is to be found in the years between 1856 and 1863, described as "a second Napoleonic age," years in which Napoleon III, as a consequence of the Crimean War and the entente with England managed to hold the diplomatic initiative. The tragedy lay in the precarious nature of his advantage, since it rested upon two very shaky props, the one the continuance of English support the other the continuance of Russian benevolence—and much of the latter was in turn dependent on that country's weakness.

When, on the morrow of the Crimean War, Napoleon III extended a hand to Russia, he was attempting to harden the European situation at a time when his prestige was high and the moment was favourable to France. Austria was virtually isolated, Prussia would dance to whatever tune was played in St. Petersburg and Britain was, officially, an ally. If Napoleon III could keep the Holy Alliance from functioning by making Russia the spanner in the works rather than the driving wheel of the whole machine, then France was well on the way to achieving a re-ordering of Europe which would be to her further advantage.

One very important factor had now emerged, namely that the Russian Empire was as much a revisionist power as was the French Empire. The one wanted to reverse 1856, the other 1815. The problem was to make England accept this factor and this was not easy. England's aim in the Crimean War had been to cripple Russia as much, or more, than it had been to maintain Ottoman integrity. Palmerston and the English government were therefore less than enthusiastic about the Emperor's plans for an alliance with their quondam enemy. When Austria, in an attempt to reinstate if not quite rehabilitate herself in the eyes of the Great Powers, reminded the statesmen at Paris of the promise of a Triple Alliance which would be directed towards the maintenance of the 1856 treaty, the English government reacted favourably. Napoleon III, on the other hand, began to shuffle in an attempt to evade a situation which would give unnecessary offence to Russia and make the task of reconciling France and Russia more difficult.[2]

In this particular case, Napoleon III, while acquiescing to please England, achieved his aim by watering down the Triple Alliance to such an extent that Russia could be persuaded to swallow what might have been too strong medicine if taken neat. But the Tsar Alexander was still piqued that the incident should have occurred at all. Since Russian policy appears to have been based, as all good revisionist diplomacy must be, upon rendering the consequences of the treaty made against her null and void, and that as quickly as possible, the Tsar's attitude is understandable. Alexander must have felt particularly miffed, since he was well aware of the strain in the Anglo-French entente, and even more aware of Napoleon III's desire for his friendship.

On the first count, Alexander had ample evidence of strain between Britain and France in the preposterous affair of the Serpents Island and Bolgrad, which provided the Russian government with a relatively cheap means (one lieutenant and seven seamen were involved) of provoking a diplomatic incident by simply being provoking.[3] As one authority has said: "The dispute ... formed the first test of the Crimean settlement. It was, on the part of Russian diplomacy, a reconaissance rather than a major engagement and revealed some disarray in the allied camp and some flaws in the Crimean system."[4]

On the second, and ultimately the vital count, Alexander had the evidence of the activities of the French Ambassador in St. Petersburg where the Duc de Morny anxiously tried to find grounds for a conciliatory approach to Franco-Russian problems in the hope that a real *rapprochement* would virtually annul the recently-signed treaty. On one point especially, the cancellation of the Black Sea Clauses, Gortchakov, The Tsar's Foreign Minister, was particularly pressing—but this was the one point on which Napoleon III dared not yield, for to give way there would really overstrain the relationship with England.

Alexander II made it plain to Morny that he was well aware of this: "Frankly, I am afraid that his relations with England dominate his whole thinking, even the public law of Europe, and I cannot hide my unease from you."[5] Morny, in agreement with the Tsar, wrote directly to his half-brother, spelling out for him the implications of an alliance with Russia. If France was to pursue an "active" or "forward" foreign policy:

> The Emperor need fear no trap on the part of the Russian government. . . . Finding itself disarmed in the Black Sea, it sincerely desires to find a real support (*un appui réel*) in France. Note well that Russia is the only power which will ratify all expansion on the part of France. I've already received this assurance; demand as much from England! And who knows, with a people as fickle and demanding as ours what it will not one day come to in order to satisfy them? Myself, I fear the English like fire. As for the Emperor of Russia, I believe I have observed him well: I believe one can count on him, he is a man of honour.[6]

Morny also pointed out that if France wanted to redraw the map of Europe for her own benefit, she would need the consent of Germany "and that would only be possible with the agreement of Russia."[7]

While Morny's "conservative" position, in the context of the Second Empire, made him a natural partisan of the Russian Alliance, it is fair to say that he clearly identified a basic problem which was bound to affect Napoleon III's European policy. But the Emperor could not break so easily with England because that would close an important option, which must be kept open, and in any event, the actual condition of Russia in 1856-7 detracted from her importance as an ally at that particular moment. Napoleon III dared not underline Russian weakness, for his real link with Palmerston was the latter's Russophobia and his fear that England alone would not be enough to cope with the Tsar's designs. Yet, at the same time, he dared not rub Alexander's nose in the mud for if France was determined to avoid an alliance except on her own terms, Russian benevolence was essential. In 1856 the state of Russia was such that this benevolence could hardly be refused. It was not just the fact that if France was not a friend who would be? It was the conditions prevailing internally in the Empire which made Alexander so effusive and forthcoming in his encounters with Morny.

Apart from Morny's conservative bias in the matter of the alliance, there was also his economic and financial interest in a country which he held to be "*une mine à exploiter*," and which an alliance would open up to those financial operators with whom Morny was closely linked. But too much should not be made of this; the hope that an alliance would lead to financial and economic exploitation was not a diplomatic concept invented by Morny, it was simply that the "railway age" in Europe had given the thing a new impetus and a new form.

In fact Morny was over-optimistic as to Russia's capacity, both as an ally and as "*une mine à exploiter*," for the economic structure of Russia was in much too primitive a condition to permit of easy penetration by foreign capital. Those who saw in the railway contracts a rich field for investment were to be disappointed, and indeed the Rothschild interests had turned down any idea of massive investment in proposed Russian railways after a visit by James de Rothschild in 1851. It was left to the Péreire *Crédit Mobilier* group, backed by Baring of London, to take up the project. It turned out to be a finger-burning occasion.[8]

The economy was in too primitive a condition to take the strain of rapid expansion, not least because of a shortage of capital and credit. The "take-off point" seems to have been still some way off and the basic problem of Russia was not how to join the glittering nineteenth-century world of capital and finance, but how to shed the *damnosa hereditas* of serfdom with its medieval economy which was strangling all progress.[9] It was the problem of serfdom and the knowledge that an attempt to solve it would no longer be deferred which conditioned much of Russia's attitude to the West at this period. Perhaps this was Napoleon III's trump card? Without serfdom and its attendant problems in the 1850's there would have been no opportunity to manoeuvre between Russia and England. Was the map of Europe redrawn because there existed an idea of "nationality" or because two-thirds of the Russian population were serfs?

In any event Napoleon III was not ready in the autumn of 1856 to go as far as Russia desired. He was not at all anxious to push England too far and he was more than suspicious of Morny's personal interest in the matter of the alliance. Walewski, the Foreign Minister, and Persigny at that time Ambassador in London, both leaned as heavily as they could on the Emperor to keep him pointing in the direction of London rather than Petersburg. And so Morny was withdrawn in June, 1857, having contracted a personal alliance with a Russian Princess, and the Emperor Napoleon remained with his hands free.[10]

How far had the "policy of nationalities" advanced by 1857? The list of achievements is meagre; an intervention in favour of the Bosnians, who wanted the right to build Christian churches and enjoy lighter taxation, was linked to the general clause of the 1856 treaty which envisaged religious toleration in the Ottoman Empire. In 1856, by the Hatti Humayan, the Sultan promised to treat his Christian subjects better, but there is little evidence to show that the Sultan intended to do anything to further this aim and even less evidence to show that the Christian signatories proposed to oblige him to do so. Apart from that, it is possible that the Hatti Humayan did more harm than good and paved the way for even more bitter struggles between Christian and Moslem.[11] It certainly did nothing for the Balkan nationalities as many there had suspected. In any event, it was not at all sure that the Balkan peoples would not rather have been "liberated" by Russia, particularly since the only positive intervention on behalf of any of them had been a joint Anglo-French occupation of Greece in 1856 to prevent the Kingdom from making good its declared intention of breaking with Constantinople. The Allies did not withdraw from there until 1857.[12]

Those who hold to the theory of a policy of nationalities usually excuse Napoleon III's apparent lack of interest in the question before 1859 on the grounds of his concentration in Italy.[13] But this is rather to equate the cause of Italy with the *politique des nationalités* to the exclusion of other peoples' interests, as if nowhere else mattered. Apart from that, there is another instance of the Emperor's somewhat cavalier attitude to nationality, in his approach to the problems of the Iberian Peninsula. In this area, Napoleon III's policy was one of Iberian Union, but this could only be done at the expense of either the Spanish or the Portuguese, both of whom disliked the other intensely. When pressed upon this point by Prince Albert, to whom he gave the idea an airing during the meeting of 1854, the Emperor had replied that he would say "... *aux Portugais, je vous donne l'Espagne, et aux Espagnols, je vous donne le Portugal.*"[14] If this were what the Emperor meant by the policy of nationalities, then it would seem, at its crudest, to have been no more than a political conjuring trick.

But in fact the real business was not being transacted in Iberia or the Balkans; it was with Russia and Sardinia that the Emperor was concerned in the period from 1857 to 1859 and the conversation at Turin and Petersburg was not about nationalities, but about frontiers, their extension and their defence. These were serious affairs but this did not prevent their being entered into gracefully. The autumn and winter of 1856 and the spring and early summer of 1857 saw many distinguished,

royal travellers on the move in Europe. In October, 1856, the Dowager
Empress of Russia, Alexandra Fyodorovna arrived at Nice to spend the
winter on the Riviera. In January, King Victor Emmanuel of Sardinia
visited her on what was at the time his own territory. The meeting was
cordial and public, so that Europe might assess the depth of amity
between the two former enemies.

In March the Tsar Alexander's brother, Grand-Duke Constantine
Nikolayevitch, reached his mother's villa via Turin, where he had been
warmly welcomed and decorated by the King. In April, Victor
Emmanuel joined the Imperial guests, one of whom (the Grand Duke)
was on his way to Toulon to launch five vessels for the Russian navy
which had been built in the port. He then continued to Paris to meet
Napoleon III while his mother, reversing roles, had gone to Turin to
meet Victor Emmanuel.

All this reads like a court and society column, but it had serious
purpose. In the middle of the last century crowned heads did not go on
tour just for a change of air and these junketings were no exception.
Apart from indicating the friendship of France, Sardinia and Russia,
they were a means of introducing a Russian plan for the establishment
of a naval station in the Mediterranean.[15] Sardinian agreement to this
plan was contingent on French consent and by a splendid piece of
timing the Sardinian request reached Napoleon III in August, just as
he was about to set out for Stuttgart to meet the Emperor Alexander.

Napoleon III intended a visit to Queen Victoria and Prince Albert
on the 6th August, *en route* to Stuttgart, with a view to discussing his
ideas for Europe. The omens for this were not good. Before the visit
occurred, Prince Albert had written "[he] may be disappointed at our
not being able to assent to his plans and aspirations."[16]

But any disappointment the Emperor may have experienced must
have been tempered by the knowledge that his position, when he went
travelling that summer, was reasonably secure at home as well as
abroad. The elections in France in June, 1857, had been favourable
and the country appeared to be weathering the first stages of the
financial crisis, which had begun in 1856. This knowledge made his
foreign policy more adventurous, and in particular he had shown an
inclination to make French power more mobile by laying down a naval
construction programme. Unfortunately for him this was, as far as
England was concerned, a fatal move and the question of the French
fleet was one which remained an irritant until the fall of the Empire in
1870. It was particularly unfortunate that during the English visit, the
Emperor treated Prince Albert to an exposé of his Mediterranean

policy, stressing that his aims in the Mediterranean were European. A fair division of the spoils were envisaged : "Spain might have Morocco, Sardinia a part of Tripoli, England Egypt, Austria a part of Syria—and how should I know . . . France herself needs an outlet for her restless spirits."[17] The Prince found all this disturbing and such projects did nothing to endear the Emperor to the English government.

It seems that Alexander II was treated to a similar dose of *rêveries Imperiales* when the two Emperors met at Stuttgart. Although the meeting was hardly as dramatic as that which had taken place between their respective uncles on a raft in the middle of the river Niemen, it was not lacking in importance. They were able to exchange Mediterranean dreams, and Alexander was enabled to acquire his naval station at Villafranca in October, 1857. No doubt Napoleon III was glad to be able to offer something to the Tsar for the real problem of the moment was not the Mediterranean, but what should be done with the Principalities of Moldavia and Wallachia, and this touched Russia much more closely than the maintenance of a few ships in the Mediterranean. The Principalities in question were, in fact, the forcing point for the next stage in Napoleon's policy.

In order to understand why Moldavia and Wallachia were important in the development of French policy, it is necessary to go back to 1853 when, as part of his diplomatic offensive during the preliminaries to the Crimean War, Nicholas I had occupied the Principalities. Combined Austro-Prussian pressure, coupled with the fact that he became engaged in war with England and France, led to the Tsar's withdrawal from the Principalities in July 1854. To his fury, they were occupied by Austrian forces as the result of an Austro-Turkish convention, and their occupation was scheduled to last until the end of the hostilities. This action, even more than lack of support in the war itself, produced the bitter resentment against Austria which was so strong in St. Petersburg, and which was even more fierce when Austria got first Prussia (in November) and then France and England (in December) to guarantee her against a Russian attack in the Principalities.

Austria had scored a diplomatic success of some magnitude, particularly as she had added to the strength of her position by getting Napoleon III in December, 1854, to guarantee her position in Italy. She, thus, thwarted a scheme of Lord Palmerston's which Napoleon III adopted in 1856, of persuading her to exchange her Italian possessions for the Rumanian principalities. Yet in Austria's success lay her own undoing. Henceforth, Russian hostility could be counted upon, while

French support was much more problematical, given Napoleon III's attitude to Italy and Sardinia's participation in the war. All that Austria had succeeded in doing, as she very soon discovered, was to isolate herself.

In 1857 she found herself forced to withdraw from the Principalities, since the Treaty of Paris was now operative, and the Principalities were declared henceforth to be neither Russian nor Austrian, but were each to have an independent, national administration with their own army. All this was to be under the blanket of Turkish suzerainty. What this meant in practice was that the area was to become the scene of a struggle for power, for the geographical position of both Principalities at the mouth of the Danube made them of considerable importance to both Austria and Russia.

Napoleon III's attitude to the Rumanian problem he expressed to Cowley, the English Ambassador in Paris, in the course of a discussion on the Turkish Empire.

> His Majesty could well understand that Turkey, Austria and Russia should oppose the Union of the Principalities, since in union there would be strength, and it must be the desire of those Powers, each for its own specific reasons, to keep those Provinces in a state of weakness; but for his own part he was convinced that the surest barrier against the future encroachments of Russia was to be found in strengthening the Principalities . . .[18]

This was all very well, but was the Emperor's motive in pressing that the Principalities be united merely that they would be a more appetizing dish to tempt Austria with in exchange for Lombardy and Venetia? Or would they really be a barrier to Russian expansion? Did Napoleon III hope that his interference on behalf of the Principalities would reconcile the inhabitants to acceptance of any further scheme he might have in mind which would involve them?

In the short run, the affair of the Principalities *was* concluded in a manner favourable to the inhabitants, in that the first elections held under the terms of Paris in 1856 were annulled, at Napoleon III's request, and the second election produced a majority which accepted a quasi-union. Finally, in 1859, the two sections elected the same ruler (Hospodar) and achieved recognition of the *fait accompli* at a reconvened session of the Paris Conference held in the same year. By 1861, Rumania was a state and France could claim to have aided much in her creation. But it was less in pursuit of an abstract theory of nationality and more in pursuit of a means of manoeuvring between

Austria and Russia that Napoleon III had lent his support. It is true, he loathed the Turks, as did most civilized rulers, but this in itself would not have been enough. Had the Principalities lacked immediate strategic significance or potential as a compensatory factor in his relations with Austria, tht Emperor might well have left them alone.

The fact that at Stuttgart Alexander had approved of Napoleon III's policy, largely because it was intensely disliked by Austria and only luke-warmly accepted by England, had increased the Emperor's partiality for the Rumanians, just as the same reason had led him to support a dynastic change in Serbia in 1858 when a pro-Russian client had been installed as King.

However, all these were incidental moves in Napoleon's plans, for he was now focusing on the question of Italy. Russian goodwill was as assured as it could be, in spite of the gaffe made by the Emperor by mentioning the Polish question at Stuttgart. The Italian problem could not be left any longer without some solution, for the simple reason that either transformation would take place under the aegis of France or there might well be a revolution and Austria would intervene, thereby setting up a chain of reaction and further revolution.

Cavour had made Sardinia not only part of international diplomacy, but also a centre for all the disaffected of Italy. For some time now, all the "progressive" interests in the Peninsula had looked to the Northern Kingdom for a sign, but the growing importance of the Italian National Society proved that a prolonged period of inaction could be dangerous for the Turin government in that it would strengthen the hand of the activist and revolutionary groups. Cavour's genuine fear of revolutionary movements and their effect upon Sardinia could be used as a weapon with which to frighten the other Powers, and it was to this end that he had informed the Austrian and other governments in Italy about plots against them. But this was to play a dangerous double game which could not last forever, for sooner or later the machinations of Sardinia would be exposed and her pretensions to "lead Italy" discredited.

A further incentive to hurry occurred in November, 1857, when elections were held in the Kingdom of Sardinia which weakened Cavour's position in the Parliament at Turin. A strong Catholic vote in Savoy and Nice was coupled with a loss in the "Cavourian party" in Piedmont itself. To add to his difficulties, an attempt was made to assassinate Napoleon III on the night of 14th January, 1858, by a group of Italian patriots led by Count Orsini. Cavour could not immediately have known that while Orsini's bomb had failed to kill the

Emperor, it had blown up all the obstacles which stood between him and his goal, for the immediate reaction in France and elsewhere was a sense of outrage.

The trial of Felice Orsini and his accomplices was an extraordinary example of the ambivalence of Napoleon III. On the one hand, the Law of General Security had been in a very sharp and repressive response to this attempted murder of the head of state, yet on the other, the intended victim clearly allowed his would-be murderer to turn his crime into a martyrdom. Orsini's speech from the dock was an impassioned plea for justice for Italy rather than an attack upon Napoleon III and it was well known in political circles that Orsini's letter to the Emperor, reminding him of his feelings for Italy, was published by Imperial favour.[19] Indeed, Napoleon III wanted to pardon Orsini and only the strongest opposition in the Council at a meeting of 12th March, 1858, prevented him from doing so. Orsini was guillotined on the 13th.[20]

Orsini created problems abroad as well as at home. He had come from England and his bombs had been made in Birmingham. The French press and public opinion clamoured for some action on the part of the English Government to prevent a reoccurrence of this type of affair and the result was Palmerston's "Conspiracy to Murder" Bill which brought him down in the Commons. Marx commented succinctly in a letter to Engels that "if Orsini did not kill Louis Napoleon, he certainly killed Palmerston." The question was, what had changed in Anglo-French relations as a result of the outburst of popular feeling on both sides of the Channel, and the subsequent change of government in London?

The new Ministry of Lord Derby and Disraeli was described by Greville as "a more decent-looking affair than anybody expected," but it was hardly strong. It had as its Foreign Secretary Lord Malmesbury, whose personal friendship with Napoleon III, dating back for many years, did not necessarily make clear what the foreign policy would be. Given the fact that "bipartisanship" was fairly well established, no dramatic changes need to be expected from the new Ministry and Napoleon III, while he had been forced to protest officially to the English Government, had let it be known privately that he had done so against his will. There seemed no reason, therefore, to expect a rupture in Anglo-French relations. It is true that much of the anti-French feeling in Britain was due to the fear of increasing French naval power because of the construction of ironclad battleships, which the British Admiralty viewed with suspicion. But this was marginalia, and food for the popular press; it had little to do with the realities of an international relationship.

Napoleon III was more than usually anxious to have no strain between England and France, for he was now resolved to move in the Italian question. In July he had gone to Plombières, a watering place in the Vosges, to meet with Cavour, and here the scheme for promoting changes in the political structure of Italy had been drawn up. Cavour himself gave a summary:

ist. That the State of Massa and Carrara would be the cause or pretext of the War.

2nd. That the purpose of the War would be to drive Austria out of Italy; the establishment of a Kingdom of Upper Italy composed of the whole valley of the Po and of the Legations and the Marches.

3rd. Cession of Savoy to France. That of the County of Nice undecided.

4th. The Emperor is confident of the co-operation of Russia and of the neutrality of England and Prussia.[21]

In a letter to King Victor Emmanuel, Cavour spelt out the meaning for his master: "Your Majesty would be legal sovereign of the richest and most powerful half of Italy, and hence would in practice dominate the whole Peninsula."[22]

The Alliance was to be sealed by a marriage between the Emperor's cousin Prince Napoleon and the Princess Clotilde, the daughter of the King of Sardinia. The point about this marriage was that the new pair would reign in the Kingdom of Central Italy, which was to be formed from what remained of the Papal States (excluding Rome) after Sardinia had taken her share, plus the Grand Duchy of Tuscany. If to this project is added Napoleon III's desire to see the Murat family restored in Naples, then a very clear picture emerges of the type of Italian state which the Emperor desired. It would have been a Franco-Italian partnership in which France would have had the predominant share. This would have effectively strengthened France's position in Europe, particularly in the Mediterranean. It would have increased her economic potential, while benefiting that of Italy, and it *might* even have made the occupation of Rome by French troops a palatable fact, since a French presence would have been less "foreign" in the Peninsula. Above all, it would have prevented the "Italian Question" from being raised again and would have drawn the teeth of the revolutionary movement, which would by then have served its purpose as a bogey-man to frighten the Powers with. There is no doubt that the fear of an alliance between Napoleon III and the forces of revolution was one which haunted the Ballplatz in Vienna, for such an alliance threatened the very existence of the Hapsburg state over and beyond the question of Italy.

In a sense, Austria was right to fear that Napoleon III's designs extended beyond Italy, but was wrong to think that he intended to unleash the forces of revolution to achieve his aim of revisionism. Quite the contrary: the Emperor proposed to carry through his schemes in accord with Russia, hardly a revolutionary, though certainly a revision-ist Power, and to this end, Prince Napoleon was sent to Warsaw in September, 1858, to negotiate a treaty with the Tsar. It would appear that Prince Napoleon muffed the negotiations and he was replaced by his own nominee, de la Roncière le Noury, who advanced as far as St. Petersburg in late September, bearing a project for a treaty of al-liance.[23] The projected treaty envisaged a substantial redrawing of the map of Europe and was in the Napoleonic grand manner. Quite apart from the setting up of the North Italian Kingdom, Austria was to be further weakened by the assistance of Hungary towards independence and by a Russian annexation of Galicia—presumably to balance France's proposed acquisition of Savoy and Nice. At the same time, Napoleon III promised to press for a revision of the Black Sea Clauses of the 1856 Treaty. The importance of these projects cannot be too heavily stressed. They implied the destruction of the entire Central European states system, for Austria could hardly survive the loss of her Italian provinces, Galicia and Hungary, except as some form of weak buffer state in a Franco-Russian dominated Europe, and they were harking back both to Tilsit and to Polignac's schemes of 1829.

The Tsar Alexander was not prepared to go as far as this. Quite apart from the internal crisis over the emancipation of the serfs which was now approaching a climax, he was worried by the effect of such proposals on both England and Prussia. As to England, he asked: "How would one explain it to England? There is no government there and the Queen is a puppet (*un mannequin*)." As far as Prussia was concerned, Alexander worried about her reactions to a scheme which, while it would certainly damage her rival in Germany, would lead to a situation not necessarily to her advantage.

The Russian government had no intention of becoming involved in a revolutionary revisionist policy. Its aims remained clear and precise: the quashing of the Black Sea Clauses, and in return for this all that Gortchakov or the Tsar would offer was a promise of mobilization. This was the gist of the proposals which were sent to Napoleon III in

November, 1858, and which he rejected. (The draft bears an anno-tation in the Emperor's hand *"Projet Gortchakov repoussè par moi."*)

It seems incredible that Napoleon III hoped to dismember Austria without opposition from England and Prussia, not to mention Austria herself, and, yet La Roncèire was sent back to Petersburg in December with virtually the same proposals. In January, 1859, Walewski, the French Foreign Minister, became aware of these extravagant projects and was horrified at their extent. To him the whole scheme was an impossible dream, which if it did not split the Anglo-French entente would hand over to Russia control of that situation.

Walewski need not have panicked, for the Russians had their own show-stopper. Gortchakov proposed that England should be made to acquiesce by giving her Egypt—to which La Roncière replied that it was to "give her the Mediterranean! We might as well give her Toulon." This was precisely what the Russian government expected as a reply and it neatly blocked any advance along the road of general revision. The Tsar made it clear that Russia would not annex Galicia, for the Polish occupation had been *à trois* and should remain so. Alexander had no intention of opening up a route to some form of independent Poland which he very well knew Napoleon III wanted since only a desire for the establishment of some form of autonomous Poland could explain the magnitude of the changes he proposed in Central Europe.

The treaty which finally emerged was vague in the extreme. Napoleon III promised nothing and Alexander II merely promised neutrality in the event of an Austrian-French war. On the Russian side this commitment was not a great price to pay for the information which they had acquired as a result of the negotiations. Firstly, they knew that Napoleon III's diplomatic position was weak, he was dependent upon England *and* to a certain extent on Russia. Secondly, it was unlikely that there would be a revision of the Black Sea Clauses in Russia's favour through French intervention. From this it followed that Russian diplomacy must look elsewhere to achieve its object.

However, as far as Napoleon III's schemes with Sardinia were concerned, the Russian alliance meant that the time had now come to finalize the Plombières project and to turn vague plans into a formal agreement. The curtain rose on the first act of this particular play at the New Year Reception at the Tuileries Palace on 1st January, 1859. In the course of making the rounds of Ambassadors, Napoleon III suddenly injected life into the usual platitudes by remarking to the Austrian Ambassador : "I regret that our relations are not as good as I desire, but I beg you to say that my personal feelings for the Emperor are always the same." Whatever Napoleon III meant by this comment, and a great deal of time has been spent in trying to interpret it, it caused a minor panic. The Bourse dropped several points—particularly marked down were Austrian government bonds—and the Chancelleries of the Paris Embassies became the scene of animated discussion.[24]

It is just possible that Napoleon III meant nothing at all by the comment than a bare statement of fact. Relations were not particularly good, for there had been the question of the Principalities and then a row over Serbia, and had it not been that diplomatic circles were on edge because of all the activity of the previous year, the whole incident might well have been unremarked. Given the premise that Napoleon III was planning something in Italy, for everyone knew of the Plombières meeting, Austria felt that she must react to the Emperor's announcement by sending several army corps to her Italian provinces. Her action could hardly be faulted, for some days later, on 10th January, Victor Emmanuel's speech from the throne at the opening of the parliament, announced that " . . . we are not deaf to the cries of sorrow that come to us from all parts of Italy." Later in the month the cries of sorrow having presumably been heard also in Paris, Prince Napoleon arrived in Turin and a formal military-political alliance was signed between France and Sardinia.

Basically the terms were those established at Plombières: the setting up of a Kingdom of Northern Italy of roughly eleven million inhabitants : the reunion of Savoy and Nice to France : the Kingdom of Central Italy to be established. But this time Papal sovereignty and the interests of the Catholic religion were specifically declared to be objects of guarantee. The "Kingdom of Upper Italy" was to pay for the war, for the waging of which France would provide 200,000 men to Sardinia's 100,000. At the same time Cavour undertook to stir up revolutionary movement in Hungary and in Serbia. This was all that remained of the "Grand Design" put forward to Tsar Alexander.[25] On his own account Cavour was negotiating with the Italian National Society so that it would bring about the union of Tuscany to the Sardinian Kingdom when the war broke out.

To the historian, the month of January, 1859, has an air of "making quick decisions" about it and it seems that many contemporaries felt the same, particularly when the marriage of Prince Napoleon to Victor Emmanuel's daughter was squeezed in hurriedly at the end of the month. The Emperor himself noted that " . . . the question had been badly managed and public opinion in Europe is steadily mounting against me and above all against you [Prince Napoleon] because they think we want war."[26]

In view of this comment, it is surprising that the Emperor did not act with more circumspection, for the situation was not spectacularly improved by the appearance of the pamphlet *L'Empereur Napoléon III et l'Italie* which was published in Paris at the beginning of February. This work gave a view of the Italian Peninsula which was highly unfavourable to Austria, in that it directly or indirectly, blamed Austria or her clients for the prevailing state of affairs, and came to the conclusion that only Piedmont could be deemed to be in a satisfactory condition. The solution to the problem of Italy, as propounded in the pamphlet, was the setting up of a confederation under the presidency of the Pope who would, at the same time, carry through the necessary reforms in the Papal States in order to fit him for his new office.

Much alarm was caused by this statement of Imperial policy, since it was taken for granted that if Napoleon III had not written the pamphlet he had certainly inspired it, and many felt that the danger of war between France and Austria had been increased.

The question is *did* Napoleon III want war? To say that the simple answer is "yes" is unfortunately not enough. He certainly wanted the *possibility* of war to be an accepted factor in the diplomatic situation which he was creating, but whether this was only an exaggerated attitude designed to produce a *démarche* remains an open question. For example, the affair of the pamphlet was followed some three days later, by the Emperor's reassuring remarks to the *Corps Législatif* that: "For some time the condition of Italy and its abnormal situation quite rightly worries diplomacy, since order can only be maintained there by foreign troops. This is not, however, a reason for thinking about war . . . peace, I hope, will never be troubled."[27]

A further indication of the Emperor's lack of real bellicosity is borne out by the fact that as soon as the alliance with Piedmont had been agreed, he had begun to counsel Cavour to adopt a conciliatory attitude. In this respect the existence of the alliance increased the measure of control he could hope to exercise over Piedmontes' policy. His reasons for moving cautiously were sound, and not least of them was the situation in Paris where his own ministers were divided on the question, the more Orleanist and conservative interests being opposed, not necessarily for the same reasons, to hostilities with Austria. Only Prince Napoleon and the Bonapartists were wholeheartedly in favour, and so lukewarm was the Emperor's attitude that it led to his cousin's resignation from the Council on 5th March.

In this context, it should be borne in mind that Prince Napoleon was aware of England's efforts to negotiate an agreement between France and Austria as a part of which Cowley had gone to Vienna at the end of February to propose terms already agreed between Napoleon III and Malmesbury (the Foreign Secretary). But Cowley's mission foundered on Austrian suspicion and resentment of Napoleon III's manoeuvres and, as a consequence, her demand that Piedmont disarm as an earnest of good faith. Although this represented a failure, in the sense of a check to direct negotiation about the central issue, Napoleon continued to work with Austria in the Peninsula over the question of evacuating both French and Austrian troops from Papal territory, for which purpose, and at the Pope's request, an agreement was reached in March.[28]

As well as this collaboration with Austria, French policy was still officially linked to England in regard to the Kingdom of Naples, for both Powers had broken off diplomatic relations in October, 1858, in an attempt to force King Ferdinand to reform his government, and this break was still effective. (It was not abandoned until June, 1859, on the occasion of Ferdinand's death and the accession of Francis II.) So, in a sense, French activity in Italy was neither confined to Sardinia nor was interference in the politics of the Peninsula being conducted in isolation. Indeed, it would be hard to find a more flagrant example of egregious intervention in the affairs of other states than the Franco-British action *vis-à-vis* Naples.

For Napoleon III the problem was not so much how to engage England, but how to make her accept a *further* commitment to the Italian question. There were indications of her increasing interests in mid-March, when Odo Russell reminded Cardinal Antonelli of the Papal promise to implement reforms in accordance with the resolutions of the Paris Congress of 1856. He informed him that England felt the time had come when Austria might be persuaded to use her influence to see that this was brought about.[29] But this could hardly be counted much of a triumph for the Napoleonic policy of further committing England to an "Italian Policy," in the sense of support for France in the Austro-Piedmontese crisis. The real *démarche* came in fact from Russia on 18th March, when Alexander put forward the suggestion of an international congress to settle the Italian question, and Napoleon straightway announced France's acceptance. Since the initiative seems to have come from Napoleon in the first place, this acceptance was hardly surprising.

The idea of the congress was not well received by most of the states liable to be involved in it. Queen Victoria noted that: "A Congress has always been an alternative to war which the Emperor has put forward: but a Congress *pour remanier les traités de 1815*."[30] The Queen would almost seem to be disapproving of a peaceful solution, but in fact, it was the *remaniement* of 1815 to which she was objecting. This objection would have had more validity had not the system already been dealt a series of blows between 1830 and 1859 often with England's connivance or participation.

Austria was not unwilling to accept the idea of a congress, but made her participation dependent on the representation at the conference table of the Italian States concerned. This virtually ruled out any hope of her appearance, since neither the King of Naples, the Grand Duke of Tuscany nor the Pope had any intention of coming. Cardinal Antonelli informed Odo Russell that " ... His Holiness will not send a Representative to appear at the bar of a self-constituted tribunal such as the proposed Congress is." What was the point? asked Antonelli, and went on to say, "[The Italian question] is simply the desire of Piedmont to extend her dominion in Italy. The question need not exist at all if the Great Powers will simply ignore it."[31]

The strenuous efforts made by the French government to get the Pope to attend the Conference, as reported from Rome to Lord Malmesbury by Odo Russell, would seem to weaken the thesis that Napoleon III was merely using the congress idea to play for time,[32] and the indication of the weakness of this argument is the mixture of rage and fear with which Cavour greeted the whole idea, compelling Napoleon III to try and pacify him.[33] This incident underlined the real flaw in Napoleon's policy, namely that he had gone too far with Cavour to be able to draw back without leaving him in the lurch and risking an exposé of all that had passed between them, an exposé which would not do much for the Emperor's position in Europe. Cavour had no power except that of the blackmailer, but this was not to be underestimated, even if his threat to go to America and publish all the correspondence was more melodramatic than practical. The fact was that Napoleon III wanted to implement his schemes, but believed and hoped they were possible without war. Cavour, on the contrary, saw war as the only means of achieving his aims—yet war could not be fought without France. So it went on.

Fortunately the Gordian knot which had proved resistant to diplomatic attempts at unpicking proved susceptible, as always, to a sharp stroke. In Vienna by April, Buol's policy was making war inevitable, for Austrian shuffling about began to irritate the Powers who could not know that this did not reflect some deep plot on the part of the Vienna government but merely a state of utter confusion. On the one hand, Buol was announcing to the Emperor Franz-Josef that France was not serious about war, which in a sense was right, but at the same time he was also advocating an avoidance of the proposed congress—a course of action which could only force Napoleon III to be deadly serious, since he had no option but war. The ultimate disaster came when it was decided to dispatch an ultimatum to Piedmont demanding her demobilization and disarmament, based apparently on the mistaken assumption that Piedmont was isolated, and without taking into account the military implications of the action. As a consequence, the Austrian general staff suddenly found itself responsible for fighting a war which it had been assumed was highly improbable because the political direction in Vienna had given the military men this impression.[34]

Thanks to Austria's action, France was in the clear. As the Empress Eugénie said to her sister: "You will know that we are about to have a war, Austria has *wished* it. . . ." "Our cause is good, our army is excellent, and *he* is full of confidence and energy." As is usual, war had, in the short run, simplified everything. For Napoleon III, Austria's ultimatum had meant a decisive change in sectors of French opinion, for until April the only support for his Italian policy had come from the radicals and the Republicans. Now from the *Corps Législatif* down to the average citizen, the bulk of the country had come to accept that the war was inevitable and right.[35]

At this stage it should, perhaps, be noted that more than sentiment was involved in French attitudes to Piedmont. Between 1848 and 1860 more than one billion gold francs were invested in various public and private enterprises in the Kingdom and that Cavour's struggle was not just with the Austrian Hapsburgs but with the Austrian Rothschilds. The latter had acquired a tight grip in Sardinian finances which Cavour tried to pry loose by using the *Crédit Mobilier*, a branch of which existed in Turin. By 1858 he had achieved some measure of success and the bulk of the money which he had found to replace that from the Rothschilds had come from either the Péreires or from French investors through loans floated on the Paris Bourse.

Among the questions discussed at Plombières between Cavour and Napoleon III had been that of how military action was to be financed. Napoleon tried to drive a hard bargain by agreeing to a loan based on the purchase of the Victor Emmanuel railway, which ran through Savoy towards the French frontier. The Emperor was anxious to avoid floating a large public loan because of the effect this might have on the diplomatic situation, but all possible facilities other than this were accorded to the Sardinian government. As a semi-private venture, the loan of February-March, 1859, was a huge success, and much of the money was French.[36] The success of the Sardinian loan helped to convince many of the rightness of Cavour's cause.

The one section of French society which looked on the war with disfavour was that which was composed of "political Catholics." This phrase must be used in order to draw a clear distinction between religious belief and political practice, for the one did not necessarily coincide with the other. For example, Thiers, an atheist, and Guizot, a protestant, were both "political Catholics" in that they opposed Imperial policy in Italy, particularly as it affected the Pope's position, because they saw and quite rightly, that the real test of the Emperor's political conservatism lay there. It was the same mentality which had accepted the *Loi Falloux* in 1850 as a bulwark for conservative education, although neither Thiers nor Guizot cared a rap about Church schools as such. It seemed as if the Imperial government had allowed too much latitude to the ultra-montane and conservative forces inside the Church in France and that it had few friends, such as the great Dominican Provincial Lacordaire, who detested Papal pretensions and the whole ultra-montane outlook. Now, when the crisis came, the Emperor found himself faced with sullen hostility leavened with occasional vituperation and, as events in Italy moved more and more quickly towards an end which he had not ever desired, the reactions of the clericals became increasingly irritating. In any event opinion could not prevent the outbreak of the war nor could it influence the course of events.

Indeed what took place in Italy in the summer of 1859 was not what anyone had either expected or planned—though Cavour, it is true, had tried to program the computer before the operation actually began. France went to war full of *élan* and confident of victory. The two battles of Magenta and Solferino, on the 4th and 24th of June respectively, appeared to justify both the *élan* and the confidence, for both Lombardy and Venetia were now actually or potentially within the grasp of Napoleon III, while Parma, Modena and Tuscany were without their rulers who had fled as the Franco-Sardinian armies advanced.

In these circumstances, the armistice of Villefranca between Napoleon III and Franz-Joseph on 11th July came as a great shock, particularly when its terms made it clear that Sardinia would only get Lombardy and not Venetia, and that the rulers of Modena and

Tuscany were to be restored. All this was to be enshrined in the setting up of an Italian Confederation under the presidency of the Pope, who was to be encouraged to reform his states.[37]

The reasons for the armistice were quite clear if looked at unemotionally. Faced with the prospect of a long campaign (for the Austrians though badly mauled, were not destroyed) and faced with a possible threat from Prussia on the Rhine where she was posing, belatedly, as champion of the Germanic confederation against French expansionism, Napoleon III was forced to weigh the general diplomatic situation against the effects of his action in Italy. In France, the rumblings of discontent from the conservatives and the political Catholics were an added factor in helping him to a quick decision. But partisans of the "Italian Cause," both then and now, have never ceased to comment on the armistice as an example of the bad faith of Napoleon III. First in this field was Cavour who, in a storm of rage, gave his resignation to Victor Emmanuel. The latter was less put about by the armistice than his prime minister and was glad enough to settle for a rich province which would greatly increase the power and economic wealth of the Sardinian Kingdom. Indeed in view of what had been achieved Victor Emmanuel's comments on Cavour were neither grateful nor flattering: "He is a muddle head who is always pushing me into some wasp's nest or other. Cavour is mad. . . . He goes off playing with follies like the rising in the Romagna and heaven knows what else. But he is finished now. He did a good job, but he is finished."[38]

Although his attitude was hardly generous, Victor Emmanuel was in a sense quite right. It was precisely because Cavour had been intriguing in Tuscany and in the other states, and in the Papal Legations like Bologna, that Napoleon III was becoming alarmed about the results of the war. Although, officially, only a provisional administration existed, in the former central Italian states, it was well known that Cavour's agents were actively pressing the case for voluntary adhesion to the Kingdom of Victor Emmanuel. It was for this reason that Napoleon, cutting his losses and abandoning any hopes of a Central Italian Kingdom, along with his claims to Savoy and Nice, had agreed at Villafranca to the restoration of the rulers of Tuscany and Modena. If this could be achieved, the situation could be stabilized and a revolutionary crisis avoided. It was one thing to have an orderly redrawing of the map: it was quite another to have some sort of Mazzinian revolution, for if Napoleon III believed in "nationality" he did not support the romantic concept of nationalism, as allied to revolution.

The whole object of the exercise had been to exclude any such possibility.

In the case of Italy this would have been particularly dangerous, since the spread of the idea of "Italy" in the Mazzinian sense would ultimately involve the whole position of the Papacy and thus complicate a great many of the Emperor's positions, both at home and abroad.

Unfortunately Napoleon III had lost control of the situation, as the Sardinian government saw quite clearly when it refused to accept the implications of the Villafranca agreement in so far as they affected either the Central States or the Legations. The Emperor was faced with the unpalatable choice of either coercing his former ally to force her to clear out of Tuscany, Modena and Bologna, or accepting a virtual *fait accompli* and persuading the Pope into abandoning the Romagna. Either way it was more than disagreeable and he expressed his disgust at the situation to the Austrian Ambassador, Prince Richard Metternich: "My thoughts were grand and beautiful, my intentions pure and unselfish. By invading Piedmont, you [Austria] gave me a good pretext to realize a desire of my life, that of giving Italy to herself. I believed that I had succeeded at Villafranca; now I see that the whole affair is more difficult than before, and I am at the end of my rope."[39]

The problem was, how to get off the rope. As in 1856 the Emperor's tactic was to draw closer to his former enemy in an attempt to keep in check a situation which, if it were allowed to develop, would be mutually disadvantageous. The terms of the Treaty of Zurich, signed on 10th November, envisaged the use of the favourite Imperial gambit of a congress to resolve the outstanding problems. The pattern of Napoleon III's diplomacy rarely varied: when bilateral or unilateral action became too risky, the danger could be lifted by multilateral action. In part, of course, this tactic was forced upon the Emperor for the simple reason that he was condemned to search for a reliable ally who would support French policy consistently and not just when it suited them to do so. The idea that such a situation might come about was not the least of the Emperor's illusions, nor the least dangerous to himself and to France. Napoleon III frequently imagined *he* was using people for the further-ance of his schemes while in fact *they* were using him for theirs.

In the case of the proposal for a congress, little tangible results could be hoped for, since French policy in Italy was already irretrievably lost. Napoleon clearly could not, as already indicated, proceed against Sardinia by force to reject her from the Duchies. Just in case he might even contemplate such an action, England made her attendance at the congress dependent on assurances from Paris that force would not be used. The sword being prohibited, there remained the pen. On 22nd December, a Christmas message for the Vatican was published in Paris, in pamphlet form, entitled *Le Pape et le Congrès*. As with the previous pamphlet, *L'Empereur Napoléon III et l'Italie*, the hand was Esau's but the voice was Jacob's. La Guerronière, the actual writer of the brochure was again directly inspired by the Emperor who himself corrected the manuscript.

The pamphlet was an acknowledgement that the Pope could not be restored to his states without the use of force and a declaration that here, as in the case of the Duchies, force could not be used. Instead, the Pope was urged to make a virtue of necessity: "The more his territory is diminished the more the Pope will be great." Here, in fact, was the very root of the problem exposed. It was clear to many, including a small section of the French hierarchy, that the temporal power was something which enfeebled rather than strengthened the Papacy. But the Pope would not see it that way. He denounced Napoleon III as "a liar and a cheat," though he went on, more charitably and perhaps more in keeping with his position, to announce his intention of praying earnestly to God that He would ". . . send grace and light to the Head of the Nation, that He may have the courage to condemn those perverse principles contained in a pamphlet lately published. . . ." In case God should fail to get through to the Emperor, Pius IX instructed the French clergy to rally the faithful in defence of the temporal power.

There is a French proverb: "Qui mange du Pape en meurt." Napoleon III did not die immediately, but the proposed congress expired straightway under a torrent of recrimination from Austria, and the Emperor discovered he had acquired an ulcer in Italy, as his uncle had in Spain. He was never to disembarrass himself of the Papacy until the Empire fell in 1870.

The Emperor's clear renunciation of force, the collapse of the Franco-Austrian entente, and the isolation of the Papacy paved the way for the next stage in Piedmont's game. Since England was stressing the harmony which existed between France and herself over the Italian question, Cavour felt that the diplomatic situation made it safe for him to resume office in January 1860. By March the Duchies and the Legations had been annexed to Piedmont after a plebiscite which was held to sound out the wishes of the inhabitants. The idea of a plebiscite was a sop to Napoleon III, but a more substantial morsel was the acquisition by France of Savoy and Nice on the grounds that Sardinia's acquisition cancelled any need for self-abnegation by her ally. France had thus broken one of the major barriers which had been put in her way in 1815 : she had recovered the Alps on her south-eastern frontier. The annexations of these areas was confirmed by a plebiscite. By an irony, Cavour may well have been glad to see them go, for Savoy in particular had been a nuisance with its tendency to return Catholic and anti-"Italian" members to the Turin parliament, where they acted as critics of his policies.

While Cavour may have been pleased, Garibaldi was not. This restless Mazzinian soldier of fortune was born in Nice and his dislike for Cavour was strengthened by this giving away of his birthplace. To Garibaldi the conservative and anti-popular nature of what was happening in Italy could not be excused by the fact that it was ostensibly leading the movement towards national unity. To the Mazzinians, the "Piedmontization" of Italy had nothing to do with their real, mystical union of all hearts and wills. It was this situation which brought about the incident of "The Thousand" in May, 1860, when Garibaldi set out from Genoa, without Cavour's knowledge or help, and invaded Sicily.

Garibaldi's invasion and the astonishing success which attended it, might have been a total disaster for Cavour, and the whole situation in Italy, had Garibaldi remained a staunch Republican and Mazzinian. Fortunately for Cavour, Garibaldi was a "king's man" in that he had a genuine liking for Victor Emmanuel who had known of his proposed adventure and who remained in contact with him throughout the southern campaign.

By September, Garibaldi was in Naples : the whole of the South had fallen, and only the Papal States stood in the way of "Italy" from the Alps to Sicily. In the Papal States there was, of course, a French garrison, and whatever Napoleon may have felt about the events in Naples and Sicily, feelings conditioned by England's tacit acceptance of Garibaldi's *coup de main*, he could not allow the Papal States to be invaded. Fortunately, it was Cavour who moved first, seeing clearly the twofold danger to Sardinian policy from both Garibaldi and French reaction if the Papacy were attacked. Cavour convinced Napoleon III of the necessity of the action and at the battle of Castelfidardo the Papal army was defeated and the Sardinian army found itself in command of the situation. Lest it should go too far, the French garrison were reinforced in October as an earnest of Napoleon III's intentions to protect the Pope from total collapse.

Nothing could now, however, prevent the annexation of the former Kingdom of Naples, which fact was accomplished after the formality of a plebiscite in October, 1860. But the feeling among the Powers of Europe was that a halt must be called to the serious revolutionary situation which the Italian events were provoking. Austria had in particular been worried by the possibility of an outbreak in Hungary, encouraged by France, in the period of May-July, 1859, and in general, the spectacle of a "national movement" in whatever form achieving a degree of success could only be both distasteful and alarming to conservative forces in Europe. On the very day that the Neapolitans voted in the plebiscite which was to unite them to Italy, the rulers of Austria, Prussia and Russia met, perhaps significantly, in Warsaw.

The principal document discussed was an Austrian memorandum which denounced France as the source of the confusion and disorder which prevailed in Europe. Unfortunately for Austria's aims, the Tsar Alexander was not as yet prepared to break with Napoleon III. Although the Russian ruler had been unhappy about the events in Naples, the Black Sea Clauses were of more importance to him that the Straits of Messina, and so Alexander was more disposed to air Napoleon III's ideas for a congress than to back Austria's desire for a promise of intervention in Italy if Venetia should be threatened. Russian policy was, as Gortchakov said, to support Napoleon as the best hope for peace and so there would be no revived Holy Alliance. To that extent France still retained the diplomatic initiative and Napoleon still kept his options open. Austria's mistake was to seek from Russia what she could only get from France, that is an alliance which would enable her to re-adjust and re-balance her European position after her defeat in Italy. Unfortunately, Napoleon's offers of "compensation" in Eastern Europe were not accepted by Vienna and Austria remained in hopeless vacillation until it was too late and her decisions were made for her. The Hapsburg monarchy virtually foundered between 1859 and 1867, wrecked on the twin rocks of internal confusion and external weakness, the one clearly dependent on the other, and both based on a chronic financial problem.[40] The solution of 1867 produced such a radical change in the whole structure, nature and outlook of the Hapsburg monarchy that it might almost be said to be a new state with old traditions rather than an old state with new traditions.

None of this, however, in the immediate term, cut any ice with Napoleon III, though ultimately France's situation was to be as drastically changed as was Austria's by circumstances beyond her control. In the period 1862-63, it seemed that France had reached the apotheosis of her European supremacy, since as yet no Power had emerged to challenge her and Napoleon was still looked upon as the kingpin of the international situation.

It was at this point that the Emperor decided to move towards a general reconstruction of Europe based upon the perfectly valid assumption that any return to the pre-1856-59 situation was impossible. In a sense, there is some truth in the interpretation which sees in the change of Foreign Ministers of France in the autumn of 1862, part of a general ministerial reshuffle, an indication of a new approach to the country's foreign policy.

Drouyn de Lhuys, who replaced Thouvenel, was an advocate of the Austrian conservative policy, whereas his predecessor was associated with a more "progressive" attitude to the Italian problem and a pro-Russian and Prussian, rather than a pro-Austrian trend. It would seem, however, that there is insufficient evidence to suggest that this particular change was a triumph for clericalism, as represented by the Empress.[41] What is certain is that in spite of his apparently powerful situation, Napoleon III was himself by the end of 1862 unable to see clearly which way to move, hence the vagueness and grandiosity of the schemes for Europe which were to be launched in 1863.

Given the difficulties of the situation it seemed better to plan for the future than to deal with the present. As far as the Italian problem was concerned, the Emperor may have felt like the criminal whose life was spared by Louis XI because he claimed he could teach the King's horse to talk. When asked what he thought he had achieved by such a preposterous claim, he replied : "I may die, or the King may die, or the horse may talk." So it was with Napoleon's attitude to the Pope and the problem of the remaining Papal territory.

As for French policy, it was surely better to look to Mexico, and to the effects of the other extra-European activities in the Near East and the Far East, than to become bogged down in the minutiae of politics. As the Austrian Foreign Minister wrote to his Ambassador in Paris ". . . The Emperor Napoleon seeks an issue, or rather awaits that chance which offers one from which he can profit, in order that he can open a way across the difficulties which encompass him."[42] It was while he was waiting that the Emperor became occupied with Mexico and other overseas entanglements.

I I

Overseas Commitments

*"Celui là fut un homme de génie ... qui
reconnut que l'équilibre européen n'est plus
comme autrefois sur les Alpes, les Pyrénées,
sur la Vistule ou sur le Ponte-Euxin, mais
qu'il embrasse le monde entier ..."*

Napoleon III, 21st January, 1864

*"Prenez garde! Il ya a aussi en Amérique
des Baylen!"*

Edgar Quinet, 1862

DURING the quarter of century of war, between 1792 and 1815, the states of Europe had undergone changes which had affected their external as well as their internal development. Those who had entered the war with overseas possessions did not always emerge with them intact and in the particular cases of Portugal and Spain the transformations undergone as a result of the wars had been far reaching.

In Latin America between 1800 and 1825 the former colonial possessions had either altered their relationship with the mother country, as in the case of Brazil, or they had broken away, as in the case of all the former Spanish possessions on the mainland. By 1825, with the exception of the island colonies like Cuba and Puerto Rico, the former Spanish vice-royalties and captaincies general had been transformed into a collection of independent republics, not only independent of Spain, but independent of one another. The failure of a plan for some kind of federation, which had been put forward by Bolivar in 1825, meant that the fragmentation would not be a passing phase and it has persisted until our own times.[1]

This mound of historical debris became a source of attraction for those states which had the means of getting there to pick through it, and in the conditions prevailing in the early nineteenth century, the only power with sufficient maritime strength to be able to establish herself in

South America was Britain. This she had done, firstly by helping the colonies in their revolt against Spain and secondly by obtaining a virtual monopoly of the trade of the new states. It was Britain which controlled the trade of the east-coastal colonies from Colombia to Argentina and La Plata, while her commercial stranglehold on Portugal was extended to Brazil. By 1825 the value of the South American trade was some eighty million dollars and represented a figure three times greater than that of her only rival, the United States of America.

In asserting her economic position in South America, the United States was not hampered by the lack of sea power as were the other European states, for she was *en place*, and while it is true that the direction of United States expansion was more landwards than sea-wards, this was as much choice as necessity. "Manifest destiny," was not necessarily an oceanic conception. For the U.S., therefore, the lines of expansion were across the Rio Grande and into California, areas which had belonged to the former Vice-Royalty of Mexico, and into the isthmus region of Central America.

Here, in this latter region, was the pressure point which led in the 1840's and 1850's to disputes between Britain and the U.S.A. and which resulted in an excessive fragmentation into "national states"—the banana republics of the future.

The great prize in this area was, of course, Mexico itself—not only because of its potential but also because of its situation. For some time much thought had been given to developing a way across the isthmus separating the Atlantic/Caribbean from the Pacific Ocean and by the 1840's it had been decided by commercial companies, on which governments kept an eye, that the isthmus of the Tehuantepec was the best place to cross as a railway portage, pending the construction of a canal somewhere in the Panama or Nicaraguan area. The struggle for control of this latter area went on between Britain and the U.S.A. until its settlement in 1850 by the Clayton-Bulwer agreement. This envisaged the construction of a canal by a joint Anglo-American company, but it was viewed with disfavour in the United States because it involved recognizing a British possession on the American continent, in defiance of the Monroe Doctrine, and the question was only settled finally between 1850 and 1859 when Britain agreed to restrict her territorial demands to the area which subsequently became British Honduras. In effect, Britain had, for the moment, checked American expansion in the region and had managed to shelve the question of the canal. If one *were* to be built, it would not be exclusively an American-controlled affair and, since the U.S. government had no wish for any other sort of canal, there was a stalemate which in fact lasted some forty years.

If, however, she had been momentarily checked in Central America, the United States could hardly complain of her lack of good fortune in Mexico. By 1848, after her war with Mexico, she had annexed Texas, California, New Mexico and the territory which became the future states of Arizona, Utah and Nevada. This amounted in all to three-fifths of the original area of her neighbour, and, given the internal conditions there, it seemed both reasonable and feasible that she should have the rest as and when she felt like it.

The condition of Mexico was deplorable; had it not been, she might have made some sort of stand against the United States. As it was, internal anarchy precluded any such course and Mexico continued to fall deeper and deeper into dissolution.

By 1850 her population was reckoned at some eight million. One million whites, three million Creoles, and four million pure Indians. These racial divisions were reflected in a caste-ridden social hierarchy in which a handful of aristocratic landowners ruled over a vast, illiterate and semi-slave Indian population. To maintain their power they relied on an army of incompetent and idle officers whose only claim to military skill lay in wearing a uniform and who in theory commanded a mass of brutalized and ignorant soldiery. Discipline was maintained by harsh punishments and payment was so irregular as to be almost non-existent. Little separated the army of the state from the army of bandits who infested the countryside and both groups shared an ability to conjugate the verb "to rob" in all its tenses.

Between 1821 and 1850 Mexico had passed from monarchy to republic, from federal to unitary state and, on the way had seen forty-six "heads of state" pass through the presidential palace. The dictatorship of Santa Anna had done no more for the wretched country than had the attempts at federal, parliamentary rule and the only thing that the political classes, Creole and white, shared as a political creed was the determination to keep the lower orders in subjection. That lesson had been learnt in 1810 when the rising of Hidalgo had shown that independence could mean a threat to social order unless great care was taken to prevent such a situation from being created. Mexican politics, even when they were called liberal, were usually socially conservative.

One of the greatest conservative forces, and the largest landowner, was the Church. Since it had the misfortune to be not only wealthy but organized it became a target for attack by those who saw in both its wealth and its organization a constant reproach to the civil "state" and who had not forgotten also that both Hidalgo and Morelos, the leaders of the peasant revolts, had been priests. The dilemma of the Mexican Church was appalling. With the Mexican conservatives for a friend, it hardly needed enemies, and yet the liberals were worse, for if the conservative element merely nibbled at ecclesiastical property, the liberals devoured it. In these circumstances, many of the leading clerics looked to the small, ultra-clerical conservative group which favoured a restoration of the monarchy and an absolutist, centralist regime.

Meanwhile the sanguinary pantomime of *coup d'état, pronunciamiento,* and civil strife continued. In 1856, a new demon King appeared, in the person of Benito Juarez who made the "secular state" the great object of his ambition and who carried through a series of laws which broke the Church's organization and its wealth, transferring the latter into the hands of what became a new aristocracy while the former went into limbo to join all the other organizations which had at one time existed in Mexico.

By 1860 Juarez had been driven out of office, fought another civil war, proposed further anti-clerical legislation, this time extending his proposals to include the break-up of the great ranches, and by 1861, was back in power in Mexico City. Here he not only took his revenge on the conservatives and the clergy, but suspended, in July, 1861, the payment of interest on all foreign bonds and on the external international debt. This merely made *de jure* a situation which had been for many years *de facto*, but it did give an excuse and a reason for interventions by those Powers which had for some time been interested in Mexico. This time the United States would not be included for the triumph of her protégé Juarez coincided with the outbreak of the Civil War, and with the Monroe Doctrine clearly in abeyance, the European Powers could feel free to manoeuvre without having to worry about intervention by the U.S.

The prime mover in the interventionist game was Napoleon III. France's interest in Latin America had been conditioned by her position after 1815 and, although she had tried to maintain a diplomatic presence in the area, most of the major events had taken place without her. During the period of the Restoration Monarchy, an attempt had been made to supply Bourbon Princes to the new states in order to prevent the growth of too many republics and, presumably, in the hope of extending French influence. But these schemes had never really had any chance of success, given Britain's position in South America, and so France had dropped out of the running in the area.[2]

In Mexico there were among the foreign settlers, mostly Spanish, English and American, some French. Like their fellow immigrants they were engaged in trade of some kind, and, like their fellows, resented bitterly the constant *va-et-vient* of government which seriously hampered their efforts at trading. Furthermore, their property, not to mention their lives, was constantly endangered by the Mexicans who, irrespective of political affiliations, considered all *gringos* as fair game. It is unlikely that any European foreign office opened the mail bag marked "Mexico" without a sinking of the heart, for it usually contained heartrending stories of plunder, rape, murder, and double dealing, accompanied by demands for intervention on the part of the government concerned.

As the crisis in Mexico reached an unusually high point in the mid-fifties, the "groans of the nationals" grew in intensity. By 1857 the French nationals were pressing for a French King, and the Duc d'Anmale was suggested. Queen Victoria was petitioned by a mixed group of English nationals and native Mexican monarchists.[3] The Spanish nationals had made such a to-do, that Juarez expelled the Spanish Minister from Mexico City on his return there in 1861.

With the exception of the Spanish government, none of the governments concerned really showed much interest in intervention in Mexico until 1860-61. Although Otway, the British Minister, informed the Foreign Secretary in 1858 that intervention was the cure and that ". . . the cause is so noble and just and so honourable to the age, when the aid required is so insignificant and when there will be no sacrifice of men or of money! . . . I beg to repeat my conviction that ten or twelve thousand men would be amply sufficient, and I can assure your Lordship [Malmesbury] that they would be welcomed,"[4] the British government spurned such an easy prey.

The French government, in particular Napoleon III in person, was likewise appealed to for intervention. In the case of the Emperor, the moves went farther and deeper than petitions, for the simple reason that it became very clear to those who were hawking the interests of Mexico around Europe, that they had found someone who was interested.

Why did Napoleon III become caught up in the Mexican affair? Like so many other activities in the Emperor's life it seems that the historians have decided for him and have then gone back to see if they were right. By and large their thesis has been the following: the Emperor, worried by the effects of anti-Papal moves in Italy, of which he might be considered the author, wanted to reconcile to his regime the clerical party in France. This party had a powerful friend at Court in the shape of the Empress Eugénie. Eugénie was a Spaniard: many of her friends were Mexican monarchists and they persuaded her to force Napoleon III into a policy of intervention to set up a Catholic Empire. This would please the Pope and the French Catholics. If a Hapsburg prince was given the throne, this would please Austria. The Italian war would be forgiven and the French Catholics reconciled.

Unfortunately for the Emperor, so the story goes, this scheme was crossed by a shady financial deal introduced by Napoleon's half-brother Morny. Morny used his influence with the Emperor to persuade him to intervene to force the Mexicans to pay their debts. In particular, they were to pay up on the bonds of a Monsieur Jecker, who had lent money to the Mexican Government. In return for his assistance, Morny would get thirty per cent of all that Jecker was able to collect.

One of the most recent comments on the Mexican affair, summating the reasons for intervention, says: "Thus France would do a service to the Catholic Church, safeguarding its interests from the anti-clerical policies which the Mexican republicans espoused, and would stand forth as the guardian of the Catholic and Latin peoples of the New World and their champion against the 'Anglo-Saxon' and Protestant influence of the United States."[5]

The argument is as neat as a new pin, but it will not do. As so often, motives are attributed to Napoleon III which it is doubtful if he had and even if he did, they are so oversimplified as to be equally wide of the mark.

Firstly, to attribute to Napoleon III the idea of creating a Latin-Catholic bloc in Central America is to misunderstand what the Emperor felt about France's mission in the world. To him, the vision was one of a world which would be based upon national groupings, so balanced as not to be competitive, held together by a common desire to promote trade, prosperity and international peace. His war would be one of words, his battlefields the green baize of the tables where met the congresses of the Powers. Whole armies of words would march at his command and his opponents could not but be overcome by logic and commonsense. They would, he always felt, understand his dream. It was a reasonable assumption in that most of his contemporaries had in their youth waded, as he had, through the flood waters of romanticism and had not emerged bone dry.

Given the grandiose views, it is doubtful if Napoleon III thought in terms as narrow as "Latin Catholic blocs," in spite of evidence that French representatives were active in both Ecuador and the isthmus of Darien in late 1861. There was, in any event, nothing inherently sinful in French operations in these regions, except to those who regarded the United States as having a pre-emptive right in Latin America based upon an acceptance of the Monroe Doctrine. Until 1861 it was not France but the United States which pursued a policy of annexation in Central and South America. The McLane-Ocampo Treaty of 1859 between the Washington government and the government of Juarez had seemed to indicate a desire for total absorption since it virtually established a U.S. protectorate over what remained of Mexico. It was not Napoleon III's intention to create animosity or hostile barriers between nations by a policy of annexation: and he at least attempted to include the United States in the plan for intervention mooted in 1860 to avoid the charge of "French imperialism." His thoughts turned to building bridges to unite peoples or digging canals to join them, and in the case of Central America, a canal was very much a part of his thinking. It had been one of the dreams of his imprisonment at a time when he had almost gone to rule in South America as President of Nicaragua. In his honour, the canal which was to be dug would have been called the "Canal Napoléon" and so his name would have been for ever associated with one of the great schemes of the world, the linking of the Atlantic and the Pacific.

In 1847 Louis Napoleon had published a brochure in an attempt to attract interest and capital to the Nicaraguan canal project in which he had pointed out the benefits such a link would bring. An immense entrepôt would be created between Europe and Asia at the junction of the two Americas, and a new Constantinople would appear which would not only be a trading centre, but a centre for civilization. Its very existence would help to develop an enormous hinterland and so a strong and balanced "*Amérique Espagnole*" would be created.

A company promoter writing a brochure is no more on oath than a man writing a lapidary inscription, but it may be assumed that much of this grandiose fantasy really did represent the thinking of Louis Napoleon at the time—and it would certainly be wrong to imagine that it played no part subsequently in the dreams of Napoleon III. What should not be forgotten is that the dream involved the creation of economic prosperity and the influence of the Saint-Simonians, in particular Michel Chevalier, was used to persuade the Emperor that such schemes were *not* just dreams. Nor were they; the Suez Canal and the Panama Canal are the proof.

Looked at in this context, the intervention by France in Mexican affairs is seen to be less crack-brained than it might at first sight appear, and, as will be shown, by 1861 there were even more pertinent and pressing economic factors at work which encouraged Napoleon III in his enterprise.

As to the charge that the expedition was conceived to appease the wrath of the French clericals and the Pope, an examination of this view reveals how very oversimplified it is.

To begin with, there is an assumption that Napoleon III was worried about the reaction of the French Catholics to the events in Italy after 1859 because they had found an advocate in the Empress Eugénie, who brought pressure to bear on the Emperor. This is far from being the case. The fulminations of Pius IX about the consequences of French policy in Italy had, after an initial period of protestation at the end of 1859, met with little real response in France on the part of the faithful or the clergy. At that time, it is true, a large section of the episcopate had thundered about "the atheism of the state," but frequently the fulminations had revealed more about the conservative nature of the French clergy than it had about their Papalism. Monseigneur Gerbet, the Bishop of Perpignan, denounced Cavour because: ". . . by the logic of things [he] must be the father of Proudhonism." He did not defend the Papacy.

As has already been pointed out (see Chapter 10 above) it was this conservatism which animated Thiers and Guizot, the "political Catholics," who did not give a rap for the Papacy's temporal power, but who saw in the attack on Papal property a means of "opening a breach to communism" and accused Napoleon III of fomenting anarchy.

The argument produced by this alliance of part of the episcopate with the Voltaireian bourgeoisie was sharply and cruelly lampooned by Edgar Quinet in 1860 when he said "The Holy Father cannot, must not, give up his temporal power. The Common Father would have no further standing among the faithful if he was no longer seigneur of 3 million Italians and 4 million *hectares*, if he no longer commanded a wretched army of 50,000 men, and if he didn't hold a lottery every Saturday. There would be no authority without dominion, no spiritual without temporal."[6]

The interesting thing was that many of the French clergy, including some of the bishops, and many of the French Catholics, shared Quinet's feelings. It cannot be too often stressed that the bulk of the faithful in France were indifferent to the Pope's problems as a temporal ruler. The Papal Zouaves contained at most five hundred Frenchmen in their ranks and, even more significantly, an attempt by the Papal authorities to float a loan in French in 1860 raised only 17 million francs instead of the hoped-for 25 million. Perhaps, even more indicative of attitudes, is the fact that Peter's Pence, the faithfuls' direct contribution to the Pope, remained at a very low level in most of France during this period and later.[7] The more the ultramontanes in France raised their head, the more Gallican sections of the French Church became, and the Pope played into the hands of the government by exacerbating the feelings of clergy and laity. For example, he refused the Cardinal's hat to Monseigneur Darboy, who had become Archbishop of Paris in 1857, precisely because he was as anti-ultramontane as his predecessor Monseigneur Sibour. The shabby treatment of Darboy, who was to die a martyr's death in 1871 at the hands of the Communards, and who was known to be an upright and virtuous *pastor fidelium* caused much resentment—a resentment which the government turned to good account by strengthening its anti-ultramontane policy and applying the Organic Articles of the Concordat with increasing rigour.

If the Roman question during this period is viewed as an aspect of international politics it can be argued that the government of Napoleon III vacillated, but it is undeniable that during the same period it showed itself increasingly disinclined to vacillate when confronted with ultramontanism in France. There is little evidence to show that Napoleon III was worried about the Bishop of Perpignan and his comments on Cavour, there is even less evidence to show that he was anxious to save the Bishop of San Luis Potosi to please the Pope and the French clericals. It is clear that the Emperor's position in the country was strong enough for him to take a firm line over the domestic problem; to have taken the same attitude over the hideous tangle of the Temporal Power, viewed as an international problem, would have been to court disaster. Napoleon III governed France, not Europe.

There is, therefore, little real evidence for the argument that motives of placating the clerics had anything to do with the decision to intervene in Mexico. If they had, they were certainly very secondary, just as was the influence of Eugénie and the Mexican monarchists.

Since 1856 various groups or individuals had hung about Eugénie hawking the prospects of a Mexican monarchy, but this salon chatter had nothing to do with policy making. Hidalgo, the main Mexican representative, was young, handsome and charming. He was decorative, and Eugénie liked him because he was, in a sense, a "fellow country-man" and they spoke Spanish together. In 1857, at Biarritz, it would seem that Hidalgo tried to interest the Emperor in Mexico, but Napoleon's reaction did not extend beyond listening courteously to

Hidalgo's exposition of the enchanting prospects which Mexico offered.[8]

At the end of 1859, when the situation in Mexico had altered because of the emergence of Juarez, there was a slight stirring of interest in Spain, France and Britain, the three Powers concerned in the area. This came about in consequence of the action of the U.S.A., whose government had not only recognized Juarez at Vera Cruz, as the legal government of Mexico, but had also negotiated a treaty which virtually gave economic control of Mexico to the Americans. Furthermore, President Buchanan's message to Congress of 29th December, 1859, following on the signature of the McClane-Ocampo Treaty, seemed to presage immediate American action against Mexico and this produced some alarm in Britain, where the settlement of the Honduras question was of very recent date. The new tone in Washington seemed to threaten an end to the consensus frontiers which had just been established in Central America.

The English government inclined towards intervention between the Mexican conservatives and Juarez in the hope that mediation might produce peace and that if elections could be held, then some form of Mexican government might emerge which would pay something to its foreign creditors. At the same time a more stable political situation might be established.

It was, presumably, the prospect of some sort of joint action which led to Russell's approach to the new French Foreign Minister, Thouvenel, who had replaced Walewski at the Quai d'Orsay in January, 1860. This move by England was fatal, for Napoleon III had always made it clear that he would not move without England's being involved and now, it seemed, this situation was about to be created. He immediately tried to enlarge the scope of the proposed action by inducing the U.S.A. to join in a multilateral approach to Mexico, but this failed, for the simple reason that the Americans had no intention of permitting any intervention other than their own.[9] However, Spain was as eager to join as the United States was reluctant and a diplomatic *ménage à trois* appeared to be on the point of emerging when the English acted on their own account. Because of the behaviour of the conservative government of Miramon, Russell broke off relations in August, 1860, and although Juarez did not actually gain power officially until January, 1861, the original scheme for joint mediation between the two sides had foundered on the simple fact that there were no longer two sides. Miramon fled, and Britain recognized Juarez in February, 1861, although the new minister, Sir Charles

Wyke, warned his government that Juarez would not pay the interest on foreign bonds any more than had Miramon.

For his part, Napoleon III continued to repulse the advances of the Mexican monarchists who, as their cause sank in Mexico City, became even more clamorous in their calls for European intervention. In Paris on 10th August, 1861, the new Mexican Ambassador La Fuente, representing the government of Juarez, was received by the Emperor who went out of his way to speak kindly to the new Ambassador and to express hope for more settled conditions in Mexico.[10]

The timing of this interview is important, for some historians have seen in the meeting between Napoleon III and the Spanish General Prim, which took place at Vichy in July, a parallel with the meeting at Plombières with Cavour. It has been assumed that a plot was hatched for intervention in Mexico, just as at Plombières a plot had been hatched against Austria. There is no concrete evidence to suggest this and any supposition of such a plot must explain why French policy remained so conciliatory to Juarez. The change to a more hostile attitude did not come until after 29th August when the French Foreign Office was informed, more or less at the same time as its English counterpart, of the decrees of 7th July passed by Juarez suspending payment on all foreign loans for two years. This altered the alignment completely. Mexican historians tend to blame a failure of diplomatic relations on the quality of the people who were sent from Europe and who did not understand Mexican problems, but it is hard to see what even a Talleyrand could have done, confronted with actions such as that of Juarez in July, 1861.[11] The results were, from Mexico's point of view, fatal, since he had succeeded in doing what had seemed impossible, and a tripartite agreement to intervene in Mexico was signed in London in October, 1861.

It seems that Napoleon's thinking had been conditioned by not only the prospect of debt collecting, but also by the prospect of establishing some form of economic concession for France in Mexico—particularly if that country could be made to provide raw cotton.[12] The outbreak of the civil war in the U.S.A. had not only immobilized that country as a factor in international politics, it had also produced a crisis in the cotton manufactures of France and England which depended on U.S. exports. The crisis was severe in England, it was even worse in France where the figures for imports at Le Havre show a drop from 365,000 bales in 1860 to 31,000 in 1862.[13] The coincidence of the cotton famine with the inevitable dislocation resulting from the Commercial Treaty with England (1860) gave rise to a situation which the Imperial

Government could not ignore. In point of fact, the Mexican affair brought return, in the shape of increased cotton supplies and the deficit was partly made up from India and Egypt, but it would be wrong to imagine that Napoleon III had not thought that it might and certainly in regions of Mexico which were suitable for cotton growing, particularly the North Coast in the regions bordering on Texas, efforts were made during the French occupation to encourage and exploit the growing of cotton.[14] In a way, the clearest and most succinct statement of Napoleon's aims in intervening is contained in the letter to General Forey of 3rd July, 1862, in which he said: "There is no lack of people who ask why do we go to waste men and money in Mexico?" The Emperor answered his own questions by going on to say: "In the actual state of world civilization, the prosperity of America cannot be without interest for Europe, since it feeds our manufactures and sustains our commerce."[15] The Emperor saw, as he said, that if there were an independent and prosperous Mexico, allied to France: "We should have restored to the Latin race beyond the seas its force and prestige; we should have guaranteed the security of our colonies in the Antilles, we should have established our beneficent influence in Central America, and this influence, creating enormous openings for our colonies, would procure for us the indispensable materials for our industries." What remains to be considered is at what stage in the Mexican imbroglio did Napoleon III become converted to the establishment of a monarchy in Mexico? Clearly it was not before the autumn of 1861, since not until that date do we have any concrete evidence to show his direct interference in this aspect of the affair.

As far as he was concerned, the real triumph was to be once more, as in the China War, engaged in an enterprise with England. The issue of what form of government should be set up in Mexico appeared as a secondary one, but unfortunately for himself, Napoleon III's indulgent attitude towards Eugénie's fantasies and his amiabilities to Hidalgo and the other Mexican monarchists, now began to form a background to a political reality. Polite interest was construed as political approbation and by the end of September, not only was a Mexican throne envisaged, but a Prince had been found to fill it. The choice was Maximilian of Hapsburg, brother to the Emperor Franz-Josef.[16]

The problem was, how to sell the idea of establishing a monarchy to the English government which was only interested in playing the bailiff? It was here that lack of candour, to say the least of it, landed Napoleon III in the soup. England's adherence to the treaty of 31st October was as much to keep an eye on the Franco-Spanish entente as it was to operate in Mexico. The English government suspected French designs in Spain and indeed it was for this reason that Russell and Palmerston, who had at first wanted to keep Spain out of the whole affair, performed a *volte-face* in the autumn of 1861 when it became clear that Spain was an integral part of Napoleon III's calculations. The English government were right to suspect that the Emperor had plans for Spain, but unfortunately they were not aware that these plans were always conceived of as being joint Anglo-French operations.[17]

The trouble was, that in linking Spain and England together Napoleon had tied his own hands completely, since he could not be honest with either. As always, he hoped that time or changes of circumstance would resolve a situation which he could not. It was another example of his propensity to regard international politics as a lottery in which, with luck, one drew a winning ticket.

No Napoleonic move of importance ever took place without the appearance of a literary *piéce justificative.* In the case of Mexico, the cardinal document is the letter from Napoleon III to the Comte de Flahault, his negotiator in London, dated 9th October, 1861, at a critical moment in the negotiations for the triple entente.[18] Since Napoleon III meant this letter to be shown to Palmerston and Russell, it may be safely assumed that it was also an attempt to "come clean" at the last moment. It summarized the Emperor's reasons for wishing to intervene in Mexico, its potential, in particular for cotton, and it also acknowledged that he had been for some time under pressure from "distinguished Mexicans" who had asked him to help in restoring a monarchy in that country.

> I told them that I had no grounds for intervening in Mexico, that my policy, especially on American questions, was closely allied with that of England, that I believed that it would be difficult to persuade the Cabinet of St. James to assist in the execution of the plan, that we should be courting a quarrel with the United States and that, therefore, it was necessary to wait for better days.

The letter then pointed out that the situation had altered; the United States was preoccupied, and the outrages of the Mexican government had provoked a determination by England, Spain and France to intervene. "Thus the only question to be decided is, what shall be the aim of our intervention?" As far as Napoleon was concerned he assumed that, since he had been informed that the survival of the allied squadrons would provoke a monarchist uprising, all that remained was to have a candidate.

Here followed a list of requirements which a candidate would need, and then: "I have put forward the name of Archduke Maximilian." Now the cat was out of the bag with a vengeance, and with no further attempt at concealment, Napoleon made it plain that the matter was settled, except that before giving consent, the Cabinet of Vienna

> ...has laid down two conditions—that the Prince shall have the aid of France and England, and that the wish of the Mexican people shall be frankly and clearly expressed.... To sum up, I ask for nothing better than to sign a convention with Britain and Spain which shall have as its ostensible aim, the redress of our wrongs. But, knowing as I do the real position of affairs, I cannot bind myself to refuse my support to those who are working for an end which I desire with all my heart, for I am convinced that the regeneration of Mexico is essential to the progress of civilization as a whole.

There are two very important points in this last paragraph. Firstly, Napoleon III did not mind what the "ostensible aim" of the convention was so long as a convention was signed. Secondly, whatever the convention stated, the phrase *"I cannot bind myself..."* made clear the decision which the Emperor had already taken. To this extent, the negotiations for the convention have an air of unreality, for although the French accepted a draft which explicitly ruled out interference in the internal affairs of Mexico, the English Cabinet, had it read the Emperor's letter carefully, would have seen that such a limitation was meaningless, given the Emperor's expressed intention that "I cannot bind myself..."

Where Napoleon III and the French government incurred odium was that they virtually assured Austria that England had accepted the implications of the intervention and so condoned the candidature of Maximilian. It was apparently not until January, 1862, that Russell and the Austrian minister in London, Count Apponyi, compared notes and discovered the extent and implications of the *malentendu*.[19]

The really interesting point is to ask, *was* it a real *malentendu*? Or was the English government's attitude slightly equivocal? It is true that both Palmerston and Russell were against any explicit statement of interventionist aims in the internal affairs of Mexico, yet was not the whole expedition entailing, as it did, the seizure of Vera Cruz, an interference in the internal affairs of Mexico? What, in any case, was to be done if Juarez ignored the Allied fleet and refused to pay a centavo? All the signatories, including the English Cabinet, must have known that the Mexicans were liable to resist an act of *force majeure*, since no one likes the bailiff's men, even when the visit has been well merited.

It has been well said that: "intentionally or not, the British, from first to last placed no real obstacles in the path of Napoleon's ambitions in Mexico."[20] This ambivalence of the London Cabinet is borne out by Palmerston himself who in January, 1862, declared to Russell that:

> As to the monarchy scheme, if it could be carried out it would be a great blessing for Mexico, and a godsend for all countries having anything to do with Mexico.
>
> It would also stop the North Americans, whether of the Federal or the Confederate States, in their projected absorption of Mexico. If the North and South are definitely disunited, and if at the same time Mexico could be turned into a prosperous Monarchy, I do not know any arrangement that would be more advantageous for us.[21]

Clarendon put it more breezily by saying: "It amuses me to see the Emperor cocking up his leg against their Monroe doctrine which ought long ago to have been *arrosé* in that manner."[22]

In fact, England's policy was one of using Napoleon III to her advantage, if he succeeded, and of washing her hands of the affair if he failed. The Emperor is frequently accused of bad faith and double dealing, but the faults were not always his own.

However, this does not totally absolve Napoleon III from the charge of pursuing a policy in Mexico which if it had in it much that was reasonable in aim, had in it much that was pure folly in execution. The initial error had been to promise Maximilian a throne, and to allow the arrangements for this to become a reality before ensuring that the situation which would make it possible already existed.

Within a short time of their arrival at Vera Cruz it became clear to the Allies that the Mexican monarchists inhabited castles in Spain and that if France committed herself to establishing a monarchy it would have precisely the same chance of survival as any other Mexican government, namely if it could exist it would. Although by 1863 French troops, now over thirty thousand in numbers, had managed to oust Juarez from Mexico City, France was alone in her project, for Britain and Spain had both given up and Napoleon had refused an offer of assistance from the Confederate States, made in 1862, in return for French support of the Confederacy.[23] By 1863 the situation was such that even Maximilian was showing signs of hesitancy about accepting his new Empire and Napoleon had to force him into acceptance, with the threat of an alternative candidate. The Convention of Miramar was formally drawn up in 1864, representing an attempt to recoup France financially for her intervention in Mexico. Maximilian contracted to pay 270 million francs which covered the cost of the French expeditionary army, estimated at 230 million francs, while the remainder was to be used to pay off the French claims, which had led to the original intervention in 1861. It should perhaps be noted that no specific mention of Jecker's bonds was included in the Convention and it may safely be assumed that Napoleon III was no party to Morny's shady deals. What the world thought of Maximilian's chances in his Empire was shown by the fact that a Mexican loan, floated in Paris and London, was a total failure in the City, and only Imperial pressure on the *Crédit Mobilier* produced an artificial response in Paris.

The obvious solution would have been to quit Mexico and abandon the project. If it was honour which needed to be satisfied, in revenge for the reverse at Puebla in 1863, then surely this had been done by 1864. But the point was, of course, that it was not so much honour as economic interest and whether Maximilian was or was not Emperor, cotton was still King, and French industry needed it.

The cotton famine, of which mention has already been made, not only affected industrial relations, in the shape of an unemployed or half-time work force, it gave ammunition to those who blamed the free-trade treaty with England and with it the whole Imperial economic policy. Since the crisis had coincided with a sharp attack by Fould and the conservatives on the financial and economic structure, the Emperor could not ignore the situation even had he been minded to. The prospect of a link between disaffected financial interests and a discontented proletariat was one which the regime did not care to contemplate.[24]

The Confederate States had, in July, 1862, offered Napoleon 22,000 tons of raw cotton, but though the offer was tempting it was refused, since the cargo would have had to be carried in French ships through the Northern blockade and could well have led to war between France and the Northern States. Napoleon would not risk this, as his refusal of help in Mexico had already proved, and he was even more determined to avoid a clash, since the "Trent" affair in November, 1861, had revealed England's determination to remain neutral. By becoming involved with the Confederacy he risked entangling himself in a very dangerous situation, which would break the tacit agreement between England and France based on a common desire to remain neutral in the war, and thus put a further strain on Anglo-French co-operation.[25]

In any event Napoleon III was loath to commit himself to the cause of the slave states, although some of his political enemies in France accused him of launching the Mexican expedition for just that purpose.[26]

In other ways all that could be done to relieve the economic crisis was done. New projects were launched to increase the cotton growing in Algeria, purchases of raw cotton were made in Egypt and in India, and an offer of French mediation between North and South in January, 1863, did something to bring down the price of raw cotton, though diplomatically it was a failure, in that Napoleon III could not persuade England and Russia to join him in presenting proposals, and neither North nor South displayed great interest.

Unfortunately, by the time Maximilian was actually installed in Mexico, any hope of stabilizing the new government was lost. The North was clearly well on the way to defeating the Confederacy, and the Washington government had made it known that it would not long tolerate the French presence in Mexico. Apart from this, the European situation had altered by 1864-65 and Napoleon's position there demanded an end to what was becoming an unnecessary and expensive failure.

In the speech from the throne in February, 1865, the Emperor announced that: "In Mexico, the new throne is establishing itself, the country is becoming peaceful, its immense resources are being developed; a happy effect of the bravery of our soldiers, the good sense of the Mexican population, and the intelligence and energy of the sovereign." No one could accept this as a serious analysis of the conditions in Mexico and the real information came in a later passage when Napoleon continued: "Thus, all our overseas expeditions are reaching an end: our land forces have left China; the navy suffices to maintain our establishments in Cochin China: our army of Africa is to be reduced, that of Mexico is already returning to France: the garrison will soon return from Rome. . . ."[27]

In truth the Frontiers of Empire were shrinking, for the barbarians were already on the road to the gates. Mexico ended in dreadful horror at the small town of Queretaro on the 19th June, 1867, with the execution of Maximilian by a triumphant Juarez, backed by the U.S.A. The Mexicans had exercised the only privilege open to the weak, the right to choose their own exploiter. The former Empress Carlotta, who had set out on a last despairing mission to Europe to collect help for the Empire, had become hopelessly insane and was to live until 1927 without ever recovering her reason. The expedition had, in sober truth, ended in death and madness, not least because as Rouher said: "*Nul ne pouvait calculer les passions de la nation Mexicaine.*"

Financially the affair had been costly : it was not just a question of non-recovery of the debts already owing, it was also a question of a further accumulation of expenditure on the army which, even had Napoleon III wished it, could not have been maintained any longer without a really serious eruption of discontent in the *Corps Législatif.*

The constitutional reforms of 1860 had given them some teeth and there were many who were anxious to use them to see how deep the bite would be. Even Rouher, who had defended the Mexican expedition as *La Grande pensée du règne*, admitted privately that "there was no serious hope of appealing for more credits." In spite of the Emperor's assurances in the speech from the throne in January, 1866, that all was well in Mexico and that, French commerce with the new Empire had risen from 21 to 77 millions of francs, no one really believed that anything could be salvaged from the wreckage.

The Emperor himself said as much when, in 1867, he announced the final recall of the French troops, "because the extent of our sacrifices seemed to outweigh the interests which had taken us to the other side of the world."

It was the same in the East as in the West. By 1866-67 the lure of China and Indo-China was also becoming resistable, though in this area the withdrawal was not total and indeed the period of the Second Empire marked only a phase in what was to be a continuing development.

French activity in this region dated back to the reign of Louis Philippe and the attempts which had gone on during that period to put France on the map. Here, as elsewhere, the Second Empire took up the task, but pursued it with more vigour and panache, and it should be said that in any analysis of French policy in the Far East, the charge of clerical activities can be made to stick much more easily than in the case of the Mexican affair. There was so little French trade in the region in the early 1850's that France's only claim to intervene was the right to protect her missionaries in South East Asia and China. Before criticisms are made of these somewhat precarious grounds for interference in the internal affairs of others, it should be pointed out that England's claim to intervene was based on the desire to protect the opium trade over which she held a monopoly, both of its production in British India and its distribution in China.

Undoubtedly Napoleon III was anxious to increase the prestige of France and enhance the commercial opportunities which the Far

Eastern market offered, but it is problematical if France would have
become so deeply involved had not England taken the initiative in
seeking help in the region. In 1853 the London government issued a
circular note to France, Russia and the U.S.A. asking for assistance in
regulating the affairs of China. This meant that England intended to
enlist support with a view to pressing for the revision of the Treaty of
Nanking of 1842, now due for renewal after the initial twelve year
period. It was not at all clear that the Imperial Chinese government
would be forthcoming in the matter of additional concessions such as
were envisaged under a new treaty, and indeed, the principal demands,
regarding the opium trade and coolie labour, would only have been
accepted by a totally defeated nation.[28]

The response of Napoleon III to the English request for co-operation
and assistance was to agree to support his ally in this disreputable affair
and it is scarcely necessary to add that the question of "the policy of
nationalities" does not seem to have arisen to disturb the Imperial
mind. The trouble was that while France's aims in the Far East were
imprecise and tentative, England knew exactly what was wanted and so
all the advantages of Anglo-French co-operation worked in favour of
the former. That is precisely why, of course, French help was accepted.

France lacked any base of operations in the Far East, her Indian
possessions, including the islands, were negligible and it was knowledge of
this which led to French attempts to establish themselves in Cochin-
China and Annam in an attempt to make France's position *vis-à-vis*
England a little less unequal. By 1856, however, it was clear that
attempts to penetrate Annam had failed. The hostile relations between
England and China, having recovered from the temporary lull brought
on by the Crimean War, were a godsend in that they did provide a
reason for interference any time the Chinese government could be
provoked into some form of action which the English could construe as
hostile. England found her excuse for the war in the affair of the
Arrow, while the Chinese obligingly provided the French government
with a *casus belli*, in the shape of the martyrdom in February, 1856, of
Father Chapdelaine, a missionary priest.

When the war began in 1857 France's position in the alliance was
stronger than had at first sight seemed likely. This was due in part to
England's embarrassment because of the mutiny which had just broken
out in India, the suppression of which was, inevitably, her prime
military objective and also in part was it due to Napoleon III's having
drawn Spain into his Far Eastern schemes and so lessened his dependence on England for bases of operations.

Spanish involvement in the affair was made possible by the fact that Spanish missionaries were active in the Far East and the martyrdom of a Dominican, Father Diaz, in Annam in 1857 was taken as proof of the necessity for the protection of these missionaries by their government. Spain was also useful, in that the Philippines provided a basis of operations for a Franco-Spanish force, thus relieving the total dependence of France on English ports and concessions, and Spain also provided 1,400 men from her Filippino army as well as a battery of artillery and two steam transports. Contemporary, therefore, with the Anglo-French war in China, went the Franco-Spanish operations in Annam and Cochin-China.[29]

It was in China that the operations first reached a conclusion, with the Treaty of Tientsin in 1858 which ended the first phase of Anglo-French collaboration in the Far East. The Emperor was well pleased with the strengthening of the entente which this brought about, with all that he hoped it entailed for his European policies. Local European opinion in China was less sure of the value of Anglo-French co-operation. The Hong-Kong *Daily Press* in June, 1858, commented sourly that: "The formation of the Alliance was ill-advised and has justified the French in augmenting their forces in these seas to an extent which, with this Indian affair on our hands, is dangerous."[30]

In point of fact the local assessment of the situation was quite wrong, since the Treaty of Tientsin did much more for England than it did for France. At the same time, the latter's Cochin-China venture was going badly, partly because the operation was under-financed and partly because of friction with the Spanish. Not till 1859 was Saigon taken and even then there seemed little hope of establishing a genuine French "presence" in the region. Napoleon III was, basically, too European-centred to devote sufficient attention to what was happening in such a peripheral field of activity, and the Italian war was of more consequence to him than the capture of Saigon. It was left to the French Ministry of Marine and French admirals to conduct this campaign.

In any event, since much of Napoleon's activity in the area was simply a means of tying himself closer to England, the eruption of further hostilities in China meant that France must look to her co-operation with England in case she should damage the alliance. Any other interests in the Far East must be subordinated to this more pressing claim. At this particular juncture, the disaster of the storming of the Taku Forts in 1859 had seriously impaired English prestige and so France was welcome once again as a support.

When the war with China was renewed in 1860, Anglo-French

relations were, generally better, not only because of the need for French help on the spot, but also because the commercial treaty of January, 1860, had drawn the two countries together. Apart from this it was now France's "second time round" in China, and her representative, Baron Gros, had already dealt wth Lord Elgin when they had negotiated the Treaty of Tientsin.

In spite, however, of increased goodwill, one of the two participants in the alliance found cause to complain of the behaviour of the other party: in China, the English military command, mostly professionals from the Indian army, complained of the inefficiency and slipshod methods of the French. In London a section of English opinion felt that there should be much greater co-ordination between the two nations to avoid waste of effort and money and to prevent the French from having the paramount position in the expedition. This was revealed during a parliamentary debate on 16th March, 1860, when Sir Hugh de Lacy Evans commented that: "The French ... have a very large army without a European war wherein to employ it, the Chinese conflict was perhaps meant as a temporary amusement or occupation for the French soldiery till something more serious turned up."[31] While the entente was subjected to this type of comment in both London and Paris, it showed considerably more signs of strain in Pekin at the level of General Grant who got on less than well with Montauban, his French opposite number. When it came to the decision to burn the summer palace in Pekin, an exercise in civilization which would bring the barbarous Chinese to their senses, the French commander dissented from the English decision, though both sides looted the palace with complete unanimity.

Given the premise, however, that Napoleon III was committed less to China than to England, the French had to soldier on, and small gain they had for it. The Treaty of Pekin was in no sense a triumph for France, while it was of great benefit to England and to Russia. Although this might be considered to be of value to Napoleon III in reconciling the two powers to him on the European scene, this was to imply a future call on gratitude, that most dubious of diplomatic coin. The actual result had been to establish England's domination along the South and Central Chinese coast and, thanks to the Russian representative Ignatiev's clever manoeuvring, to establish Russia along a vast slice of North Chinese territory. Ignatiev gained the Trans-Ussuri territory for his country without firing a shot.

As far as Napoleon III's Far Eastern policy was concerned, the only gain in China was a certain amount of prestige and, under the terms of the Treaty of Pekin, a share of the China trade. It was clear that France would never amount to much in a region where England and Russia had all the advantages, and the attempt to make use of Cochin-China was very much a *pis-aller* half-heartedly pursued.

The Treaty of Saigon, made in 1862, left France as the only interested Power, since Spain was bought off by a cash payment, but French attempts to extend their influence remained under the control of the Ministry of Marine and Napoleon III himself played little part in these developments. The opening of the Suez Canal in 1869 came too late in the Empire's history to bring about a dramatic change in this attitude, and it was left to the Third Republic to reap what the Second Empire had, sparsely, sown.

The Emperor may have felt that "the European equilibrium embraced the entire world," but in fact he never really thought himself out of a European situation, and he knew that France's position as a Power was not dependent upon what happened on the Yangtse and the Mekong but on what happened on the Rhine and on the Vistula. From 1863 onwards, both these regions dominated Imperial foreign policies and the problems which arose there influenced greatly the decision to withdraw from more distant areas of the world.

12

The Vistula and the Rhine

*"Je n'ai pas fait la guerre pour la Pologne,
l'intérêt français ne l'exigeait pas et je ne la
ferai dans aucune éventualité analogue."*

Napoleon III, 1864

IN 1795 a major European state disappeared from the map when
the former independent Kingdom of Poland was finally par-
titioned by Austria, Russia and Prussia. The Polish nation had
disappeared to be replaced by the Polish question, for the absence of
any buffer state between the Powers of Austria, Russia and Prussia,
whose frontiers now marched together, affected the structure of the
entire European states system. In spite of Marx, it was not communism
which was the spectre haunting Europe, it was Poland, *la Pologne
errante* which rattled its chains from time to time through the corridors
of the European chancelleries.

What was quite clear to all who thought seriously about the Polish
question was that to re-establish a Polish State would be to cause a
major disruption in Europe, since such a re-creation could only be based
upon an alteration in the existing power structure. The two decisive
moments in the evolution of the Polish problem had occurred as a result
of just such an alteration. In 1807, the creation of the Grand Duchy of
Warsaw was only possible because Napoleon I dominated Prussia and
had achieved an uneasy accord with the Emperor Alexander I of
Russia. The disappearance of the Grand Duchy in 1814-15 was the
result of a restoration of the "classic" situation in which France had
been driven out of Central Europe and had lost her *point d'appui* in
Poland. Without outside support, the chances of a Polish state re-
emerging were minimal and the peace makers of 1815 had in any case,
no intention of allowing such a situation to arise. The basic concern was
to re-establish a balanced partition in which Russia should not be
allowed to achieve an over-dominant role. Alexander I was checked,
though it necessitated the other allies using France as a counter-weight
against him. The frontiers of the Congress Kingdom of Poland which

emerged in 1815 represented a compromise between Russia's territorial claims and her geographical needs for defence purposes, and the political aspirations of the Polish ruling classes. The arrangement was also convenient in that it enabled Alexander I to exercise his liberal views abroad without imposing any real limitation on his autocratic powers at home.

As far as Austria and Prussia were concerned, they were again co-partners in the partition, although the actual areas held, particularly in the case of Prussia, differed from those they had acquired in the earlier partitions. These frontiers were, in fact, to last for one hundred years, for the Polish state did not re-emerge as an entity until 1918–19, but the nineteenth century witnessed attempts by the politically active sections of the native Polish ruling groups to reassert their right to rule. In furtherance of this aim, a constant barrage of propaganda was kept up stressing Poland's right to exist as an independent nation and in 1830–32 a serious revolt had been carried out against Russian rule. The repression which this revolt brought about and the subsequent policy of russification pursued by the Petersburg government only served to increase the vehemence with which Polish exiles argued their case.

In 1830 the Polish insurrectionists had looked to the "Western Powers" England and France for support. Since neither of these states held territory which belonged to Poland they were the only hope, for Austria and Prussia were unlikely to assist in a rising which, if successful, could only call in question their own right to hold Polish territory.

As far as England was concerned, Lord Palmerston was willing to send a diplomatic protest to the Tsar, but had no intention of taking any action which would lead to hostilities. In this instance a breach in the 1815 settlement, unlike the dissolution of the union between Holland and Belgium, could only be to England's disadvantage, and was never envisaged.

In France, the new government of Louis Philippe dare not become embroiled except verbally, though, unlike England, France would be bound to welcome any breach of the 1815 settlement which could work to her advantage. But France was dependent on England's goodwill and dared not antagonize her patron and so the most that Paris would offer was an expression of indignation and a manifestation of sympathy with the Polish cause. The crushing of the revolt led to an enormous influx of Polish exiles into France and Paris became a centre for the Polish political émigrés. This meant that in the period between 1832 and 1848 the "Polish cause" became part of the stock in trade of the

French radical movements so that both Lamartine and Blanqui found themselves commenting on Polish affairs in 1848 in order to satisfy popular clamour.[1] Among French political groups support of Polish aspirations was popular for the simple reason that it represented not only an attack on 1815, but also an attack on the Tsar, who could be identified both as the main upholder of the Vienna settlement and as the arch apostle of anti-liberalism and anti-revolutionism. Patriotism and radicalism could join hands over Poland if they could not do it about very much else. None of this, it must be said, had the slightest effect on the situation in Poland where Russian policy was pursued without any consideration of what the rest of Europe thought. Its attitude was remarkably similar to the English government's attitude to Ireland; the problem was a domestic one.

So long as the European situation remained fairly static, the Russian government was quite entitled to consider the Polish problem as non-existent, except as an exercise in administration. Problems could only arise if the European states system was threatened with change and it was largely the threat of such changes, arising from Napoleon III's foreign policy, which led to the crisis of the 1860's.

The Emperor knew perfectly well that any radical redrawing of the European map must involve some consideration of the future of Poland. He was equally aware that the Polish question was a potential upas-tree and one that he could not afford to touch without taking prophylactic precautions. The problem which had arisen in the Danubian principalities and Italy, and the even more recent problems in Mexico had made Napoleon III more circumspect by 1861 than he had been in earlier years. Those who see in the Emperor's hesitations in the last decade of the Empire the effects of ill health and confusion might also consider the effects of experience as making for a more cautious and hesitant approach.

It was not Napoleon III's lack of interest in Poland which had made France's policy hesitant in the period between 1856 and 1863. The Emperor wanted to move, as indeed he had made clear during the Paris peace conference in 1856, when it was clear that the Austro-Russian entente, which had lasted since 1815, was in full dissolution. Such a dissolution must have its effects on the situation in Poland as elsewhere. Napoleon III's problem was how to turn it to his advantage.[2] The Emperor's expressed interest in Poland may well have helped to persuade Alexander II that he should begin his reign by conciliatory gestures in Warsaw such as the amnesty for Polish *émigrés* and political prisoners granted in May, 1856. In any event, given the near-crisis situation inside Russia, it would have been folly for Alexander not to conciliate Polish opinion in an attempt to remove one possible source of trouble. To tackle the problem of emancipation of the serfs while dealing with a hostile and recalcitrant Poland would have been an impossibility.

Alexander's policy in Poland gave some sort of public satisfaction to the expressed intentions of Napoleon III to help Poland, without committing either too much, but they did nothing to satisfy the Polish political groups. Neither in Paris, where the "white" faction centred round Prince Adam Czartoryski at the Hotel Lambert, nor in London where the "Reds" sought a military uprising as the answer to the question, was there any diminution of hostile propaganda against Russia. In Paris, the efforts of Czartoryski and his group were strongly supported by Prince Jerome Bonaparte who was, as ever, as outspoken in his comments as his imperial cousin was reticent. Prince Napoleon pressed for an active Polish policy involving revolution if necessary. The Emperor worked for an accord with the Tsar so that a revolutionary situation could be avoided. The experience of Italy, where changes made to avoid a revolutionary movement had, by 1860, produced a revolutionary change, made Napoleon III cautious.

The trouble was that in aiming for a Tilsit-type agreement with the Tsar, Napoleon III, unlike his uncle, had not the victory of Friedland behind him. All that he could hope for was that Russian diplomatic needs would make her co-operative, but by 1859-60 Russia knew that her real need, the revision of the Black Sea Clauses of 1856, would not be achieved with French assistance. Napoleon would not break with England to please Russia and England's insistence of the inclusion of the Black Sea Clauses had skilfully tied Napoleon's hands for the future. It was for precisely this reason that Drouyn de Lhuys had opposed the Clauses in 1856, seeing that all the advantages in such a situation accrued to England. Yet, in accepting the English conditions, the Emperor was not merely being sentimental about his ally, he was being realistic in that he knew opposition could mean the loss of that ally and he dared not risk this.

It was the knowledge that her diplomatic position was not as weak as she had first thought, coupled with initial successes of Alexander's reforms in Russia culminating in the emancipation of February, 1861, which led Russia to a more "forward" policy in 1860-61. In the Far East, in China and Japan she scored considerable successes.[3] In Persia and in the Balkans there was a revival of Russian activity.

Most significant in this renewal of diplomatic activity was the *rapprochement* with Prussia which dated from the meeting of Prussian and Russian representation at Breslau in June, 1860. At this meeting, the Tsar obtained a promise of support in getting rid of the detested Black Sea Clauses, and from then on the Berlin-Petersburg axis became a factor to be reckoned with in any diplomatic calculation. Russia needed to buy time, in that the emancipation edict needed not merely to be proclaimed but also to be implemented, and so Gortchakov let it be known that Russia's aim was a Franco-Prusso-Russian entente. Such an entente was virtually a non-starter in diplomatic terms, but it had the advantage for Russia of occupying the participants and of temporarily preventing them from carrying on any other diplomatic offensive. Above all, it was basically disadvantageous to France, since it not only took the pressure off the Russian government, but led Napoleon into supporting Prussia's claim for federal reform in Germany. These claims were directed against Austria, but indirectly were a threat to France's position unless Napoleon III could be absolutely sure that he could control the future course of events in Germany if Prussia moved against Austria. France was by now virtually without a firm ally, not only because of the situation just outlined, but also because England had taken up a more hostile attitude. Palmerston had written to Russell in February, 1861, that: "... the whole drift of our policy is to prevent France from realizing her vast schemes of expansion in a great number of quarters." Although this had not prevented collaboration in Mexico, there is no doubt it did reflect Palmerston's view on French activities in general. As far as he was concerned, the Emperor was too active in too many spheres and recent developments in the Middle East had angered the English government. In this area, Napoleon's plans were intimately linked with the project to construct the Suez Canal which had been a matter of consideration in France since 1855. Only the Emperor's reluctance to offend English susceptibilities had held de Lesseps back from launching his scheme at that time, but this reason could not be allowed to dominate French plans for the area for ever. After 1856-57 France's prestige stood higher than Britain's at Constantinople, largely because the French army had made a better showing in the Crimean War, and so the Emperor was under pressure from de Lesseps and others to push ahead with the great dream of Michel Chevalier and the Saint Simonian expansionists of making the Mediterranean a "French lake."

In pursuance of this aim, France had intervened in Syria in 1860, in defence of the Maronite Christians who were being attacked and massacred by the Muslim Druses. Napoleon saw a chance to establish a pro-French regime in the area adjacent to the line of the Suez Canal, on which preliminary work had already been begun, thus giving France a firm foot in the south-eastern corner of the Mediterranean.

In 1860 an anonymous pamphlet appeared in Paris entitled *Abd-el-Kader, Emperor of Arabia* in which the author (quite obviously Napoleon III) advocated the setting up of an Arabian state under the sceptre of the former Algerian rebel leader, whom the Emperor admired but had no intention of restoring to Algeria. This new Empire would be French in outlook and structure using the *Code Napoléon* as the basis of its laws, and introducing the metric and decimal systems to enable it to trade freely and easily with more advanced regions. Even more important, the pamphlet urged that this new Empire should become the guarantor of the free navigation of the isthmus of Suez as envisaged by the treaties of 1856.[4]

Anxiety about what France's policy in the area might lead to had induced Palmerston to collaborate in the Syrian expedition on the principle that co-operation was an effective means of exercising some control over French policy. Unfortunately for Palmerston, the French, while obeying the English desire for a withdrawal of forces, which took place in June, 1861, left behind a pro-French ruler in the Lebanon to protect the Christians and England incurred the odium of, apparently, leaving a Christian people to the mercies of a very precarious political situation in which a small number of Christians was marooned in a sea of Muslims.

Furthermore, on a wider scale, the policy of Palmerston was a failure since it did not prevent the Sultan's acceptance of the Suez Canal project as having an official existence and work on the construction of the canal was now begun in earnest. Palmerston's attitude to the scheme never varied from one of absolute hostility, and from 1861 to 1869 the question of the Suez Canal helped to envenom Anglo-French relations at a time when Napoleon III could well have done without any such complication. With a substantial part of the French army overseas, in Mexico or in the Far East, Napoleon III's position was not as strong as Palmerston held it to be. It may well have been the realization of this which had led Napoleon to replace Thouvenel by re-installing Drouyn de Lhuys at the Quai d'Orsay in October, 1862. The stress was to be on conservatism in foreign policies which meant that France would incline towards Austria in an attempt to balance off the Russo-Prussian entente, but whatever Napoleon III intended to do with French policy was bedevilled by an event over which he had no control. A fortnight into the New Year, on 15th January, 1863, an insurrection broke out in Warsaw.

The insurrection had been threatening for some eighteen months and, as is so often the case, was due less to repression than to reforms which had not gone far enough to satisfy the discontented. Part of Russia's "forward" policy had been an attempt further to strengthen her hold on Poland to avoid any chance of trouble if Russia were faced with a showdown elsewhere in Europe. The sending of the Marquis Wielopolski to Warsaw in 1861 to carry out a programme of reforms by Imperial decree was an indication of Alexander II's determination to achieve some sort of peace in Poland. The constitution of the Congress Kingdom which Nicholas I had abrogated in 1832 was partly revived, though without any Parliamentary structure, and the Russian government appealed for the support of the Polish ruling class. The answer to this came with a claim for the revival of the Polish nation ". . . in the territory designated for her by God, and sometimes by history." In more mundane terms, this meant the frontiers of 1772. It was quite unacceptable to the Russians and it would have been equally unacceptable to Europe as a whole. The Polish revolutionaries were firm believers in no bread as opposed to the half-loaf. That, in itself, was not the least of their problems.

The news of the Warsaw outbreak did not cause an immediate stir in the rest of Europe, since the Russians indicated that it was a domestic problem which could easily be handled. Of all those likely to be involved, the most relieved to hear this was Napoleon III. In an interview with Metternich, the Austrian Ambassador, the Emperor said : "One can well have sympathy with this or that people's national aspirations, it is the revolution which, pushing itself in between (*en s'interposant*), spoils everything. It is because I do not wish, and cannot, traffic with revolution that I have so much hindrance today; it is revolution which loses the best causes, which destroys all the sympathy one could have, which makes Italy odious to me and disgusts me with Poland."[5]

In these circumstances, and well aware that public support for a war on behalf of Poland would not be forthcoming beyond the point of speeches and resolutions, Napoleon III had to apply himself to achieving a diplomatic victory. The attempts to do this exposed both the weakness of France's position in Europe and, by implication, the Emperor's position as an arbitrator in European affairs.

It should be remembered that the initiative in making Poland a European affair came not from Paris but from Berlin. In February,

Bismarck sent General Alvensleben to St. Petersburg to negotiate a Prusso-Russian convention which provided for military co-operation on the frontiers of the two states in dealing with the Polish rebels. It is useless to argue what Bismarck achieved or what he thought he wanted to achieve by this convention. There is no point in wasting time on the question "Did it split Russia and France?" as Bismarck claimed. The one thing it undisputably did was to make the Polish affair a European affair, nothing could have been more serious than that.[6]

The French response to the Alvensleben Convention was immediate. On 15th February, a week after the signing, Drouyn de Lhuys saw both the Prussian and Russian Ambassadors and warned them that France could not now stand by as a spectator in the Polish affair. He informed Golz, the Prussian Ambassador, that any difficulties which might have existed between England and France were ironed out by a common attitude to Poland.[7] At the same time, the French government made plain that any intervention would not be in any sense armed intervention on behalf of the insurrectionists. A speech by Jules Favre in the Chamber demanded full support for the Poles. Billault, former President of the *Corps Législatif*, answered that: "The Emperor's government is too sensible to give a illusory diet of empty words to bolster up these revolutionary passions..." Billault, in fact, had pinpointed the weakness in all the clamour about Poland which, as he said on another occasion in the Senate was a "policy of a great many words and very little action." This was not only true of France. England, for her part "... showed an unbridled liberalism in her language and an equally unbridled circumspection in her behaviour."[8]

The Imperial policy was therefore announced as one of intervention, but it would be pacific. This was one occasion on which *L'Empire, c'est la paix* was resolutely applied as a working maxim.

The obvious diplomatic manoeuvre must be to align England with France. This would not only smooth over the recent animosities and restore Napoleon III's sheet-anchor in diplomacy, it would also enable him to seek for an entente with Austria and would be a public admission of the "conservative" nature of the Emperor's approach as opposed to Bismarck's "revolutionary" policy. It was now Bismarck's turn to indulge in fantasies about redrawing the map of Central Europe. In conversation with a deputy of the Prussian *Landtag*, one Behrend, Bismarck outlined a scheme for the occupation of part of Poland by the Prussian army and the establishment of a Polish Kingdom which would consist of the existing Prussian Poland plus the area of Galicia which belonged to Austria. This Kingdom would be ruled over by a

Hohenzollern Prince and would therefore, be linked to Prussia by a dynastic union. When this news reached Vienna the Austrians protested violently against this threat to their own part of Poland and Bismarck was compelled to renounce the scheme and indeed to deny that he ever mooted it.[9]

This conversation took place within a week of the Alvensleben Convention. If it was merely a joke on Bismarck's part it ran the risk of seriously misfiring. It would not have been found remotely funny either in Paris or St. Petersburg. Indeed, it may well have been knowledge of Bismarck's European fantasies which led to the extraordinary incident in Paris on 21st February in which Metternich had a conversation with the Empress Eugénie at the Tuileries. As they talked, the Empress roamed over the map of Europe, pencil in hand, drawing in frontiers. While thrones fell, dynasties were transplanted and fundamental problems were dissolved by the feminine touch. Metternich's dispatch makes it plain that this was the most grandiose exposé of Imperial ideas he had yet encountered and he thought it should be taken seriously. Since the scheme did, in essence, favour Austria, who would cede Venetia but receive, after a war with Prussia, Silesia and areas south of the River Main, it could be seen as an attempt to re-inforce the Emperor's bid for an Austrian alliance. But can this fantasy be taken seriously?[10] Given the general trend of Napoleon III's thinking at the time, such a scheme for the recasting of Europe could only be meaningful if one accepted that the road to a conservative policy lay through the creation of chaos. The Emperor was a dreamer, but he was not a fool and, in fact, when Metternich saw him three days after the *voyage à la lune* with Eugénie the conversation, although about an alliance, was sober and restrained, even hesitant.

In face of this new development in the Polish crisis the French attitude was, inevitably, to seek for a diplomatic grouping to bring pressure to bear not only on Alexander II but even more, since Alvensleben, on Prussia. The only possible allies were Austria and England and Austria's position was difficult, not merely because she now viewed every situation from the point of view of its possible repercussions on her situation in Germany but because she herself possessed part of Poland. In an attempt to "go it alone," Austria rejected the idea of joint mediation proposed by France, in spite of appeals by the Pope to Franz-Josef and the frank admission of Napoleon III to Metternich in Paris that he wanted an entente with Austria. It was perhaps, inevitable, that Austria should be distrustful of Napoleon, in view of what had gone before in 1859-60, but given the fact that Napoleon's *real* diplomatic offensive was directed against Prussia rather than Russia, the Vienna government would have done better to stoop in order to conquer.

Austria would not commit herself. In March there were exchanges of draft agreements between Paris and Vienna so vague as to be meaningless. Expressions of good intentions were no substitute for a delivery of the goods and Rechberg summed up the Austrian attitude to the whole manoeuvre by saying "... the risk [in a French alliance] was certain, and the advantages problematical."

Why did Austria refuse? Was it the possible effects of an Austro-French alliance on what remained of the structure of the 1815 settlement? Finally to break this would be to expose the Hapsburg monarchy to all sorts of pressures. Was it because she feared to compromise her "German-ness" by an alliance with France and so weaken her standing *vis-à-vis* Prussia in the eyes of the lesser German states who feared Napoleon's Rhenish ambitions? Or was it fear for Venetia whose possession gave the Empire its only access to the sea? This latter point undoubtedly weighed heavily in Vienna since it was one of the principle arguments used by Rechberg in his conversations with Metternich. A body politic so liable to suffer compound fractures could hardly be expected to welcome the prospect of amputation.[11]

Quite apart from political considerations, there was the fact that in matters liable to affect the economy the Austrian government could not afford to take chances. By the early sixties the state of the finances was extremely alarming, since there was still a chronic deficit and the amount owing in loan was some seven and a half billion francs. These were spread over one hundred different types of loans, bearing sixteen different rates of interest, all contolled by the Rothschilds, either directly or through intermediaries. In 1863, the Péreires tried to take up a loan for the *Crédit Mobilier*, but failed to defeat the Rothschild interest though they did manage to make it an expensive victory for their opponents.[12] It is significant that the French government had been behind the moves of the *Crédit*, clearly because the idea of loan and alliance were linked, and so the failure was as much diplomatic as financial.

As far as the Austrian government was concerned, the basic situation remained one of financial instability and this undoubtedly did much to condition Austrian policy, particularly since the finance minister promised a balanced budget if war could be avoided for five years.

Unfortunately, the choice of peace or war for Austria did not lie with the finance minister or even with the foreign minister at the Ballplatz.

Austria did not live alone in Europe and the crisis caused by the Polish insurrection left her in much the same state as she had been in 1856; virtually isolated and therefore vulnerable.

Napoleon III, foiled in his attempt to associate Austria with him, in a diplomatic move over Poland, was forced to bid for England's support without any strong cards in his hand. Palmerston was suspicious of Napoleon's aims in Poland particularly because he believed that to allow French influence on the Vistula was to put France again on the Rhine. England could derive no advantage from a situation which could lead to a resurrection of a "Napoleonic" Europe. The battle of Waterloo had not been a sham fight. Any collaboration which Napoleon III received from England would be given on a basis of tying him down rather than turning him loose. In his desire to hold to the entente with Alexander II, the Emperor had been too clever. By indicating that the action was against Prussia rather than Russia, he had alarmed England, who as has been said, suspected that the Vistula flowed into the Rhine. The diplomatic note which finally emerged from the three capitals of London, Vienna and Paris on 17th April, 1863, was quite clearly directed against Russia. England would not have it otherwise, nor would Austria. By such methods they would, with luck, ease Napoleon III out from his relationship with the Tsar.

From that point of view the initial Russian response was disappointing. Gortchakov was more forthcoming than Napoleon III could, in the circumstances, have dared to hope and certainly gave no indication that the Tsar would consider the note as a reason for breaking with France. Gortchakov knew the value of protest notes: "If they sent me forty notes on the affairs of Poland they would cause me no more embarrassment than the clutter they make in the archives of my ministry."[13]

It is doubtful if any of the participants in the note had any illusions about its effect and Napoleon III might well have been able to pursue a peaceful diplomatic campaign had it not been that election year in France demanded a more "busy" response to Poland. The liberalization of the Empire meant that the elections of May–June, 1863, for the Legislative Body gave rise to more political activity than France had seen since 1852. Indeed the elections showed that the Empire had entered a new phase in its political evolution. This was revealed both by the government's attitude to the elections and by the electorate's voting pattern. In the case of the government, the controlling hand of the Prefects was much less evident than in previous elections and the official candidates frequently got off to a bad start because they lacked the organizational support of the *Préfecture*.[14] What the elections did produce was evidence of a tendency to criticize sharply various aspects of Imperial policy except the Emperor's attitude to Poland. Even before the elections an observer had noted that all classes in France, workers and bourgeoisie, clericals and anti-clericals, even the Empress and Prince Napoleon, agreed on being indignant about Poland. Only Blanqui, in the Sainte Pélagie prison, appeared curmudgeonly in his attitude. To him, the Polish insurrectionists were "clerico-feudal brutes," whose ideas were on a par with those of the "planters of the South" (of the United States). "If Poland were to become reconstituted by its own efforts, the Jesuits would immediately be the masters."[15] To Blanqui, the Republican party in France with its cry of "support for Poland" had taken leave of its senses. Had he forgotten the day in 1848 when the Paris crowd had called to him in the Assembly *"Parlez-vous de la Pologne"*? Whether he liked it or not, and no matter how irrational it might seem to him, popular feeling did support Poland and neither the Emperor nor the Republican party could ignore this. In the period preceding the June election, the reports of the *Procureurs Généraux* indicated how widespread was the feeling throughout France that something should be done for Poland.[16] The Emperor, sensitive to public opinion, could not ignore this, nor could the Republicans be allowed to appear more Bonapartist than Napoleon, particularly since Prince Napoleon had himself indicated his irritation with Napoleon III's purely diplomatic manoeuvres as early as March, 1863. Anticipating Trotsky, the Prince had ended his harangue with the statement that France's attitude to Russia was "not war, nor was it peace." The Emperor's immediate response to this *gasconnade* was a sharp rebuke.[17]

The net result of this stir in opinion was to make it plain that further action on Poland was essential, but it must be peaceful. Napoleon himself wanted it that way and so, he was convinced, did the people who were noisy but not bellicose in intent. Given the failure of the attempt to lean on Prussia, further action could only mean diplomatic pressure on Russia. After a great deal of horse-trading, which mainly served to reveal how divergent rather than congruent were the policies of Austria, England and France, a further note was presented on an individual basis to St. Petersburg in June 1863.

It should be added that the period between April and June had also revealed the extent of the disarray which existed between Austria, Prussia and Russia, where tentative attempts to breathe life into the corpse of the Holy Alliance foundered totally. Poland worried all of them, but this was not sufficient to bind them in a common front against

France. Prussia wanted Alexander II to break with Napoleon, but the Tsar was not prepared to abandon the entente on which he still rested his hopes of revising the 1856 settlement. In any event, it was hardly the moment to inaugurate changes in Russian foreign policy. Austria wanted a guarantee of support against France's pressure for a union of Venetia, but neither Prussia nor Russia would give any assurance on this point.

In any event, a basic stumbling block to co-operation was the increasing tension between Prussia and Austria over the problems of the Germanic Confederation in which both sides were now openly jockeying for leadership. The threat of a crisis in Germany had much to do with preventing the English Government's supporting France in any of these moves against Russia. Russell had defined the attitude of the English Cabinet in a dispatch to Lord Cowley in Paris saying: ". . . it must not be supposed that in case France were singly to make war for Poland, Great Britain would admit her own helplessness and retire within herself. She would insist on certain conditions in favour of the integrity of Germany and against encroachments on the part of France before she consented to be neutral."[18]

This raised a very serious situation for Napoleon III. Not only would England avoid a promise of neutrality, but she warned of possible hostility. When, therefore, in July, the Russian Government rejected, as was expected, the Note of June, France was faced with the prospect of military action in isolation. The only offer of a military alliance which Napoleon III had received was from Charles XV, the King of Sweden, who in March and June of 1863 had proposed mutual military co-operation in an attack on Russia.[19] To Charles, the aim of such an alliance was the re-acquisition of Finland, which had been lost to Russia in 1815, and, which he felt could have been acquired in 1854-55 had not Sweden missed her opportunity.

The vital day of decision for France was 5th August. At the *Conseil* held at Saint Cloud, the main business was to resolve the question of peace or war with Russia. On 20th July the French forces had taken Mexico City and this was (illusorily) regarded as a definitive end to the campaign. Billault, as Minister of State, wrote that: "The taking of Mexico pleased me enormously especially since I hope it will hasten the moment when the burden and difficulties of this expedition will become less heavy. In Europe we need our liberty of action, not because I believe in war, I sincerely hope it can be avoided, but the situation is difficult."[20] This difficult situation was the result not merely of the

European problem, but also the consequences of the reforms of 1863 which were beginning to show their results in some unexpected quarters. It was clear to all that under the new constitutional structure there was need to exercise control over the law-making activities of the *Corps Législatif* now that the latter had acquired great powers. This type of arrangement was implicit in Article 51 of the Constitution, so there was nothing underhand about the idea, but it necessitated employing men in the *Conseil d'État* who could cope with defending ministerial policies before the legislative body if this should prove necessary. It was, therefore, of considerable importance for the making of policy that the June elections had resulted in a strengthening of the conservative group in the *Conseil d'État* just at the time when Napoleon III was intent on stressing the role of the *Conseil* in the governmental machine, and needed the support of those such as Morny, Fould, Baroche, Boudet and Billault. At the Council of Ministers on 5th August, they were all vehemently on the side of negotiation with Russia and against war.

In this attitude they had the support of Rouher, the new Minister of State, who had informed Walewski, a "pro-Pole," that: "No matter how valid your feelings for Poland may be I can tell you that a war, whatever it may be, is not to the taste of either of the bourgeoisie or to the populace of the countryside."[21] One can surmise that the same language was used at Saint Cloud for, although the Emperor and Drouyn de Lhuys (the Foreign Minister) were for a more positive action, the "peace party" seemingly carried the day in a discussion which began at nine in the morning and finished at four o'clock in the afternoon.

Viewed from this angle any thought that there was any serious intent behind Napoleon III's apparent attempt to "go it alone" with the support of only Sweden and possibly Denmark must be dismissed as fantasy.[22] Even in his wildest flights of fancy the Emperor cannot have envisaged a European war in which France had for allies only two minor states; and it may be pertinent here to recall his remark about war for Poland that: "... *l'intéret francais ne l'exigeait pas*".

By the autumn this fact was clear to all the other Powers who had seen that as far as Poland was concerned, Napoleon must either put up or shut up. As usual, faced with an impasse which implied military action, the Emperor turned to a congress to point the way out. On 4th November he appealed to the European sovereigns to meet for: "... the treaties of 1815 in almost all their articles, are destroyed, modified, ignored or threatened. From this arises obligations without control, rights without title and pretentions without limit. ... I propose therefore, to you to control the present and to assure the future by a Congress."

The Note, which was addressed to the sovereigns of Europe was interesting, for it explicitly stated what Napoleon III held to be the basis of his power, his determination to behave in a "conservative" fashion in Europe. Although "called to the Throne by Providence and the will of the French people" and therefore in a position where ". . . it is less permitted to me than to any others to be unaware of the rights both of sovereigns and of people," the Emperor stressed that whatever his origin his aims were not revolutionary. "If I take the initiative in such a move, I am not yielding to a moment of vanity; but since I am the sovereign to whom one most attributes ambitious schemes I have it in my heart to prove by this frank and loyal proceeding that my only aim is to arrive without shocks at the pacification of Europe." Paris was suggested as the meeting place for: "Europe would see, perhaps, some advantage from choosing this capital, which has so often given the signal for upsets, become the seat of a conference destined to lay down the basis of a general pacification."[23]

Any consideration of this Note must involve consideration of the speech from the throne on the following day (5th November) when the Emperor addressed both Houses. In the speech, Napoleon stressed that France had no need to resort to force to assist the cause of Poland. There had been no threat to her frontier: ". . . the only circumstance which would oblige us to act without prior consultation." And so: "without rushing to arms or keeping silent, one way is open: that is, to submit the Polish cause to an European tribunal." The congress would not only deal with Poland: "Has not the moment come to reconstruct on new bases the edifice which has been sapped by time and destroyed little by little by revolutions? The treaties of 1815 have ceased to exist. The force of things has everywhere overthrown them, or tends to overthrow them. They have been broken in Greece, in Belgium, in France, in Italy as on the Danube. Germany agitates to change them; England has generously modified them by the cession of the Ionian Islands, and Russia tramples them underfoot at Warsaw." The Emperor went on to explain that through the congress passions would be calmed, peace would be assured, disarmament could begin. "Two ways are open: one leads to progress by conciliation and peace; the other, sooner or later, will lead to war through an obstinate determination to maintain a past which has crumbled."[24]

The appeal for a Congress marked the supreme test for Anglo-French relations. If England refused to participate, the project was doomed for only England's adherence could assure that Austria, Prussia and Russia would attend. The time had come to discover whether the treaties of 1815 were as dead as Napoleon III had proclaimed them to be and whether the Powers would be prepared multilaterally to agree to a revision of the European states system. The crisis in French policy had, now, been reached, for the response to the Emperor's Note would be made clear to all whether any major Power had an interest in seeing France redraw the European map. As far as England was concerned, the answer was "no." England's policy towards France had been that of using her when it suited but of closing ranks against her when it did not. The Crimean War had been of benefit, French help in China had been useful, Mexico had not cost much and given French success, could have been profitable. But what was to be gained: ". . . from the meeting of a Congress of Sovereigns and ministers without fixed object, ranging over the map of Europe, exciting hopes and aspirations which [they] might find themselves unable to gratifiy or quiet." Queen Victoria thought the idea of a congress was "an impertinence." Palmerston told Russell more specifically that: "If the Congress gave Moldo-Wallachia to Austria, and Venetia and Rome to Italy, incorporated Sleswig with Denmark and separated Poland of 1815 from Russia and made it an independent state, not touching the question of the Rhine as a French frontier, or the relieving of Russia from what was imposed upon her by the Treaty of Paris, such a congress would be a well-doer by Europe."[25]

Unfortunately such a congress would also be a non-starter in Europe, for the simple reason that the changes it envisaged could really be made only by threat of war or the actuality of war, and this would involve the closest Anglo-French alliance and a re-starting of the Crimean campaign. From this England had nothing to gain; she had boxed in Russia and achieved stability in the Near East in 1856 and so France had nothing to offer her. With England's less than lukewarm response to the plan for a congress there was little hope of its success.

By the end of 1863 France was isolated in Europe. Russia had been estranged because of Poland, England had snubbed the Emperor's schemes while Austria remained no more or less hostile than she had been. The impossibility of a Franco-Austrian entente had been underlined as recently as December, 1863, when, trying to salvage something from the wreck of his congress proposals, Napoleon had proposed a meeting of Prussia, Russia and Italy to redraw the map of Europe at Austria's expense. The weakness of the Emperor's position revealed to what an extent France had lost the diplomatic initiative. She must now wait upon events, since she could not create them, and if she were to pursue any "forward" policy she must move with the power which showed signs of actively pursuing a revolutionary foreign policy.

In August 1864, Bismarck had made it clear to Gramont that : "The day when one is obliged to start out on the adventure, it is we who can, better than anyone else, set out with France by beginning not with promises but by giving her a reward for her help."[26] It is true that Bismarck's conversation could be likened to the astrologer who promises that "something to your advantage will soon occur," but there is no doubt that in Paris much was expected of Prussia as an agent in re-ordering central Europe. At this point Bismarck had entered upon the scene in order to preserve Prussia from the threat of internal reform, but he had seen that in order to do this he must take control of the national movement in Germany and embark upon a foreign policy which would preserve his dynasty and his state by revolutionizing the Central European states system. The days of speeches and resolutions were over in Europe, and with them went Napoleon's utopian schemes. Bismarck was about to demonstrate the truth of Frederick the Great's maxim that "diplomacy without war is like music without instruments."

Bismarck's first moves involved the re-opening of the Schleswig-Holstein question. This was the problem whose complexities, as one historian has noted, "could have been handled by any competent solicitor," but it inspired Palmerston's comment that only three people had ever really mastered the affair; one was Prince Albert and he was dead; the other was a Danish Professor who had gone mad; the third was himself, and he had forgotten it. It was unfortunate that Palmerston had forgotten what it was all about. Had he done his homework properly the course of European history might well have been altered. Certainly he might himself have appeared in a less contemptible light when his bluff was called by Bismarck in an issue arising out of the Schleswig-Holstein problem.

At the first rumblings of the affair in July, 1863, Palmerston had announced "that if any violent attempt were made to overthrow [the rights] and interfere with the independence of Denmark, those who made this attempt would find in the result that it would not be Denmark alone with which they had to contend."[27] This sort of windy rhetoric was not, of course, meant to do anything except boost Palmerston's stock with the electorate and the House of Commons. Familiarity with Palmerston's bombast bred contempt in too few of his listeners. Among those who took this particular outburst seriously were the Danes, and when they found themselves threatened by Prussia and

Austria in January and February, 1864, because of the Schleswig-Holstein dispute, they decided to resist. In the ensuing war they held out until April, quite alone.

The war with Denmark did produce a flickering among the dying embers of the Anglo-French entente. In June, 1864, the Emperor instructed his foreign minister Drouyn de Lhuys to ask Cowley to: "... forget past jealousies and rancours and come to an understanding that is necessary to us both." The English Ambassador transmitted the message to London but Palmerston was obsessed with French power and with the supposed aggressive intentions of Napoleon on the Rhine and in Italy, and so nothing came of it.

It was too late now to hope for a change in English policy for in July, 1864, occurred one of the debates in the Commons on foreign policy which have a decisive effect upon events. This particular debate was on the question of non-intervention in Europe and it produced a coalition between the Radicals and the Tories. The occurrence of such a coalition could be likened to the appearance of a bird of ill omen in that such an unnatural union is usually a harbinger of disaster. 1864 was no exception. Cobden, as radical spokesman, defined non-intervention as "no foreign politics," General Peel, for the Tories, announced, amid waves of applause, that he was "opposed to all treaties and guarantees which render it necessary to interfere with the affairs of others."[28] It is only fair to say that given the recent disaster in English foreign policy and the threat of more to come unless Palmerston and Russell died, this attitude is fairly comprehensible. This was, however, no consolation to Napoleon III, though it certainly cheered Bismarck who saw it as a heaven-sent opportunity to deal with France in isolation. If England were prepared to ignore alterations in the European balance and refuse to accept any contractual obligations with any other Power, life would be much easier all round.

It would appear that by the autumn of 1864 Napoleon III had got the message from across the Channel. He now shaped his policy accordingly and he began by clearing, or attempting to clear, some of the lumber from the diplomatic attic. In September a convention was signed with Victor Emmanuel in which the Emperor pledged himself to withdraw his troops from Papal territory within two years, in return for an Italian promise to respect the integrity of the Papal States and to protect Rome. Napoleon described the Convention as "a work of peace and conciliation," but Pius IX was of the "not peace but a sword" school of theology, and his answer to this attempt to turn the poacher into a gamekeeper was a thundering denunciation not just of the

September convention but of the modern world. The *Syllabus Errorum* represented an attempt to preserve the integrity of Papal territory through the practice of total obscurantism. The heresies condemned in the *Syllabus* were universal in their form, but they clearly had particular local instances. Never had the Pope seemed more like an Italian bishop, and the ludicrousness of the document produced, particularly in France, a still greater revulsion against Papal pretensions. In the long run the *Syllabus* did much to make Napoleon's Italian policy more acceptable in France, though it had been suggested that it led to an estrangement between Eugénie and her husband. This seems unlikely, and it may well have been that she was more irritated by his affair with Marguerite Bellanger which had been going on for some time and which, because of its physical aspects, she feared would undermine the Emperor's health. Her particular *violon d'Ingrès* at this time was a grandiose scheme for rebuilding the Church of the Holy Sepulchre at Jerusalem, a scheme which judging from the plans would have been an architectural disaster, apart from any political effects it might have had.

The Emperor, however, as the September convention had proved, was not so embroiled in amatory exploits as to neglect foreign policy. In October, 1864, Count Vincent Benedetti was sent as Ambassador to Berlin and the Emperor began his manoeuvre to prevent any *rapprochement* between Austria and Prussia which he feared might now be a possibility after their joint action against Denmark. In fact, Bismarck was not remotely interested in an alliance with Austria as the proposals he put forward prove. At no time could they have been acceptable and they were simply a means of keeping Austria entangled without committing Prussia to anything. They had the additional merit of getting Napoleon III involved.

While he kept Austria in play, Bismarck worked hard to gain French support, an exercise which was facilitated by Napoleon III's anxiety to remain a spectator of German affairs until his intervention could be effectively turned to France's advantage. Bismarck tried to catch Napoleon in May, 1865, at a time when the war between Prussia and Austria seemed imminent, by indicating that France should look for part of Belgium and French-speaking Switzerland. The Emperor was absent from France on a visit to Algeria, but even had he been in Paris it is doubtful if Bismarck would have received a satisfactory tug on the line. The bait was not attractive.

Bismarck had now come to closer quarters with Austria without having the satisfaction of knowing how France would react. It was this which led to the Convention of Gastein of August, 1865, whereby

Austria and Prussia agreed to administer each his own Duchy, Austria in Holstein, Prussia in Schleswig. This produced a reaction in France where, tongue in cheek, Drouyn de Lhuys's circular denounced this breach of the Treaty of Vienna and the Treaty of London of 1852. In fact the reason for the French determination was the fear that Gastein might prevent a clash between Austria and Prussia and a feeling that Bismarck had done more than just "paper over the cracks." Could it be that a reconciliation was possible? If so, that would be an end to any hopes of France's profiting from an upset caused by an Austro-Prussian conflict.

The Emperor need not have worried. Gastein was only a holding operation for Bismarck and the Prussian Cabinet was convinced that only war would resolve the German crisis.[29] Gastein bought time in which to try again for French support and it was this which lay behind the visit to Biarritz in the autumn of 1865. Napoleon III's own summation of what took place at the meeting with Bismarck is probably as valid as any other. "He [Bismarck] talked a great deal ... but in general and vague terms. I could not disentangle exactly what he wanted, and he did not make any formal propositions. For my part, I did not express to him any personal desires whatsoever."[30] Once again Bismarck had been frustrated and he was to remain in this condition until in March, 1866, he tabled the card Napoleon had been waiting for. It was Venetia which was the trump, and in March, 1866, Bismarck began the negotiations with Italy which led to the Italo-Prussian treaty on 8th April. What is significant is the fact that the French Ambassador in Berlin, Benedetti, was a party to the negotiations between the Prussians and the Italians. The Foreign Minister, Drouyn de Lhuys, wrote to remind Benedetti that the Imperial policy was one of neutrality and that: "We remained absolutely ignorant of the treaty of Alliance, offensive and defensive ... which has been made between Bismarck and the Minister of Italy."[31] This disclaimer was of no consequence, for the deed was done and at last Austria would be forced to abandon Venetia which she had refused to sell or exchange. At last Napoleon III would be free of Italy.

With the signing of the Italo-Prussian alliance on 8th April, 1866, a crisis point in French policy was reached. Austria must now realize that she could only buy off France by the cession of Venetia, for only France could persuade Italy to make the alliance with Prussia void. This could be done quite easily by allowing the very short time limit on its implementation to expire for if war did break out within three months of signing the treaty, it ceased to have any force.

At this stage it was essential for Napoleon III to assert his position. He must see that Austria ceded Venice, and to ensure that Prussia did not manage to gain control of policy, he must assert France's determination to be "active" rather than "passive" as she had been since 1864. It was essential that Bismarck should not be allowed to feel confident of French support, for this would upset Napoleon III's plans to act as mediator in what he hoped would be a diplomatic crisis.

It was for this purpose that he made his famous speech at Auxerre on 6th May in which he announced: "I detest the treaties of 1815." The whole speech was couched in "Jacobin" terms and delivered in a carefully assumed tone of anger and resolution. Some historians have seen it as a reply to Thiers' speech in the *Corps Légistatif* of 3rd May in which Thiers had predicated the use of strong language to keep Prussia in her place. It may well have been that the Emperor was annoyed by this type of intervention at a most critical juncture in his policy, but it is doubtful if the Auxerre speech was simply designed to put Thiers in his box. Just as Rouher's speech in the Legislature on the 3rd May warning Italy not to go it alone had been directed at Rome, so the Emperor's speech was meant for Berlin and Vienna, to reassure the one and upset the other.

On the 4th and 5th of May Austria had behaved as Napoleon hoped she would by offering to cede Venetia, but only if France could persuade Italy to be neutral to an Austro-Prussian conflict. Unfortunately, when Napoleon approached the Italians, they refused to accept because to do this would be to desert Prussia—"a question of honour and loyalty." In point of fact the Italian administration looked forward to a successful war which would bolster up sagging "national" morale in the Kingdom of Italy and produce enough patriotic fervour to damp down increasing discontent and anti-Piedmontese feeling. Napoleon was, therefore, in a state of considerable irritation when he made the Auxerre speech but irritation was no substitute for policy and it was essential that he still try and keep control of the situation.

To a great extent he succeeded, by creating a general unease as to what France's policy might be. Only on 26th May was the secret of Imperial policy revealed when a circular went out from Tuileries inviting the Powers to a congress to discuss Venetia, Schleswig-Holstein and the Germanic Confederation. Once again the great dream of peaceful change was re-animated. In truth it was difficult to see how else Napoleon could have acted for it must be remembered that all through this period of 1865-66 there were clear indications that the bulk of public opinion was pacific.[32] In any event, the Emperor had no wish for war, but the congress scheme had no chance of success once Austria made her acceptance conditional on the exclusion of any territorial aggrandizement by any participating state. Reluctantly, therefore, Napoleon abandoned hope of a peaceful solution and shifted his tack so as to ensure that the outcome of an Austro-Prussian conflict should not be detrimental to France's interest.

On 12th June, the day that she broke diplomatic relations with Prussia, Austria signed a secret agreement with France. By this Austria agreed to cede Venetia while Napoleon promised French neutrality and expressed his determination to keep Italy neutral if possible. In return for all this, Austria would, providing she won the war, accept the creation of an independent German state on the Rhine. Franz-Josef had indicated to the French Ambassador, Gramont, that Austria would expect Silesia for herself and an increase in the area of the middle states of Bavaria, Württemberg and Saxony.[33]

The war changed all. The total defeat of Austria and her allies radically and definitively altered the balance upon which everyone's calculations had rested. After Sadowa a new European situation existed and it was Engels who, writing to Marx in July, 1866, pointed out that Bismarck could not stop now. The German bourgeoisie would, said Engels, insist on the re-establishment of a German Empire in the Southern States, but without German Austria.[34] Engel's view was based as much on economic as on political factors and it was certainly true that much of the commercial and economic expansion of Prussia's *zollverein* area was an added attraction to support Prussian policy. The lines of communciation favoured Berlin and Hamburg rather than Vienna and Trieste and the rising German bourgeoisie were able to link patriotism and profits—always an irresistible combination. Bismarck was to find himself overborne by it.

Engels was not the only observer who was aware of the implications of Sadowa. In Paris, the news stunned Napoleon III for it was immediately clear that one of the premises of his policy, that of acting as mediator in a drawn battle, had now been removed.[35] The Emperor had to act quickly in case Bismarck and the Prussians pressed home their advantage and Austria disappeared not only from Germany but from Europe. The question was, should France proceed by threatening a military demonstration or by trusting to a diplomacy based on Bismarck's fear of the consequences of military action?

On 5th July the Council of Ministers met at St. Cloud. It was perhaps the most fateful meeting held during the whole of the Empire's existence and this is not simply the judgement of hindsight. The

Empress who was present, believed that: "the destiny of France and
our dynasty's future are at stake." Napoleon had already announced,
on 4th July by telegram to William of Prussia and Victor Emmanuel
that "the startling results [of Sadowa] force me to abandon my role of
complete abstention." What did this mean? The problem was that the
Emperor did not himself know the answer. He needed time, of which
there was little to spare.

At the meeting Drouyn de Lhuys, who had spent the morning with
the Emperor, was anxious for military intervention. So was Eugénie,
supported by Persigny and Magne. It seemed that the Emperor would
accept and that France would move behind a show of force, but at the
end the counter-party carried the day. Rouher, supported by Baroche
and La Valette, persuaded the Emperor not to sign the act of mobilization largely because of Rouher's intervention. It was not just that
Rouher—already dubbed "*Le Vice-Empereur*"—was a powerful voice, it
was that he struck exactly the right note, to tune in with Napoleon's
own hesitations: "Is your Majesty absolutely certain of being completely free *vis-à-vis* Prussia. Have you not favoured the alliance with
Italy? Have you not, in some way, taken sides against Austria? And
would not the dispatch of an observation corps to the Rhine, which
would be absolutely to the advantage of this latter Power, be to
abandon the promises made to Prussia?"[36]

The short answer to all these questions was that they were now
irrelevant to the situation but Rouher knew how to play on that
weakness for intellectual speculation which so often hampered the
Imperial will. Apart from this Napoleon was ill, and for the first time
his actual physical condition affected his capacity for decisions. He
made the wrong one, and France opted for peaceful mediation.

Bismarck knew that a move would come either soon or not at all.
Once he was sure that Napoleon would only talk he facilitated the
Emperor's passage to peaceful mediation, by indicating that Prussia
would accept France's good offices. The terms of settlement he proposed
were seemingly moderate. The Germanic confederation of 1815 would
be dissolved. Austria would be excluded from Germany which, north of
the River Main, would be confederated under Prussian aegis. To disarm
any fears Napoleon entertained about this being too much of an upset
in the equilibrium, Bismarck agreed to guarantee an "independent
existence" for the German states south of the Main. As for Venetia,
Italy would have it.

It seemed to Napoleon that this outcome was to France's advantage.
A cardinal point of the 1815 settlement had gone, Venetia had been

acquired by Italy, and the "German" state was tripartite, thereby providing France with an opportunity to exert her influence on the middle portion of the South German and Rhenish area. In fact none of this was so; Austria was ruined, Italy was still disatisfied, and the South German states were neither economically nor politically open to any French influence. Not only that, Bismarck may have felt that he had finished his task but, as others had noted, the German nationalists had other ideas. His success was his undoing, it was also to be Napoleon III's.

13

The Time of Trial

*"Le Pays est assujeti à une grande épreuve,
dont il est, quant à présent, bien difficile de
préjuger l'issue."*

Napoleon III

*"Des points noirs assombrissent notre horizon.
Nous avons eu des revers."*

Napoleon III 1867

IT has already been indicated that among the factors which led
Napoleon III to decide on a non-military approach to Austria in
July 1866 were the influence of Rouher and the Emperor's own
physical condition. These were by no means the only factors; others will
require examination, but these two are sufficiently important as to need
further elaboration.

In order to understand the influence which Rouher wielded it should
be remembered that his position was virtually that of a prime minister.
Indeed the wags had not only dubbed him *"Le Vice-Empereur,"* but
referred to the *Rouhernement.* His position sprang directly from the
need to defend the government's policies before the *Corps Législatif*
after the constitutional changes of 1861-63, a task which required
someone who was both able and fluent. Rouher, an Auvergnat, was a
man of considerable ability but little charm. Although devoted to the
Emperor and the regime he was essentially an authoritarian who had
rallied to Louis Napoleon in 1850-51 because he saw him as a force for
order. His sympathies were not really with the liberalization of the
Empire and his constant and obvious attempts to restrict the Emperor's
liberal intentions by his attitude towards the *Corps Législatif,* combined
with a talent for not suffering fools gladly, led him to clashes with the
deputies.

It was unfortunate that Billault, the minister who might have balanced
Rouher, had died in 1863. Billault had been president of the *Corps
Législatif* and was a parliamentarian rather than an administrator. No

less authoritarian than Rouher (he was another who had rallied in 1849-50), Billault was more flexible, and less imbued with a desire to dominate. Indeed it may well have been Napoleon III's aim to make of Billault his "prime minister" rather than Rouher, and it is possible that if this had worked he might have been able to keep more control of affairs than the latter. Significantly, Billault's designation was "*Le Sous-Empereur*," a title which implied a difference between his position and that of Rouher *vis-à-vis* the Emperor. His sudden death in September, 1863, was a severe blow, particularly if one remembers how limited the Emperor was in his choice of men. Ollivier noted that Billault was: "... of a quick mind, flexible, committed, well tried in [public] business, very much master of his thoughts and speech."[1] There were too few of this sort in the political cadres of the Empire.

So, Napoleon was left with Rouher. Rouher who was, if not anti-Bonapartist at home, certainly anti-Imperialist abroad. Throughout the German crisis of 1865-66 he had never ceased to applaud the policy of abstention, and his position in July, 1866, was at least a logical continuation of this attitude and it was also a measure of how secure he felt in his position as *Vice-Empereur*. Not the least of the reasons for this feeling of security in office was the Emperor's physical condition, for in 1865 Napoleon really was ill. It was not just that he could no longer sustain an evening of sexual pleasure—he had twice collapsed while visiting his mistress—it was a much more serious malady. In July, 1865, his physician, Dr. Larrey, had diagnosed the stone, and in August and September he was prostrated by frightful pain accompanied by severe haemorrhages from the bladder. Since an operation for the stone was in those days usually fatal, he dared not contemplate surgery and so he was forced to conceal his condition, forbidding his doctor to tell even the Empress. The course of the disease could not be arrested without surgery, but because he dared not risk death with the Prince Imperial still only ten years old, the Emperor condemned himself to four years of agony. Only after the fall of the Empire did he dare to risk the operation, and it killed him.

Given the lethargy and vacillation induced by living in a state of constant discomfort, interspersed with crises of acute pain, Napoleon III's general physical condition undoubtedly affected his capacity for making decisions. All who came in contact with him noticed how ill he seemed to be. In the autumn of 1866 Eugénie said: "I find a man sick, irresolute, exhausted. ... He can no longer walk, no longer sleep, and scarcely eat." Some observers felt that the Emperor's pain increased if he found it convenient. Cowley commented that: "I should say it is in

energy not in intellect that he is the worse for wear." But *au fond*
Napoleon was ill and certainly the events of the autumn of 1866 bear
marks of irresolute thinking. Not only that, the policy of France was
certainly being directed, if not made, by Rouher.

It was a bad moment for the Emperor not to be fully in control of
foreign policy. The only way in which anything could have been
achieved from the disaster of Sadowa would have been for France to
maintain a resolute, consistent and bold approach in face of the new
power Prussia had acquired. Benedetti, instructed to inquire about what
compensations France might expect for accepting Prussia's *fait
accompli*, made this plain. It must be done ". . . while conserving our
calm and friendly attitude, but at the same time speaking a language
which permits no illusion."[2]

France had aspirations to an adjustment of the Rhine area which
would give her the frontiers of 1814. It was further hoped that
Luxembourg might be added to this region and also the area of Mainz.
This was the scheme as sent to Bismarck from Vichy in August,
presumably drafted by the Emperor, who was there seeking health
from the mineral springs, accompanied by Drouyn de Lhuys. Bismarck
received the proposals with irritation and counselled Benedetti to
recommend that his government seek compensation in Belgium.
Evidence of Prussian resistance led to pressure from Rouher and
La Valette upon the Emperor to abandon a policy which was so
dangerous. The pressure was successful and in August Drouyn de Lhuys
resigned to be replaced at the Foreign Office by the Marquis de
Moustier.

Rouher's argument about the compensation policy was that the time
was not ripe : "Let us keep ourselves ready in the future, to profit better
from events." The point was that Benedetti, now in Paris, had talked
with the Emperor and warned him that unless France was really
prepared for a use of force she would need to move very carefully.
Napoleon knew quite well that neither was the army ready for war nor
was the country prepared to accept it. French opinion wanted the fruits
of victory without paying the price. Now once again, as in June,
Napoleon had to say "*je ne peux pas faire la guerre.*" Rouher was
resolute for peace and had poured cold water on the Luxembourg idea
by saying : "And it's for a shanty like that we should get into conflict
with Germany."[3]

The trouble was that France could not simply do nothing. All
Europe expected some reaction to Prussia's triumph and so Rouher
produced a plan which was the greatest blunder of all. Benedetti was

instructed to tell Bismarck that: "... the extensions of Prussian supremacy beyond the Main could not fail to be a natural occasion, almost obligatory, for us to seize Belgium, but other occasions may present themselves."[4] This implied that France would decide when the time was ripe and evidenced the fact that both Napoleon and Rouher, presumably, felt France was still master of the situation. She was not. Bismarck called the tune, and he now had in his pocket a compromising text in which a specific demand had been made for Belgium. He was to produce it with considerable effect, in 1870. Since Rouher's plan came joined to a proposal for an alliance between France and Prussia Bismarck was even surer of French weakness. What did Prussia need with France now that Austria had been defeated? Napoleon III had thrown away, or allowed to fall from his hand, the only card he had held, namely what would France do in the event of a Prussian triumph? Bismarck now knew she would do nothing. On 21st August he telegraphed to St. Petersburg: would Russia keep Austria neutral if war broke out between Prussia and France? On 24th August came the reply: "Your excellency may take a firm line against France."[5]

Russia saw not only a chance to spite Austria but a chance to revise 1856. She had now survived the serious internal crisis caused by the emancipation question, and the Polish revolt had enabled her to measure the disarray among the forces likely to be ranged against her in Europe. Alexander and Gotchakov were on the move again and it was not likely that there would be any comfort for France in the direction their policy took.[6]

Until 1866 it was possible for Napoleon III to imagine that the chance circumstances which had enabled him to manoeuvre in Europe had resulted from the power of France. Now Austria was broken and a prisoner of the Magyars, England was detached, Russia had survived her crisis, and Bismarck was set on a real revisionist course. Given these changes in Europe, it was pathetic to read the language of the French circular of September, 1866, which sketched a vision of a united Western Europe holding its place in a world increasingly dominated by the two great powers of the U.S.A. and the Russian Empire. The vision was splendid; and it was set against "a background which seems devoid of any menacing possibilities." As if to emphasize that France would not tolerate any "menacing possibilities," the last section of the circular pointed out that: "The results of the last war contain a grave lesson, one which has not been gained at any cost to the honour of our arms. They indicate that we require to improve without delay our military organization for the defence of our country—The nation will not fail to

perform this duty, which cannot be taken as a threat against anybody."
The circular was a strange potion whose ingredients were partly
Bonapartist and Imperial mixed with the Proudhonian view that war
was anachronistic, a view which interestingly enough, even Marx
denounced as "grotesque."

What was the reason for this more martial ending to the circular? In
the first instance it was clear that any further withdrawal on France's
part would irreparably damage the position of both the Emperor and
his country in the eyes of European opinion. Apart from that, public
opinion in France was uneasy and the Emperor told the Prussian
ambassador that: "The country demanded of his regime a statement on
its attitude towards the changes which have taken place in Germany.
Any further hesitations would arouse passions."[7] Whatever policy was
to be followed a reorganization of the armed forces was clearly essential.
At the root of the proposed reforms which began to be formulated in
the autumn and winter of 1866, was the question of rearmament. In
1866 it was still possible to purchase exemption from military service, or
to ballot for conscript service. The former method pleased the rich, the
latter invested the conscription with the element of a lottery which, if it
did not exactly please the peasants and workers, at least gave a sporting
chance of exemption. 100,000 men were engaged annually and once in
service was for seven years.

It was now proposed to raise the effective strength, not the paper
strength of the army to 800,000 and this doubling of the effectives
meant that every Frenchman would have to serve six years with the
colours. It was hoped that reduction in length of service would
compensate for the loss of exemption and the ballot. It did nothing of
the kind and indeed provoked an outcry in the country at large. The
frothy belligerence of July and August which had been noted by the
Procureurs in their reports to the central government now gave way to
alarm at the prospect of Frenchmen actually having to put their money
where their mouths were. By a bitter irony, the provinces which had
displayed most verbal bellicosity against Prussia were now equally voci-
ferous against the army reform plan, thus proving what Napoleon III
had known perfectly well, that the apparent warlike feeling in the summer
of 1866 was really spurious. The one thing the Emperor never lost was
his capacity for appreciating the feelings of the public and he saw,
frequently more clearly than his ministers, what their real sentiments
were.

However, if in the summer he had been able and even willing to go
with public opinion, now in the autumn he must square up to it and try

to carry it with him if France was to put herself in a better situation. The government began to strike a note of alarm throughout the country by inserting syndicated articles in newspapers, and by seeing to it that the speeches of ministers contained in them references to the necessity for France's military re-organization. The public were hard to convince, partly because they disliked the proposals and partly because they were encouraged to dislike them. The encouragement came from the opposition to the Empire which had been growing steadily since the elections of 1863. In 1865 and 1866 there was plenty to feed on. Apart from the failure in Europe the Mexican affair ending in disaster and the summer of 1866 saw Napoleon confronted by the Empress Carlota, sent by her husband to beg for an end to the French withdrawal and a guarantee of support. The refusal to help finally unhinged Carlota's already tottering reason and after a terrifying scene which broke Napoleon for several days (it was during the height of his illness), Carlota left for Rome to appeal to the Pope. The events there, soon known throughout Europe, displayed Napoleon in the most atrocious light as a hardhearted adventurer who abandoned his protégés when the going got tough.

Apart from political disasters there were acts of God. The harvest of 1865 was poor and that of 1866 was feeble, partly caused by excessive rainfall, which also produced serious and devastating floods. This led to a degree of economic dislocation which was reflected in the disturbed state of public opinion, which, as has been indicated, was mercurial in this period. There was also a recession in French industry which, although it was now recovering from the cotton famine ended by the final victory of the Union in the American Civil War, was susceptible in other sectors. It was the metallurgical industries which were now depressed partly because of under-investment, caused by a reluctance to put out capital at a time of international instability. Steel production and iron production dropped considerably from 1863 to 1866 as did profits in the industries associated with both products.[8] Napoleon III encouraged the practice of granting naval contracts to private firms as well as to the Imperial dockyards in an attempt to encourage these depressed industries.

Partly also the crisis in capital was brought about by the struggle between the Rothschilds and the *Crédit Mobilier* which was reaching its crisis in 1867 and which led to the collapse of the Péreires.[9] A further factor in slowing down the movement of money, at a time when France was literally stuffed with gold, was the fear of the government's warlike intentions. It was not only the peasantry and the workers who feared the consequences of a renewal of an active imperial foreign policy, it was also the *Notables* and the financiers.

No matter how conservative the government might appear to be it could not succeed in calming the Bourse. In the autumn of 1867 when Magne returned to the Ministry of Finance the Bourse slumped—although Magne was closely linked to Fould and the orthodox financiers of the peace party.[10] The Emperor rightly saw that only by getting on to the gold standard could France tap the enormous gold reserves which she now had, but the orthodox viewed even this purely financial policy with suspicion, feeling sure that it was only a prelude to some other crack-brained scheme of the Emperor's.

Their fears were not wholly imaginary in that Napoleon, although ill and not always on form, had not abandoned his reforming programme. In 1864 the workers had been granted the right to strike and the right to form trade unions. This was perhaps one of the most important pieces of social legislation passed during the Empire and was seen by Napoleon as the counterpart of the parliamentary reforms of 1860-63, designed to benefit the political classes. To the latter, the law of 1866 was repugnant, and suspicion of the Emperor's intentions was not allayed by his patronizing of the workers' International in the same year. To add to the disgust of the bourgeoisie, the government encouraged workers to express their views in newspapers and pamphlets, and there is some indication of the success of this *vis-à-vis* the workers in the fact that both the bourgeoisie and Blanqui were unceasing in their denunciations of government policy.[11]

Unmoved by criticism and condemnation the Emperor continued his hesitation-waltz with the people. The *Manifesto of the Sixty* in 1864 which stressed that the workers had the right to express themselves electorally through their own candidates and not through bourgeois representatives was a triumph for his ideas about how universal suffrage would be used by the people. Even more re-assuring to the Emperor was the fact that the manifesto stressed: "We shall march to the conquest of our rights peacefully and legally, but with energy and persistence." Energy and persistence were held to be worthy of reward and so in 1865 further reforms were designed to ameliorate the conditions of imprisonment and make less arbitrary the nature of, and reasons for, detention. Both these measures were designed to help the poorer sections of society.

As if to balance this out, the classes were catered for by the *Senatus Consultum* of 18th July, 1866, which increased the *Corps Législatif*'s right to propose amendments, though it can be argued that the reservation exclusively to the Senate of the right to discussion of the Constitution was a warning to the Lower House not to go too far. Finally, in 1867 the Chamber was granted the right of interpellation, by which time it was determined to use it and found that there were plenty of questions to ask. The more the Emperor appeared to be losing his grip, the more the opposition pressed its attack, and since the events from 1865 to 1867 did nothing to strengthen Napoleon's position their attitudes became more trenchant. It is important to remember that the Emperor was not opposed to change or evolution in the sphere of government, the whole purpose of the Empire and indeed its history to date, gave evidence of that. The problem was, at home as abroad, in which direction to go, once the possibility of alternative routes was opened up by abandoning the policy of direction from above.

In the meantime, government had to go on, and it was this fundamental necessity which was the source of Rouher's power, a power which he exercised with ever increasing authority and even independence. Allain Targé, a radical critic, hostile to the Empire, reported that on one occasion Rouher had even refused to come when requested by the Emperor and that *Badinguet*, (a pejorative nickname for Napoleon III) accepted the minister's insolence. "Rouher can impose himself. The Emperor has so successfully created a void of talent and personalities that in order to keep the *Corps Législatif* under control he has to put up with Rouher." This was precisely the point. The more the Empire became parliamentary, the more essential it was to exercise control so that it did not become transformed into a parliamentary Empire which would serve as an anteroom for the Orleanists.

Since Thiers' election to the Chamber in 1863 the voice of Orleanism could be heard once again, and it was Thiers who put forward the programme for the "essential liberties," bourgeois in character and anti-Bonapartist, particularly in its Saint-Simonian aspects. But Thiers and his group never forgot the fear they had experienced in 1848 and so there was a limit to their harrying of the Empire. Awareness of this problem kept the opposition divided and explains their oscillation between collaboration with the moderates and non-socialist Republicans like Jules Favre, and their acceptance of support from the clerical conservatives and "political Catholics." The opposition, in particular Thiers and Favre, had attacked the government in 1866 and its foreign policy and in the autumn and winter over the proposed military reforms. The question of these reforms linked together both the opposition in the Chamber and the opposition in the Council of Ministers which centred round Fould and Magne. The latter were drawn in through worries about the financial implications, and the coalition might have been dangerous had it held together. But in the short run, both Fould and Magne came to heel and were of little real value to the opposition group. Much more worrying was the possibility of a liaison between Thiers and the oppositionists with the mass of the country if they could find a common cause. Ollivier wrote to Walewski on 1st January, 1867, that: "On the morrow of an agricultural inquiry, in which the country made it plain that it wanted a reduction in the [annual] military quota, an increase in the military establishment of France constitutes a capital fault. It is to furnish to the adversaries of the government a lever, which they have sought vainly for ten years in order to stir up the masses of the people."[12]

In reality it was becoming increasingly easy to move sections of the masses for the simple reason that many areas of French society were becoming restive. It was nearly twenty years since the Emperor had taken power as President and a new generation had emerged which neither feared nor revered 1848. In a way it was this movement of opinion which the Emperor was trying to swing into. He sensed it and perhaps understood it better than those who surrounded him. The problem was how to get there and who would help him. This was the thinking which lay behind his "where to find the man" comment made at this time. It was not just the death of Morny in 1865 which had left an irreplaceable gap. It was the knowledge that Persigny was not able enough, as the 1863 elections had shown, and that Billault had died in 1863 just when he might have been useful. True, Baroche, Fould, Magne and above all Rouher were still there, but not one of them was sufficiently progressive in outlook to fulfil the Emperor's need and some of them were too inclined to Orleanism for the Emperor's taste. To a certain extent Prince Napoleon was radical in outlook, and had he been prepared to work seriously with his cousin he might well have done the Empire a service. Unfortunately, age did not bring maturity in the Prince's case and he remained a liability rather than an asset because of his tendency to say too much in public without due regard for the consequences.

In his correspondence with the Emperor à propos of the reforms of 1867, the Prince denounced the establishment of a ministry which appeared to him to cancel out, by its compositions, the value of the reforms. In particular he denounced Rouher as a man totally unsuited to direct the "new course" in the Empire because he was so identified with previous policies. Needless to say these comments were publicly repeated by the Prince and were used as a stick with which to beat the ministry, so that, as so often before, the man who might have been a crutch for Napoleon III was merely another cross.

Napoleon, long-suffering as always, pointed out in a mild rebuke that: "Your observations would be correct if my government were a parliamentary government like that of Louis Philippe. Then when one changed ministers one changed the entire policy." This was not the case today, he continued, because "...I am responsible for all that the ministers do and say...." "Apart from that, in the actual circumstances having no man either at the [Ministry of the] Interior or at the [Ministry of] Foreign Affairs who could use words with skill, it was absolutely necessary to keep M. Rouher as Minister of State since he was thus authorized to deal with all questions."[13] Rouher was the best minister Napoleon had—as indeed Rouher himself had pointed out in a long and highly interesting memorandum which he had sent to the Emperor at a time of proposed changes in the 1867 ministry. The burden of this analysis was that none was so good as he. Napoleon was obliged, *faute de mieux*, to concur.[14]

Indispensability did not mean that Rouher was omnicompetent; in the field of foreign affairs, in particular, his attitude and tactics were neither wise nor helpful, and as the implications of Sadowa became increasingly obvious, tentative attempts had to be made to obtain for France some sort of *quid pro quo* by negotiation with Prussia. The alternative was a virtual abdication of any position for France in Europe.

Bismarck had always hinted at Belgium and, as has already been noted, Rouher had accepted this as an ultimate aim of French policy but not an immediate possibility. In view of the alarm which any hint of such a move caused in Brussels and in London, this was a common-sense attitude. Unfortunately for France, Rouher's lack of diplomatic skill and lack of perception had led him to send the draft scheme of proposed annexation to Bismarck in August, 1866, in spite of Benedetti's reluctance to present the text. Benedetti may not have been the world's greatest diplomat, but he did see the danger inherent in providing Bismarck with a document which could be used to France's disadvantage should the necessity ever arise.

The refusal to deal at that time with Bismarck over Belgium did not, however, preclude any move by France for compensation elsewhere. The obvious choice was Luxembourg and, although Rouher had dismissed it as a "shanty" he could not completely ignore the Emperor's desire to provide public opinion with some sort of fillip to France's prestige.

Once the project for army reform was launched as the first step in a move "forward" policy, the government took up the question of Luxembourg. Since the winter of 1866 Napoleon had been negotiating with the King of the Netherlands for the sale of the Grand Ducal Appanage of Luxembourg. This method of increasing prestige by purchase was not a particularly exciting one and indeed it smacked more of the reign of Louis Philippe than of Napoleon III, but it was realistic, given France's military condition, since it seemed devoid of international complications. All went splendidly. The King of Holland was willing to sell, the Luxembourgeois were agreeable to being trans- ferred; all that Holland required was a guarantee from France against Prussian aggression. In return for this France would have acquired an area which would help to round off her north-eastern frontier and give her part of the defensive line of the Ardennes. All seemed to be going splendidly when suddenly the treaties of 1815 appeared on the scene. Under one of the terms, Prussian forces garrisoned the fortresses in Luxembourg as part of the "encirclement" of France. This meant that ultimately Prussia must become a party to the negotiations. Before matters had got to this point the session of the Legislative Body and the Senate began in Paris, with all that implied in the context of the January reforms. As has already been indicated, the opposition were eager to flex their muscles, and to Thiers and the opposition, Rouher's foreign policy was a gift.

The Emperor as usual, read his speech from the throne which rehearsed the arguments of the La Vallette Circular of September, 1866, namely that France had nothing to fear from the new situation across the Rhine. Fishing about for some justification of this attitude, Napoleon invoked the nationality principle, with reference to the St. Helena texts, which had predicated agglomerations in Europe. "The transformations which have taken place in Italy and in Germany are preparing the realization of this vast programme of the union of the states of Europe in one single confederation."[15] But although the speech was optimistic in tone it was noted that the Emperor read badly with pauses and hesitations, and it was coldly received by the Chambers. "His Majesty's speech is applauded very little," Ollivier remarked and another observer noted that the reception was in general icy, and there were few of the cries of *"Vive l'Empereur"* which normally accompanied the event.

The attack on Imperial policy was launched by Thiers on 14th March. He denounced the government's playing with the nationali- ties question and invoked the balance of power as the real basis for international settlement. The Prussian triumph in Germany should never have been permitted and the government should have moved to prevent it. "It would have only had to utter one word to stop the war : the Chamber asked it to do it : it did not do it. . . ." This statement was manifestly untrue. Thiers knew perfectly well that he had himself opposed any action in the summer of 1866 and his speech was merely an exhibition of parliamentary tactics which bore no relevance to the situation. It may well have been the element of cant in Thiers' speech which led Rouher to reply so trenchantly, and disastrously, on 16th March.

Rouher's speech was a defence of the German policy which, he said, had created a Germany of "three slices." The North German Confederation had twenty-two million inhabitants, South Germany had fifteen million, and Austria had thirty-three. This had broken the Germany of 1815 which had been confederated to keep France in subjection and the new arrangement was therefore favourable to France. Rouher's analysis was as faulty as Thiers, and what is more, he knew it. Bismarck had already blown the "three slices" theory sky-high by secret alliances with the South German states. This had been told privately to the Emperor by Ambassador Benedetti, who had been told it by Bismarck before leaving Berlin on his arrival in Paris on 9th March.[16] When he spoke of it in the Chamber it was certainly known to Rouher, but in case the point had been missed Bismarck announced it in the *Landtag* in Berlin within three days of Rouher's speech. French policy was shown to be based on an illusion. As far as the opposition was concerned it was further proof of the incompetence of Rouher and the Emperor and a serious row occurred in the *Corps Législatif* on 17th and 18th March when Favre, for the Republicans, and Thiers for the *Notables* delivered scathing attacks on the Minister. For the first time in the history of the Empire the *coup d'état* of 2nd December was publicly resurrected and produced a violent scene in which Rouher lost his head completely and Walewski, the President, lost complete control of the Assembly. Never was the Emperor seen to be so badly served in a bad situation.

Worse was yet to come. Bismarck knew well that once the news of the alliance between Prussia and the South German states was announced, France would abandon any hope of pursuing a revisionist policy in Europe at the side of Russia, for clearly this could never be to her advantage. In these circumstances, Bismarck played another card and threw the whole Luxembourg negotiation into the light of day. Not only did Prussia make it plain to the King of Holland that she would not tolerate a cession. Bismarck had himself been attacked in the *Landtag* by arrangement with the German nationalists, who extracted from him an assurance that "the Royal Government would watch over the interests of the nation," and would not agree to any weakening of the national position.

In an extraordinary way Bismarck is like a distorted mirror image of Napoleon III. Having brought France to an impasse whereby she must either accept abandonment of compensation through the acquisition of Luxembourg or go to war to get it, the Prussian minister agreed to accept a European conference to settle the question. The conference at London involved the major powers and was virtually the congress Napoleon III had sought so vainly for years. The meeting, however, took place in London not Paris. France was not the convenor, but an invitee, and the results were in no way to her advantage. It is true that Prussia abandoned her rights in Luxembourg, but France did not acquire the area. Like Belgium, Luxembourg was neutralized under international guarantee. Napoleon's feelings were summed up in his comment to his minister Magne: "I trusted Bismarck and he has betrayed me."

Not only had Bismarck betrayed Napoleon, he had outsmarted him, and he had made it plain that there would be no *rapprochement* between France and Prussia, and there would be no compensations for Napoleon now or later. Napoleon might pretend to find the settlement of the Luxembourg affair satisfactory and to pretend also that France and Prussia were like "two friends, who happen to disagree in a café and find themselves obliged to fight, they don't know exactly why." The brutal fact was that *Il avait travaillé pour le roi de Prusse* and public opinion knew it.[17]

It has been argued that the Luxembourg affair was of capital importance in what it revealed: "The dream of Franco-German amity was shattered for ever: it could not be revived by Jules Ferry in 1884 nor at Locarno, nor at Montoire."[18] It was certainly evident to Napoleon III that Franco-Prussian amity had taken a sharp knock, and he now cast about for a means of containing Prussia through alliances. The question was, as always, with whom?

The participation of the English government in the settlement of the Luxembourg question in the summer of 1867 was no evidence of their desire to return to a continental involvement. Indeed, Lord Stanley, the foreign minister went out of his way to assure the Commons in May that this was an exception to a general line of policy which the government had accepted. In view of this there was little hope of

Napoleon III reviving the entente. As for Russia and Austria, there were difficulties which were, in fact, to prove insurmountable.

However, in the summer of 1867 Paris was *en fête*. In one of those hymns to materialism so dear to the heart of the nineteenth century, the great Exhibition of that year was designed to show not just the progress of France, but the progress of civilization. The exhibits were splendid, each country contributing the best to its respective pavilion. They ranged from aluminium (France), through the rocking chair (U.S.A.) to a monster cannon by Krupp. This last exhibit was awarded a special prize. The Exhibition was a royal and Imperial occasion in that it brought together a collection of the major and minor sovereigns of Europe. Napoleon III may have hoped to do a little diplomatic business on the side, but the sovereigns came and went, and France was without any firm supporters in spite of amicable exchanges.

Bismarck had come with his King and neither of them had been shown any hostility by the public. They were more fortunate than Tsar Alexander II who was hissed, greeted with cries of *Vive la Pologne, Monsieur*, and finally shot at by a Polish *émigré*. Alexander's would-be assassin missed. The firing squad at Querétaro did not, and news of Maximilian's execution, by the order of Juarez, reached Paris from Mexico on a day in June when the Emperor was scheduled to award prizes at the Exhibition and did so, white-faced and in obvious distress.

In August Napoleon and Eugénie went to Salzburg to meet Franz-Josef, but it was not merely a desire to condole that took them there. The Emperor of Austria had no doubt added his brother's death to the list of grievances which he held against Napoleon III, but diplomacy is based less upon sentiment than upon an exchange of marketable goods. What France needed to show was that she was capable of undoing the effects of the treaty of Prague—at least in Germany—if she wanted some return from Austria-Hungary. It could hardly be expected that Napoleon III would pressure Italy into abandoning Venetia and so Germany was the only possible theatre of operations. The trouble was that even if France now came out into the open, and clearly pledged herself to the revision of the Treaty of Prague she would have to deal with a dual monarchy, for Beust had just concluded the *Ausgleich* with the Magyars and the new state of Austria-Hungary had emerged.

This was as much a blow to the Germany of "three slices" as had Bismarck's alliance with the South German states been. Beust, Franz-Josef's minister, a Saxon who had been driven out of his state after Bismarck's victory in 1866, hungered for revenge on Prussia. To him, and to his master, the agreement with Hungary was only a temporary concession, an intermezzo, to be reversed when Prussia was humbled and Austria master in her German house again. But there was no chance of any of this coming about. At the first sign of movement by Austria Bismarck had signed up the South German states and blocked any further moves in that quarter. At the first sign of an Austro-French *rapprochement* the German liberals in Austria, who admired Bismarck's work and envied it, made common cause with the Magyar nobles and, for different reasons, combined to thwart the French advances for an alliance. From now until 1870 Napoleon II pursued with net and pin a butterfly so delicate as to have virtually no substance.

In the autumn of 1867 Beust offered an Austrian alliance against Russia, or a combination of Russia and Prussia. That was the only combination which would fit in with the internal situation of the dual monarchy. It was no use to Napoleon III, though it was not viewed with any great feeling of disappointment by Rouher and the ministry who still maintained an attitude of peace above all.

This was manifested not merely in their lack of any support for an "Imperial policy," but in their virtual opposition to the army reform laws as finally presented by *Maréchal* Niel in the summer of 1867, after the dismissal of *Maréchal* Randon in January had led to a watering down of the original proposals.[19]

Even the watered-down version was too much for the Chamber—and it was not only the opposition who attacked. When the Empress said to Niel: "I hope you will manage to raise the war budget," he replied, "Yes, if M. Rouher does not oppose me in the wings." And when Rouher assured the *Maréchal* that he would support him in the Chamber, Niel merely replied that it would be enough if he stopped opposing him in his private and backstairs conversation.[20]

Whatever the reasons, the laws were the subject of debates until January 1868, a fact which should be borne in mind when assessing the extent of the liberty of discussion which the French Chambers now had. Like most debates between professionals and amateurs, great heat was generated and little light thrown on the real problems of military reform. The Republicans' opposition was based on their fear of a political army. Theirs feared expense and announced with the conviction of total ignorance that Prussia's military forces were far from formidable. In 1870 both Favre and Thiers were to denounce the Imperial government for its great neglect of France's defence.

The debates left France with a compromise army. In order to acquire the million men that the Emperor wanted, the annual contingent was to be increased so that by 1875 in case of mobilization, France would be able to dispose of 800,000. The balance was to be made up by reforming the *Garde Mobile* which was to be a sort of "citizen army," training for a fortnight a year but able, in theory, to be in the field with little delay. In fact, the *Garde Mobile* was never properly organized or armed and in 1870 its units, if they managed to get to the front, displayed as much reluctance to fight as the ministers had displayed in 1868 in allowing their formation.

The only visible sign of French military preparations was the acquisition of a new rifle, the *Chassepot*. Accurate to 1,600 yards and breech-loading, it was a "magnificent" weapon and superior to the Prussian "needle-gun," which had been so effective at Sadowa. By an irony of history the *Chassepot* was not tried out against the Prussians, but against the Italians when, in October, 1867, Garibaldi launched an attack on the Papal States and the Roman Question re-opened.

Garibaldi's expedition never had any chance of success except in the mind of its instigator who believed that the whole world hated the Pope and priests as much as he did. He found no support in the Papal states whose inhabitants knew enough about the condition of the Kingdom of Italy, particularly its fiscal structure, to make them chary of rushing into union.[21] Apart from that, Napoleon III had decided that the Pope must be protected and had dispatched a fleet to Civita Vecchia for that purpose. To the Emperor it must have seemed that he was now living through history twice and the thought can hardly have cheered him.

Rouher's plan was to oppose Garibaldi with a joint Franco-Italian force, drive him out, and then summon an international conference to settle the Roman problem. The Italians refused to be caught in any such operation and when Garibaldi was defeated at Mentana on 5th November it was by a joint Franco-Papal force. General de Failly telegraphed: "*Les Chassepots ont fait merveille.*" It was natural for the general to want to record a triumph of fire-power, particularly of a new weapon, but it was a serious political error and one which the government could well have done without. The opposition went into action. The "Italianists" had already denounced the intervention as presaging the ruin of the dynasty: "The *raison d'être* of the Bonapartes, their legitimacy is to personify the principle of the French Revolution and the mission of that Revolution is not to uphold theocracy." So said Senator Bonjean, statesman for the anti-Papalists and radicals in the Senate. From the other side, even "liberal" clerics like Archbishop Darboy of Paris, no lover of Pius IX, was compelled to defend the Pope's right to live in peace and the government's obligation to defend Rome.

The comments of Bonjean and Darboy were the small change of opposition and were in no way significant. It was left to Rouher to bring about the catastrophe in his speech in the Chamber of 5th December, 1867 in which he delivered himself of the famous "*Jamais! Jamais!*" peroration. "Italy will not seize Rome. Never, never will France accept this violation of her honour and her Catholicity. . . ."

The Deputies of the clerical right raised their hands to Heaven at this superb disavowal of twenty years' policy; the Legitimists, Berryer and Chesnelong rushed to congratulate the minister. The Radicals and the "Italianists" found themselves aligned with the Republicans in crying out against this statement. They were right to do so, for the best verdict on Rouher's action is the letter which the Legitimist Falloux wrote to Thiers: "What a victory for you, and what a triumph for the Moral Order throughout Europe." For the genuinely Catholic Falloux to congratulate Thiers, the Voltairean bourgeois and political Catholics, reveals much about the opportunist nature of the opposition to the Empire. Even the liberal and anti-Papal Catholic, Montalembert wrote to Thiers on 10th December: "Behold parliamentary government restored, thanks to you." It was not in fact, restored just yet, but it would certainly not long be delayed.

It is said that the only rebuke which Napoleon III delivered to Rouher after the lamentable scene in the Chamber of 5th December was to remark to him in mild tones: "In politics one must not say 'never'," The story sounds authentic. It would be characteristic of Napoleon III to be mild in rebuke, but it would be a mistake to imagine he had not registered the immensity of the minister's blunder. The problem of who was to replace him was still there, and if the events from 1865 to 1868 had proved conclusively that the Empire needed new men and a new course, they had not yet produced the men to cope. Unfortunately events would not wait on the men and the time of trial was not yet ended.

14

Change and Re-founding

"On reconnait la bontè de l'arbe aux fruits qu'il porte, a dit l'Evangile; eh bien! Si l'on fait un retour vers le passé, quel est le régime qui a donné à la France dix-sept années de quiétude et de prospérité toujours croissantes?"

Napoleon III, January, 1869

"L'Empire et la Liberté."

Emile Ollivier, 1869

BY 1868 there were clear indications that the political structure of the Empire must be changed and that the changes must be far-reaching. The virtual defeat of governmental policy on two important issues, the army reform and the Italian question, showed to what extent the Legislative Body had begun not only to make its opinions felt, but to make them prevail. That was exactly what Montalembert had meant by his comment to Thiers on 10th December, 1867, about the restoration of parliamentary liberty.

Apart from activity in the Chamber the opposition press had taken advantage of the confusion to publish attacks on government policy, such as the army reforms, and on the whole structure of the Empire. This led to prosecution under the press laws which in turn led to increased criticisms, described by Baroche as of "an extraordinary licence." Since the journals had increased not only in numbers but also in their circulation, they provided a stimulus to public debate.[1]

The government was hampered by the fact of its being caught in a contradictory approach for the letter of January, 1867, had promised a relaxation of the press laws of 1852 and the Emperor neither would, nor could, go back on this. Consequently, the law of May, 1868, considerably eased restrictions while reserving to the government certain pressure points on which it could lean if need be. The press took advantage of the new situation to increase both its numbers and its polemics.

In June, 1868, the right of public meetings was conceded, hedged about it is true with restrictions as to what might be discussed. But the restrictions mattered less than the principle and the opposition found ways of defeating the prohibitions on meetings specifically designed to discuss politics or religion by holding reunions thinly disguised as "literary evenings."

With the newly acquired right of discussion in both press and public meeting, the opposition was determined to make the government's present life difficult, while at the same time preparing for the elections which must come in 1869. In the summer of 1868 groups within the government even considered holding the elections earlier than the scheduled dates to prevent the opposition from establishing itself. For some weeks the ministers seriously debated this question, but the absence of the Emperor, who was ill and had to go to Plombières, prevented any resolution.

In the circumstances, the only thing the government could do was to proceed by law against journals and journalists who offended. This avenue had not been closed by the May laws of 1868, but it was a dangerous route to take, for the bulk of the magistrates was Orleanist or Legitimist in sympathies and frequently dismissed the case or fined the offenders derisory sums.

From the government's point of view, journalists were an irritant. Much more serious were the by-elections results in which the opposition candidates triumphed, as in the case of the Republican Grévy in the Jura in August 1868. His poll was double that of the official candidate and the result was, as Baroche noted, *pénible* for the Emperor. In view of the by-elections, any thought the government might have entertained of advancing the date of the general election was totally abandoned.

The Emperor's dilemma was agonizing. With every move he made towards liberalization he discovered fresh difficulties. Like a man in a minefield each step was a major decision and each one might be the last. Napoleon III sought, as always, a democratic Empire in which opposition existed but was not destructive. He had hoped that after eighteen years a new generation would have emerged which would be critical but not revolutionary. Napoleon had hoped that the social democracy for which he had striven, and continued to strive, would have unmasked the "false democracy" of the bourgeois liberals and Republicans and that the workers would never again allow themselves to be deceived, but the Emperor underestimated the political agility of the bourgeoisie, the Liberals and the Republicans and overestimated the Empire's success with the workers.

Eighteen years of the Empire had not destroyed either the *patronat* or the *Notables*, nor in spite of all its efforts to educate them, had it created a working class with sufficient political awareness and economic strength to resist the siren songs of the Republicans. The trouble was that the years from 1866 to 1868 were years of difficulty for the working population because of the economic crisis and because the cost of living had reached a point it had not known since the bad years of the fifties.[2] It had been calculated that a worker's salary in the Paris region in the year 1867 was barely adequate to cover his basic necessities, and in 1868 it was worse.[3] These conditions provided fertile ground to be worked over by the opposition, which was almost bound to be that of the traditional Republicans, given the feebleness of "socialist" ideas among the French working class. Apart from the followers of Proudhon, who so irritated Marx at the meeting of the International in 1867, the only other socialist group of any consequence was that made up of the Bonapartist workers.

The "Manifesto of the Sixty" in 1864 had proposed for consideration the view that the working class should have their own political representatives. It rejected the Marxist concept of class conflict, and by implication accepted the "unionist" or "integralist" view of society as advocated by Napoleon III, but it did mark a new phase of workers' politics.

What the government was determined to avoid at all costs was a fusion between the bourgeoisie, in any of their political manifestations, and the workers. If the elections of 1869 were to be held with any hope of success for the regime, there must be no violent dislocation of the social structure which had existed, in spite of all its limitations, since 1852. In this situation, as in 1852, all turned upon the Emperor himself. Only he could hold the balance and prevent a fissuring of society. The difficulty was, of course, that as the Emperor was older, and ill, the very changes he had brought about tended to work against him; that he had now no men who really believed in his policies; and finally, that France's European situation was dangerously exposed.

The opening of the legislative session in 1869 produced a speech from the throne which, in its tone, seemed to imply that the Emperor was fully in command once again. Napoleon referred to the fact that the laws voted in the last session had given rise to "a factious agitation, and produced a reappearance of passions which one had thought extinct; but, on the other hand, the nation, deaf to the most violent appeals, counting on my firmness to maintain order, has not felt its faith in the future shaken."[4]

The opposition was not at all put out by the Emperor's firm

language. They sensed that the Empire, certainly in anything like its present form, was on the run. In February, 1869, they hotted up the chase by attacking the financial structure as evidenced by the activities of Haussmann. The Prefect of the Seine had not been over-careful in acquiring legislative sanction for the sums he needed for rebuilding Paris, as required since 1863, and Thiers now turned his oratorical talents against Haussmann.

In this context Thiers represented orthodox finance which, having destroyed the Péreires and the *Crédit Mobilier*, was now after the blood of its sister institution the *Crédit Foncier*. The destruction of both these institutions would immensely strengthen the hands of the *Haute Banque*, both politically and financially, which was the reason for the attack. That Haussmann had borrowed money from the *Crédit Foncier* was beyond dispute; to charge that he had done so as part of a criminal financial swindle was absurd. But Jules Favre the Republican, made common cause with Thiers and the *Notables* and produced his *Comptes Fantastiques d'Haussmann*, the title a pun on the *Contes Fantastiques d'Hoffmann*. Favre's campaign, linked to that of Thiers, produced a law restraining the activities of both Haussmann and the *Crédit Foncier*. *En route* they had achieved an even greater victory, for Rouher had made a bad showing in the debate and was clearly destined for a fall. Even the Emperor avowed that this time Rouher had "manoeuvred very badly."

Unfortunately the Emperor was not manoeuvring any more adroitly abroad than Rouher was at home, as France's European situation was not improving. The Austrian alliance still eluded him and the proposed conference to settle the Papal problem had not mollified either the Italians or the Pope. The only diplomatic breakthrough was a move to set up a triple alliance of France, Austria and Italy which reached the stage of a draft treaty in May, 1869, but which fell to the ground because it was not really about anything which any of the proposed signatories wanted.[5] The Emperor could offer no *coup de théâtre* in foreign policy to help the regime through the elections. A fumbling attempt to acquire control of the Belgian railways had likewise foundered in the early summer of 1869, and the main effect of this abortive financial and strategic *coup* had been to reveal to Bismarck England's continued determination not to become involved in any continental disputes, significantly, even if it involved Belgium.[6] The activities of France in Belgium were, of course, a bonus for Bismarck in that when the time came he was able to allege a continuous intent on the part of France to annex the neighbouring kingdom.

The government entered the electoral contest of 1869 with little to offer the electorate. What is more, both the will and the way to bring home the official candidates was lacking. Just as the sand at the bottom of the hour glass appears to run out swiftly, so at the end of the Empire the pace of events seems unusually rapid. The disarray of the government at the centre was reflected in the hesitancy and confusion with which it approached the election. Since there was no Bonapartist party, all would depend on whether the regime could, or would, use the method of backing the official candidates by employing the administration. Once it rejected this the field became free to all.[7] It should be remembered that the government did not totally renounce all interference in the course of the elections, but the influence was sporadic, and in geographical terms, scattered.

The opposition fell roughly into two groups. The "Liberal Union," a compound of Legitimists, Orleanists, and moderate Republicans, with a new group of radical Republicans led by Gambetta. It was in Gambetta's famous "Belleville Programme," his address to his electors in that *arrondissement* of Paris, that the radical Republican aim was most clearly stated. The ideas were essentially bourgeois and anti-clerical mixed with a little utopianism, general disarmament, and a pinch of economic reform "which must be constantly studied and investigated in the name of the principle of justice and social equality." The manifesto ended with a stern call to *Liberté, Egalité, Fraternité!* There was nothing new in any of it, even though Gambetta and his associates did represent the second and more "advanced" wing of the opposition.

Turning from the opposition one finds that there were also two governmental wings: the Bonapartists who wanted to see a renewal of the "Faith of '52" with its authoritarianism, and those who saw that the evolution towards a more parliamentary Empire was inevitable. Like the opposition groups they had little new to offer and indeed one critic of the last few years of the regime saw this lack of programme as the cause of so much disaffection. Persigny said in a letter to the Emperor in June, 1869, that it was the democratization of the Empire "which represented precisely the shabby bourgeois system of little shifts, little expedients without belief, without conviction, without any moral basis, and without grandeur, which characterized the government of Louis Philippe and the public has just condemned it from one end of France to the other."[8] One must recall the Emperor's comments: "... only Persigny is a Bonapartist and he is mad," but one should at the same time note that the government had not had a resounding electoral success.

In one sense Persigny was right in that the leading Orleanists and legitimist candidates had been rejected, and with them had been rejected the clericals. The bulk of the deputies elected were still loyal to the Empire and the government could take pleasure in the fact that its majority was almost one and a half million. This meant in arithmetical terms, that there had been only a drop of half a million in the "loyal" vote. Two things, however, must be weighed against this. Firstly, the opposition had polled 3,300,000 and had increased by half since 1863. Secondly the number of abstentions reached thirty per cent throughout the nation. In some regions it reached forty per cent, though this was generally in districts where only the official candidate stood. Abstention might, therefore, mean either satisfaction or disgust.

The most important group among the opposition was that of the thirty Republicans. United in their opposition of the Empire, they were not, as Prince Napoleon commented, ". . . able to define the system which they would construct on the ruins of the actual state. That is their irredeemable weakness . . ."[9] It was true that Gambetta had been more specific than any of his fellow radical Republicans, but he was only one voice in thirty.

In any event, the Empire could easily overcome violent or threatening opposition. What it could not survive was the support of its friends. When Ollivier announced the establishment of a grouping, liberal and dynastic in its aims, the regime was bound to yield. Ollivier addressed the government thus: "Concede liberty: you are the masters and you can [do so] without weakness, and tomorrow this great current of opinion which rolls without ceasing, even more impetuous and menacing, instead of swallowing you up, will tranquilly carry your fortunes . . ." The manifesto of the 116, demanding that the government "give satisfaction to the feelings of the country by associating it more efficaciously in the conduct of affairs," was also Ollivier's work. By it, he hoped to proceed to the post of chief minister. If Ollivier could add nine more votes to his 116 signatories the government would find itself in a minority in the Chamber—a situation for which there was no parallel in the history of the Empire. In these circumstances, whatever Napoleon wanted, his hand was forced. Rouher resigned and the Emperor accepted his resignation. With him went Baroche and with them both went the end of an era which had begun with their rallying to the Prince President in 1849.

The next move must be to let Ollivier in, but the Emperor would not give way immediately and prorogued the Legislative Body while he formed a caretaker ministry under Chasseloup-Laubat. He was now resolved to liberalize and on 8th September the *Senatus Consultum*, perhaps the most important since the foundation of the Empire, ordered that the Legislative Body be freed from virtually every restriction placed upon its deliberation. Ministers would be appointed by the Emperor, to that extent it would still be a ministerial government responsible to him, but they would meet with the Emperor in the chair as a virtual Cabinet. They could be from either the Senate or the Chamber and the only restriction was that although accountable to Parliament, they were still responsible to the Emperor.

These reforms cleared the way for Ollivier. In October there was a last fling by an old conspirator when Ollivier travelled to Compiégne secretly and entered the Palace late at night, heavily disguised, for a meeting with his sovereign. Rigid Bonapartists likened this to the nocturnal encounter between Annas and Caiphas.

As political encounters go, it was reasonably successful, in that Ollivier was accepted in principle although he could not make his proposed practice stick. Napoleon would not accept a "parliamentary ministry" nominated by his new protégé, including it is said, the appointment of Prince Napoleon as Minister of Marine, but basically the terms agreed favoured a liberal slant. From December onwards the Emperor groomed Ollivier for stardom by sending him state papers and discussing with him all important matters. Finally, on 2nd January, 1870, Ollivier was nominated as head of the Ministry.

It was a heterogeneous collection of men who took office, but given the condition of French political life at that moment, it could hardly have been otherwise. Ollivier had himself made the transition from Republican deputy to minister of the Emperor not only because of vanity and ambition, although he had his share of both, but because he had become convinced that the future of France could be worked out within the existing structure. Indeed he felt, as did many others, that the only alternative to putting the Empire on a new course was a revolutionary procedure, and at this he, and many more, drew back. Even the traditional right-wing had not desired the death of the sinner but only that he might turn from his wickedness and live. All that they wanted of the old Adam was that he should still promise order in 1870 as he had in 1850. This was Napoleon's last and only trump card; he would still answer for order. It was partly this consideration which conditioned the ministry formed by Ollivier in that the appointments to the Ministries for War and Marine were the Emperor's. However, more important was the fact that the new reforms had produced a reconciliation between the liberal right and the Bonapartists. To that extent the whole affair was a regression in that it marked, for the Emperor, a *rapprochement* with a parliamentary system he detested. In that sense the reforms of 1869-70 announced the emergence of the Orleanist Empire and with it an acknowledgement of the defeat of much that Napoleon III had hoped and worked for.

In the new ministry, six out of the eight men were from the traditional right. They were not only rightists, they were in the case of Buffet, the new Minister of Finance and Daru, the new Minister of Foreign Affairs, clerical in their sympathies. When Rouher and Baroche had gone, they had taken with them Duruy, the anti-clerical and progressive Minister of Education. His successor Segris was a man of no political attachments. He was neither hot nor cold, and in his political youth Louis Napoleon would have spewed him out of his mouth. The Minister of Public Works, the Marquis de Talhouet-Roy, was a monarchist; the minister of Agriculture and Commerce, Louvet, was an anti-free trader and an Orleanist who married off his family into Legitimist circles. At the Interior there was Chevandier de Valdrôme, son of a peer of Louis Philippe.[10]

With such a galaxy of new Orleanist faces in the ministries, it was not surprising that the governmental receptions were attended, for the first time in twenty years, by the old guard, like Guizot, Thiers and Odilon Barrot, who once again emerged from the obscurity into which the *coup d'état* had relegated them.

What of the Bonapartists? The authoritarian, the mamelukes, the *Arcadiens*, or the faithful as they would have styled themselves? They felt themselves betrayed by the acceptance of the Orleanists who represented all they hated. To men like Duvernoy, David, Granier de Cassagnac, Echasseriaux, the great days of the Empire had come with the democratic programmes of the late fifties and early sixties, with its attempts to draw in the workers by social reforms, and by the indentification of the regime with an anti-clerical policy, typified not only by the Italian policy abroad but by the scholastic reforms of Duruy. Duruy's attack on the conservatism of the Sorbonne and his determination to begin a policy of laicisation of education were immensely popular with this type of Bonapartist, not just because of an innate anti-clericalism, but because it represented a side-swipe at *les grands* and *les bien-persants*. At ground level this sort of Bonapartism was earthy and rancorous, not just because it was peasant but because it was the politics of the narrowed eye that measured up squire and priest and hoped to see them humbled. If Napoleon III had wanted to found a party to support him, here was his raw material. Perhaps it was his awareness of what it was really like which precluded him from doing this, as well as his aversion to party as a source of disunity in the state.

That there was little or no party organization is borne out not simply by the growth of opposition, but in its success. Of what use to expand if you do not win seats at elections? To counter this, the local authorities had urged the government with ever increasing vociferousness from 1866 on, to work on the masses by propaganda. It was true that at a certain level of society the Prefect operated as an agent for the regime by his social pattern. Balls, receptions, soirées, brightened the life of the provincial bourgeoisie, but they did nothing for the people at large, and in the major cities they cut no ice at all.

The government tried to fulfil an educative role, in the propagandist sense, but it found it hard to sustain a concerted effort and confined its activities mainly to the periods immediately preceding elections and plebiscites. This urgent task once accomplished, the level and intensity of the propaganda dropped.

However, in so far as this type of Bonapartism still had a political expression, it was far from negligible in that it had at least eighty to ninety deputies in the Chamber, but as a group they had little real power against the coalition of Ollivier's third party. Their moment of excitement came in July, 1870, when they clamoured loudly for war with Prussia, hoping that victory abroad would lead to a victory at home and that the Emperor would disembarrass himself of the "parliamentary rabble."

Now that Ollivier was in power, it remained to be seen what policies would be produced. As far as the new minister himself was concerned, his intentions were impeccable. "He proposed to tackle the most fundamental problems at their roots . . ." and he designed a series of commissions to investigate under six headings what he considered to be the major problems of government. These included the question of decentralization, a *leitmotiv* of government in France since 1815, including a separate status for the city of Paris. Education was to be looked at from two aspects: the question of the university's monopoly, already attacked by Duruy, and the question of establishing technical education. Public works and communications were to be examined with a view to helping the country's expansion.

Contemporaries, and later commentators, have pointed out that there was little new in this programme. This was true. There was also an interesting fact that it resembled very closely the prospect put forward by Prince Napoleon to the Emperor in his Memorandum of May, 1869, in which he had outlined a plan for government action.[11] In some ways, Prince Napoleon went further than Ollivier in that he recommended a cut in salary for functionaries and an elected Senate.

While it was not part of Ollivier's programme to turn the Senate into an elective Senate he was determined to ensure that there would be no backward moves towards an authoritarian Empire. The *Senatus Consultum* of 20th April, fixed the constitution of the new Imperial structure by putting together in a coherent form all the piecemeal decrees of a decade. This new constitution did transform the Senate into a simple second Chamber. No longer had it the custody of the Constitution, nor had it any powers other than those normally given to a Legislative body. This *Senatus Consultum* was, in fact, the last of its kind.[12] Of the authoritarian Empire, all that was left was the plebiscite which the Emperor now insisted be used to ratify the new constitution.

Before the dispute which arose over Napoleon III's determination to hold a plebiscite, a procedure highly distasteful to the Orleanists, there had already been signs of friction between the sovereign and the ministers. The Orleanists were conservatives *and* protectionists and their advent to power meant an attack on the free-trade policy pursued by the Emperor. Early in January, Thiers denounced the Free-Trade Treaty of 1860 as a blunder "equal to that committed in Mexico and Germany," and demanded an end to these utopias. Ollivier was himself not an opponent of free-trade, but his position was not such that he could hold out against his colleagues and he found himself reduced to silence in the Chamber while Thiers and Rouher disputed the free-trade problem. Finally, when he could no longer avoid uttering, he lamely acknowledged that the government intended to set up an enquiry to look further into the matter. Here was parliamentary government with a vengeance. As Baroche remarked: "It seems to me that all that can't go on for long."[13] Certainly a delicate situation had arisen for within weeks of the new system a fundamental question had been asked, to which an answer must be given; whose will would prevail if the legislators wanted something which the Emperor could not accept?

It was this dilemma which led to the attempt to define by a new constitution who was who in the Empire. If on the one hand the Emperor was prepared to accept changes he was on the other hand determined to show that France's loyalty was to him and to the regime rather than to constitutional forms. Napoleon was making his defiance, and as he said to Prince Napoleon, "I may founder perhaps, but I will be on my feet and not rotten."[14]

This determination to re-assert the Empire's claims to be based on popular sovereignty appeared to be a deliberate renunciation of the *rapprochement* between the regime and the liberal right. Two of the ministers, Daru and Buffet resigned, their Orleanist principles revolted by what Thiers called "a Caesarian procedure." For the others on the right the decision was nothing like as clear cut, for the simple reason that various factors inclined them, in spite of themselves, to vote "yes" in the forthcoming plebiscite.

Since the end of 1869 there had been increasing evidence of a renaissance of the "social question" in that the working class were becoming restive. This restiveness, not confined to pamphleteering and meetings was an inevitable consequence of removing restrictions on publishing and the holding of meetings, but extended to industrial action. Strikes became increasingly frequent, not only in their incidence but in their violence. At the mining area of Aubin in October, 1869, there had been clashes between strikers and troops in which fourteen miners had died and others had been wounded. In the region of the Loire, in parts of Alsace and in the Lyons area around St. Etienne, there had been in the winter of 1869-70 industrial disputes, strikes and, inevitably, clashes with the "forces of order." The most serious strike occurred at the Le Creusot works where the stoppage lasted into 1870 before it finally broke for lack of support and funds.

As yet the workers were feeling their way and one commentator is of the opinion that: "In 1870, even at Le Creusot, the change in attitude of the workers expressed itself less in establishing a position against the Empire, and for a defined social order, than as a more lively sympathy for the lot of his comrades and from a new sense of his strength."[15]

The same commentator points out the lukewarmness of the support given by the Republican deputies in the *Corps Législatif*, and it is certainly remarkable that in the case of the Le Creusot strikers the only support which came was verbal and not financial.

The violence of this new wave of industrial unrest worried and alarmed the *Notables*, who feared a reoccurrence of the atmosphere of 1848-49. It helped to enhance their dilemma about their attitude to the plebiscite. Dare they vote "no" and open up once again the possibilities of revolution by rejecting the Empire? Their situation was not made any easier by the fact that the Imperial government frequently intervened to protect the workers, and often at the workers' own request, and by the knowledge that the Emperor himself made no secret of his determination to ease the workers' conditions.[16] Not without reason did the workers in many regions say in May, 1870: "We vote 'yes' for the Emperor because the bosses vote 'no'."

The question put to the French people on 8th May, 1870, was in the following terms : "The people approves the liberal reforms carried out on the constitution since 1860 and ratifies the *Senatus Consultum.*" This was an extremely clever formula, since it combined two separate things : approval of change in a liberal sense with an acknowledgement of the popular democratic basis on which it all rested. Who could vote "no"? The liberal right, as already indicated, could hardly deny the validity of the liberal reforms, and quite apart from any fears of revolution it might have, the authoritarian right, the "pure" Bonapartists, could hardly deny the validity of the *Senatus Consultum.* Even the Republicans were put in a quandary by the ambiguous nature of the proposition and could only decide finally in a negative way on the grounds that nothing could absolve the regime from its past misdeeds.

There can be no doubt that the opposition groups expected a very powerful negative vote. The elections of 1869, apart from anything else, gave them grounds for this. Up until the last few days before the poll newspapers of various shades from Legitimism to Republicanism encouraged their readers to vote "no." At the last moment many changed ground and urged a "yes" answer because : "The plebiscite of 8th May is a pacific but relentless struggle of order against revolution."[17]

The result was a stupefying victory for the Emperor : 7,350,500 "Yes" against 1,582,500 "No." The figures meant that eighty-two per cent of the total vote had been in the affirmative and that the relationship between majority and opposition was five to one, instead of six to four as it had been in the elections of 1869.

On 9th May the Emperor spoke about the results.

> The Plebiscite had as its aim simply the ratification by the people of a constitutional reform, but in the midst of the conflict of opinions and the enthusiasm of the battle the debate was lifted to a higher plane. This is not to be regretted. The adversaries of our institutions turned it into a question between the revolution and the Empire. The country decided in favour of the system which guarantees order and liberty. Today, the Empire is strengthened in its foundations. It will show its strength by its moderations. The government will not depart from the liberal line it has marked out for itself.

More succinctly, the Emperor had said, "I have my figure." He had vindicated in a most striking way his own personal triumph and his faith in the people. It was no good pretending that the vote was meaningless or that the plebiscite had been a trap for illiterate fools. It had happened, and as Gambetta said, "the Empire is stronger than ever." It had, in fact, precisely fifteen weeks of existence left to it.

15

Thrones and Candidates

*"C'est en Espagne qui se noua le drame qui
s'achèverait sur notre frontière de l'Est."*

P. de la Gorce

"That crown of thorns."

Lord Clarendon

*"Il reviendra vainqeur: ou il ne reviendra
pas."*

Offenbach, *La Grande Duchesse de Gerolstein*

ONE of the sideshows of European diplomacy in the nineteenth century, although it was not a new entertainment, was a guessing game, the object of which was to find out who would next rule in Spain. In the period between the war of the Spanish succession which had ended in 1713 with the Treaty of Utrecht, and the abdication of the Bourbons at Bayonne in 1808 the game had ceased to be modish, but once Napoleon had unsettled the Spanish by installing his brother Joseph as their King, the situation never really righted itself.

The problem of the Spanish succession was bedevilled by the fact that it was rarely settled without interference by some outside Power, usually France and/or England. It is true to say that the Pyrenees were France's natural frontier, it did not necessarily mean that other French statesmen thought the actual demarcation line should run on the French-speaking side of the mountain range. Louis XIV had hoped to abolish the mountains, Louis Philippe so it was said, would have liked them to be twice as high. By the reign of Napoleon III a new attitude had arisen since they were being surveyed for railroads. Whatever the dynasty, France looked upon Spain as a natural field for her activities both political and economic, and it could not, therefore, be a matter of indifference to her who ruled at Madrid either in the eighteenth or in the nineteenth century.

As for England, her view of Spain was that it ought not to fall too strongly under French influence and certainly that it should never become a French colony as Portugal had become an English one. English policy was, therefore, directed to preventing any untoward extension of French power in the Peninsula and a *modus vivendi* had been established by the Quadruple Alliance of 1834. Like most Anglo-French accords of the reign of Louis Philippe, the Quadruple Alliance was more in the interests of England than of France but, given the circumstances of the time, coupled with England's firm grip on Portugal and Gibraltar, there was little that France could do but accept the situation of enforced co-operation.

In both the Iberian Kingdoms, by the 1830's, grown men had been kept off the thrones to which they (and others) felt themselves to be the heirs in favour of infant girl children. The ostensible reason was that the men, Miguel in Portugal and Carlos in Spain, were given over to reactionary politics while from their tenderest years the little girls had given overt signs of inclining to a "liberal" policy of a type favoured by Lord Palmerston and, with more reluctance, Louis Philippe. The resulting civil war in both countries had enabled England to maintain her commercial hold on Portugal, Brazil and the former Spanish colonies, while the French were allowed to gnaw the barer bones of Spain's economy by becoming entrepreneurs and risking their capital in various commercial enterprises.[1] By 1850 they had achieved a considerable degree of control over many areas of the economy and with the advent of Napoleon III in France it was felt that French policy would become once more a "forward" one in the Peninsula.

In Lisbon the Portuguese were quick to sound the note of alarm that Napoleon III would follow Napoleon I in interfering in the affairs of the Peninsula and that England must take great care to prevent any Franco-Spanish combination which would upset the balance achieved by the Quadruple Alliance.[2] England's relationship with Portugal depended not only upon the Quadruple Alliance but upon the more binding treaties of Alliance of 1642 and 1661, a fact which was alternately the cause of joy and woe in Lisbon where "dependence" often had a different meaning.

The existence of this special relationship between England and Portugal was to colour Napoleon III's activities in Iberia during the whole of the period. There was certainly a French policy in Spain during the Second Empire, but it was a French policy in alignment with England and that accounted for much of its hesitancy and vacillation. Napoleon III was quite well aware of how touchy English governments were when it came to French activity in Spain and so while French commercial activity began to increase steadily with the general movement of French capital and enterprise after 1850, the Emperor took great care to see that no political offence was given. This did not imply however, that the ultimate aim of French policy did not envisage an extension of political power through economic activity, in particular by railway construction, and with this went the hope that such a development might help to ease Portugal out from under the weight of England.

The French idea was to construct the railways in the Peninsula so as to make Lisbon the chief port for Brazil and "the Americas" and thus prevent the Spanish from developing Cadiz. Brazil was sufficiently important for the French export markets, it was fifth in the table of countries to which France exported, for it to be a commercial prize worth having. Apart from this, a land route through France and Spain to the sea at Lisbon would break England's maritime monopoly and would help Portugal to achieve a measure of political freedom—under the benevolent eye of France.[3] Such a policy would certainly lead to a commercial struggle between England and France in the Peninsula, a rivalry which already existed between various financial interests of both nationalities, but it need not necessarily involve a political clash.

As far as Portugal was concerned, English capital already had a firm grip on the finances of the state, although the agonies of the Portuguese bond-holders in London make one wonder why they persisted in throwing good money after bad. This was particularly so after 1852 when the Portuguese government officially suspended payment of interest on its public debt,[4] and the fury of the English investors reached such a peak that all transactions in Portuguese bonds and shares were suspended on the London Stock Exchange.

It was during this particular crisis, when the Portuguese Government was fishing for a loan, that the *Crédit Mobilier* offered its services to Portugal, presumably in the hope of establishing itself there, just as it did in Spain with the *Credito Mobiliario* in 1855. Also at this time Emil Péreire pointed out to Napoleon III the necessity for railway development in the south-west of France because of "the considerable influence which France possesses, and which she must wish to increase in the Mediterranean and the Spanish Peninsula."

The French project to expand financially into Portugal did not, in fact, come to anything, although it took place against a background of speculation as to whether England or France would agree on a sort of financial condominium in the Peninsula or whether they would fall out in disputes over such a problem. In late 1854 there were expectations in both Lisbon and Madrid that one of the after-effects of an Allied victory in the Crimea would be a redrawing of the map of Europe. "In this new Tilsit the Peninsula would be the apple of discord just as Turkey was in 1807." As far as any suggestion of altering the political structure in the Peninsula by uniting the two Kingdoms, the French Minister at Lisbon, the Marquis de Lisle de Siry thought that: "This is a dream, like those [projects of unifying] Germany and Italy. They will always serve to feed the speculations of certain minds."[5]

It was precisely these speculations which did feed the mind of Napoleon III who was closely concerned with the question of Iberian union and whose interest in its possibility provided a background to what went on in the Peninsula until 1870. The more unstable the situation in Spain became, the more the Emperor was tempted to try to find a solution which would produce not only stability, but unity.

By the period 1854-56 it was clear that the question of the Spanish succession had come round again when Queen Isabella found herself confronted with a revolution, in which she only succeeded in saving her throne by acceding to a military revolt led by generals Dulce and O'Donnell. These events led to speculation as to whether Isabella might not be exchanged for something better and if so what? Various alternatives were canvassed varying from a republic to an acceptance of Carlism, passing through, among others, the idea of a union with Portugal. The partisans of this cause assumed that French support was essential to achieve this end, since England would never accept any alteration in the *status quo* as established by the Quadruple Alliance. But Napoleon III, whatever his long-term interests, was not prepared to upset the balance in Spain during a critical period of the Crimean War. The French Ambassador in Spain was informed that: "The will of His Majesty is to maintain that which is. . . . Any Union would be to create a powerful bloc at the gates of France." At the same time, the minister indicated that for the moment the Emperor felt that any type of government other than monarchy of Isabella would only be *funeste*.[6]

Although this was the first time since the affair of the Spanish marriages that France had become involved in a crisis over the Spanish succession, it was not unexpected that it would happen, in view of French interests in the country. Nor was Napoleon III's attitude to its solution so clear as Drouyn de Lhuys' memorandum might lead one to think. In November, 1854, at Boulogne, the Emperor had startled Prince Albert by bringing up a plan for Iberian Union which envisaged establishing the young King of Portugal, Pedro V, on the throne of the two countries.[7] Presumably the Emperor had hoped for support in such a project, since the young Portuguese King was the son of Ferdinand of Saxe-Coburg and Maria II of oPrtugal and was part of the royal Mafia which Prince Albert's family were establishing throughout Europe. In this particular case family ties were, however, not enough and Napoleon III received no encouragement from Albert in this project.

This check did not discourage Napoleon III from keeping the project in mind, nor did it discourage the partisans of Iberian union, who existed in both Spain and Portugal. The more squalid Isabella appeared, the more there were cries for her replacement and these frequently took the form of acclamations for *"Dom Pedro V,"* with which the Queen was greeted on more than one occasion. A scheme was put forward to marry off the young man to the Infanta, the Princess of the Asturiasi, which would give the hope of a union by dynastic marriage, but this failed. When a Spanish marriage project was revived again in 1860-61 it was rejected by the King of Portugal, who had recently lost his young wife in tragic circumstances, because the Princess was "ugly" and "rickety." "If I take a wife I shall take a woman" was his comment, but the problem was not simply one of a lack of physical attraction. France and England were interested in who married whom in the Peninsula.

In the years between 1855 and 1858 there are various indications that Napoleon III maintained an interest in the schemes of the Iberianists, but in 1858 an unexpected and colossal row blew up between Portugal and France, directly involving England. This was a dispute over the French ship, the *Charles et Georges*, which had been arrested by the Portuguese authorities in East African waters, as a slaver. The French government refused to accept the actions of the Portuguese as being covered by the anti-slave trade conventions claiming that the ship carried "indentured labourers" who were willing to accept the "contracts" offered to them. The Imperial government thereupon demanded the release of the ship and the crew and threatened to send warships to the Tagus to carry this threat into effect. When the Portuguese still refused to give in, their minister was instructed to ask for his passport and to break off diplomatic relations.

Well before this crisis point had been reached the Portuguese government had appealed to its "oldest ally" for help, but had received little real encouragement from London. Indeed it was made clear that Portugal must put up with the consequences of her action, even though she had been in the right, and make the best deal she could with

France. So in the end the Portuguese, seeing themselves alone, gave in completely and the French ship was released. The affair did little to enhance the reputation of any of the parties concerned, except the Portuguese who had tried to enforce international law and had been bullied into allowing it to be broken. The French in particular came out badly, not only because the ship was in fact a slaver but, even worse, because the bulk of its cargo was made up of very young Africans, many only children,[8] and so their official plea of "voluntary contracts" was manifestly a lie. One immediate effect of the case was to lead the Emperor, who was horrified by the report of the *Procureur Impérial*, to order an immediate cessation of the traffic in indentured labourers, which Napoleon quite rightly stigmatized as slavery under another name.

On a wider diplomatic front, Anglo-French relations had not been improved by the incident, nor had Anglo-Portuguese relations. As far as the Lisbon government was concerned it had simply been crushed between the millstones of two Powers who cared only for their relationship with one another and nothing for the rights of nations. As the King of Portugal put it: "The small are never right, and from this I am duly convinced that diplomacy is the most laughable and ridiculous thing invented by our so-called civilization."

It was the aftermath of this incident, combined with fears over a general upset in Europe caused by the Franco-Austrian crisis of 1859, which produced an interesting and abortive attempt by both Spain and Portugal to draw together in a pact of neutrality which would enable both states, singly and collectively, to neutralize the Peninsula in European affairs.[9] They would then, it was hoped, cease to be the playthings of the Powers.

The likelihood of this plan succeeding was quite remote, simply because the economic interests of England and France precluded their being indifferent to any such scheme. Apart from this, a secondary consideration was the strategic factor and the background of the Quadruple Alliance of 1834. The Portuguese would have liked to draw closer to Spain but were afraid of England's reaction unless they could count on French support. In view of recent events, this was most unlikely.

Indeed by early 1860 there were strong rumours in both Madrid and Lisbon that Napoleon III, in return for the Basque provinces of Spain, would give Portugal to Spain by way of compensation.[10]

It was inevitable that the events in Italy between 1859 and 1861 should have repercussions in Spain and Portugal and so at the end of

1860, and through the early part of 1861, the Iberian Unionists began to agitate more forcefully in both Lisbon and Madrid. It was suspected that Napoleon III was involved in this because of frequent calls made by the Duke de Saldanha at the Tuileries. Saldanha was a prominent figure in Iberian political life, one of the "men on horse-back" who had dominated the Civil War period in Portugal, who was still a power with the army. In so far as he was committed to anything other than finding a means of paying his debts, Saldanha was an Iberianist, hence the suspicion that something was brewing in Paris. Certainly at this period Napoleon III was determined to try and breathe life into Spain and, to this end, he worked towards giving her a place on the international scene in association with France. This was the thinking behind the participation of Spain in the Cochin expedition of 1860 and it certainly coloured the Emperor's thinking on Mexico.

In spite of the comings and goings of various Iberianists at the Tuileries, there is, however, no concrete evidence to support the view that Napoleon III was at this time actively intervening in their affairs. But with the sudden death of the young King Pedro of Portugal in December, 1861, and the accession of the only surviving male member of the Bragançase, Dom Luis, there was a revival of the Emperor's interest. It would seem that the marriage of the new Portuguese King to Victor Emmanuel's daughter, Maria Pia of Savoy, was considered a triumph for the French interest at Lisbon, just as the marriage of Luis's sister, Maria Antonia to Leopold of Hohenzollern was regarded as a triumph for the Anglo-Coburg faction.

The intervention in Mexico, which although Portugal did not participate, might be seen as the Quadruple Alliance in action overseas, gave a fillip to those in Spain who sought French support in putting Spain once more on the map. At the same time there were moves in the Peninsula to stress the affinity of the Latin nations and it was asked why should not Europe, which recognized a Kingdom of Italy, recognize a federated Iberian Empire? This would put an end to an unnatural division and produce a much more viable economic unit in which France would have a dominant position and "highly profitable market." Apart from any economic considerations, the growth of a Latin bloc would help France's strategic position in the Mediterranean.[11]

By the mid-sixties an enormous amount of French money was tied up in Spain.[12] The steady growth of railways in Spain was largely due to French enterprise and French capital, and Spanish bonds were supported by the Paris Bourse during periods when they found little favour

anywhere else. France's economic position had reached a high point of
development but this economic expansion took place against a background of ever-increasing political instability which took the form of
uprisings and *pronunciamientos* in the finest Spanish tradition. Such
political instability was an irritation and a nuisance to those groups who
wanted stability in order to achieve greater economic expansion. By
1866 it was becoming clear that Isabella's tenure of throne was liable
to be terminated and discussions about her successor had already begun
in various quarters.

In Lisbon, the French Minister was convinced that Dom Luis of
Portugal was actively interested in the succession and that behind the
scenes he was engaged in negotiations with various Spanish politicians.
On one occasion the King stressed how suitable his candidature would
be from the point of view of Napoleon III who would not accept the
Duke de Montpensier (the Orleanist Prince or any other ruler liable to
be hostile to France's interests in the Peninsula.[13]

The attitude of the French Foreign Ministry, particularly under
Walewski and Drouyn de Lhuys was to discourage any such visions, for
fear of upsetting England by producing another gaffe like that of the
Spanish marriages. Officially, the Emperor followed the same line but,
as has already been pointed out, it would be a mistake to attribute total
consistency to Napoleon III, given his *penchant* for grandiose schemes
and it is clear that he was taken up with the idea of Iberian union even
if only spasmodically. There is an interesting petition, received in the
Imperial Cabinet on 18th September, 1867, signed by many representatives of commercial interests in France which *inter alia* begs the Emperor
to act in the Peninsula by producing a united country in which Spain
would acquire Portugal and Gibraltar. This type of fantasy seems to
have been at least momentarily taken seriously, if an underlining of this
passage may be so interpreted.[14] It was litlte wonder that the French
Ambassador in Madrid, Mercier de l'Ostende, told his minister in Paris
(the Marquis de Moustier that in all the disturbance in the Peninsula
"they always make use of the Emperor's name."[15]

However, all this was fairly nebulous and had it not been for the
final crisis of Isabella's reign, which cost her the throne in September,
1868, all questions of Iberian union and candidature would probably
have remained speculative. With the actual declaration of a vacancy on
the Spanish throne a very different situation arose, and it was quite
clearly one in which France would have a more than tangential interest.
Causes both proximate and remote; historical, economic, political, and
strategic factors all combined to make the Spanish candidature a matter

of vital importance for Napoleon III. That is precisely why Bismarck chose it as a means of provoking France.

The Emperor's personal interest in the events which began in Spain in the autumn of 1868 is proved by his request that all dispatches from Madrid should be sent to him in cypher. At the same time Imperial policy was made clear by a telegram from Biarritz instructing the Minister for Foreign Affairs that : "Great care is to be taken to see that no interference occurs in the internal affairs of Spain. In every case, you must act in concert with England."[16] It was this determination to act in concert with England which conditioned many of the Emperor's subsequent moves in the question of the candidature. Although there is ample evidence to show that Napoleon could not resist the temptation to try and promote the Portuguese candidacy, and with it union of the crowns of Spain and Portugal, it is equally clear that he would only push the policy if England would acquiesce.[17]

This attitude seemed further to complicate what was already a very tortuous situation, and one fraught with danger for France. What is more, it could be argued that in pursuing the chimera of Iberian union Napoleon III delayed the choice of a candidate just long enough to enable Bismarck to assess the real value of the Spanish crisis as a means of provoking France into war.

This is not to imply that the succession question would have been other than marginally less complex had Napoleon not entangled it with the question of the Iberian union. Even without that additional complication the list of possible successors to Isabella was far ranging in its suggestions. In October, 1868, it included Prince Alfred (of England), the King of the Belgians (who would relinquish his country to Napoleon III), Prince Amadeos of Savoy, and King Luis of Portugal. This list made as yet no mention of Leopold of Hohenzollern-Sigmaringen, though it was already being pointed out in Spanish newspapers that his wife was sister to the King of Portugal and that, therefore, he had Iberian connections.

In the winter of 1868-69 the question of the Portuguese candidature was seriously discussed in Madrid, Lisbon, and Paris. Part of the trouble in coming even to a first resolution was the existence of two Kings in Portugal, Luis, the reigning monarch, and his father Dom Fernando, husband of the late Queen Maria II (who had died in 1851). Both Kings were aware they could become involved in the Spanish candidature, but neither wanted to be committed to any discussions until they had assurances of support from France, or at least a lack of opposition from England. In Madrid, General Prim, the

"King-maker" and Olozaga, felt the thing was possible, that is the accession of a Portuguese monarch: "providing that one can count on the help of France and England." The answer to this dispatch, annotated in the hand of Napoleon III, was to instruct Mercier de l'Ostende (by telegram) to sound out the English Minister to find what England's reactions would be.[18]

Clarendon's reaction from the Foreign Office was to warn off the Portuguese from becoming involved, but for once the Portuguese were not prepared to bow to the will of their ally. In Lisbon matters were now moving quite quickly, for the King had dismissed the government of the Marquis de Loulé and had appointed the Duke of Saldanha to form a new ministry. In view of Saldanha's "Iberian" background this was seen in many political quarters as a positive step in the direction of a Portuguese-Spanish combination. When Saldanha was transferred to Paris as Minister, the task of forming a new government being entrusted to another Iberianist, it was assumed that this was to tie the whole thing up with Napoleon III, and that a Portuguese candidacy for Spain would soon be officially announced.

This was exactly what was being attempted. In April, 1869, Saldanha left the Paris Legation and went to London to see the Foreign Secretary, Lord Clarendon. He informed Clarendon that: "... on his arrival in Paris he had been charged by the Emperor of the French to press upon the King of Portugal the acceptance of the Spanish crown which would certainly be offered to him by the constituent Cortes." Saldanha professed to believe that if the King refused, Spain would be so offended that she would attack Portugal. In such an unlikely event, Clarendon said, England would support Portugal.[19] He did not, however, rise to the bait and say that the best way to avoid such an occurrence would be for the King of Portugal not to refuse the profferred crown.

At the same time as Saldanha was trying out the terrain in London, General Prim was making enquiries from the Spanish side by testing the reactions of the English Minister in Madrid, and this diplomatic offensive would seem to have been inspired by the Tuileries. All that could be got out of Clarendon so far was an assurance to the French that England would not support Montpensier "... the most deplorable of all" [possible candidates], but that England would not commit herself.[20] Neither Saldanha nor Prim could elicit any more positive a response to their inquiries.

This led to despondency in both Lisbon and Madrid and to an outburst from Serrano, the Spanish Foreign Minister who said: "We have nothing to hope from England. Only with France can we obtain those things which we want: Iberian union, the restitution of Gibraltar and the maintenance of our African possessions."[21]

Unfortunately, for all concerned, France was not disposed to move without England, but since Clarendon and the English government would give no clear indication of their choice, Napoleon III was obliged to go on hesitantly pushing the Portuguese candidature in the hope that he could persuade either Luis or Fernando to accept the Crown and then persuade England to accept this solution. Luis had, it would seem, abandoned any further thought of the crown for himself and from now on the hopes of the Iberianists and the French were concentrated around his father Dom Fernando. Unfortunately, Fernando hesitated and shuffled and could not be brought to resolution. At times it looked as if he might, particularly after his morganatic marriage in June, 1869, to the German-born actress Elisa Hensler. This marriage was highly unpopular in Lisbon, particularly among the society of the Portuguese capital, whose members combined a high degree of indulgence towards themselves with great severity towards the lapses of others. This particular union was considered to be an outstanding example of *mésalliance* because the lady's reputation in Lisbon was not based wholly on an appreciation of her theatrical talents.

There were constant attacks in the Portuguese press on Fernando and his wife and it was even suggested on one occasion that the Comtesse ". . . would feel more at home in the bed of Queen Isabella than in that of Queen Donna Maria of blessed memory." The transference of Fernando to Spain, it was suggested, would be a relief for both the Portuguese treasury and the state.

So infuriated were Fernando and his wife by this type of snide comment that their interest in the Spanish throne revived and the autumn and early winter of 1869-70 were taken up with further discussions between Lisbon, Madrid, and Paris about the possibility of the King's acceptance. Fernando would only accept, literally, at a price. Sums of money were discussed, and at one stage the French Minister informed his government that Fernando's acceptance was assured if France would guarantee him a sum of 12,000,000 francs in case the Spanish rejected him. The King averred that he could not accept the prospect of a beggarly old age.[22]

This transaction was indignantly repulsed by the Quai d'Orsay, with a comment that it was "outrageous" and the negotiations foundered once again.

By 1870 the frustrations of the pro-unionists was such that in May

they carried out a *coup d'état* in Portugal, led by Saldanha, to force
Fernando to accept the Spanish throne in spite of himself. This
scheme was hatched in Paris between Prim's representative Olozaga
and Saldanha. The proof of this is in a letter from Lord Howden (a
former British minister in Madrid) to Lord Lyons, the English
Ambassador in Paris. Howden's letter is dated June, 1870, but it states
specifically, *à propos* of the question of Saldanha's activities in the
autumn of 1869 : "The whole business was arranged eight months ago
between Olozaga and that turbulent old charlatan, Saldanha, before the
latter left Paris with, of course, the latitude as to time and executions
which such hazardous attempts require. I can speak of this with
personal assurance, as it was about this time, when it was supposed that
I would go to Madrid (as Minister) and the whole scheme was
presented to me with a view to obtaining my complicity."

Given Napoleon III's relationship with both men it would not
perhaps be too fanciful to imagine that the Emperor knew what was
afoot.[23] Certainly, on the day that Saldanha carried through his *coup* in
Lisbon a personal letter from Napoleon III was delivered to Dom Luis
by Adolphe Ollivier, brother of the French minister. This letter, written
as the Emperor said, at the request of the Spanish Ambassador,
endorsed Fernando's candidacy. This was at least marginal support for
Saldanha's aims.[24] Clarendon was of the opinion that Napoleon had
been even more anxious to find a solution favourable to himself after
January 1870 in case the Duke de Montpensier was chosen, particularly
since : "... his [new] government having Orleanist proclivities will
probably not share their master's fears about the danger to France of
Montpensier wearing that Crown of Thorns."[25]

But whatever the solution was to be, it was clearly by the early
summer of 1870 not going to be a Portuguese one, and it is sad to
reflect that while an *opéra bouffe* was going on in Lisbon a *grand
guignol* was being prepared at Potsdam and Varzin. Already the
Hohenzollern candidature had been tabled officially in October, 1869,
in a pamphlet by Don Eusebio de Salazar entitled *Soluciones de la
cuestión Dinastica*, after Leopold had been sounded out as to what his
response would be. Bismarck had certainly kept an eye on the whole
question of what was to happen in Spain knowing full well not only
France's traditional interest but, in view of her recently expanded
economic advantages her particular interest in obtaining a favourable
solution. That is why he had supported Montpensier in 1868 since this
was a candidature bound to cause great annoyance in Paris not only at
a political, but at a personal level, since Napoleon III could only

view with disfavour the prospect of an Orleanist King of Spain.[26] It was only when Leopold emerged as a "better buy" from Bismarck's point of view, because of Napoleon's very sharp reaction to the suggestion of his candidacy, that he dropped Montpensier. It may well have been that he was also aware of English coolness towards the Montpensier solution and he had no wish to involve England in this particular game.

Quite certainly Bismarck knew in the spring of 1869 that France was hostile to any suggestion of a Hohenzollern candidate. Benedetti, the French Ambassador in Berlin, had been instructed to inquire into rumours of Leopold's "Kingworthiness" in March, 1869. He had received an assurance from the Prussian Foreign Ministry, though not from Bismarck personally, since he was absent, that there was no question of any such proposal. The visit of Leopold to Berlin in April-May, 1869, seemed to give the lie to this assertion, however, and Benedetti was told by his government to watch carefully. The Emperor himself instructed Benedetti that: "The candidacy of the Prince of Hohenzollern is essentially anti-national : the country will not tolerate it and it must be prevented."[27] Napoleon's suspicions were well founded. In spite of Prussian demands, the Spanish envoy sent by Prim, Don Eusebio Salazar, had discussed Leopold's candidacy with Bismarck, as indeed Bismarck admitted in May, 1869, when asked directly by Benedetti. It must have been reassuring for Bismarck to find that he had picked the right candidate. Every French inquiry underlined the importance of Leopold.

Bismarck had already in 1867 expressed a hope that France would attack Germany since this would have a beneficial effect on the move towards national unity.[28] The Prussian minister had announced to Benedetti that as far as unification was concerned *le courant de notre eau nous y porte fatalement,* and Bismarck was aware of the necessity of keeping the current flowing strongly, so long as Prussia could canalize and direct it. As the year of 1869 drew on, it was clear that there were contrary winds rising in various parts of Germany and Bismarck was impressed by the need for action to avoid being driven off course.

In Prussia itself, the immense military machine, although it had paid handsome dividends, was costly to maintain and in 1869 there were indications in the Prussian *Landtag* that the Catholics were making common cause with the "Greater Germany" liberals, and even the anti-clericals, on a joint programme of anti-militarism and economies in expenditure. The attacks by these "traditional" groups were reinforced, even though feebly, by the new Social Democratic Labour Party founded at Eisenach in 1869, whose leaders, Bebel and Liebknecht, hated Bismarck, the Prussian state and all that it stood for.

In Würtemburg and Bavaria in spite of the military alliance made in 1866, there was ever increasing opposition to "Prussianism" and a "Protestant *Reich*" and in the spring of 1870 Bismarck lost an ally in Bavaria when Hohenlohe was turned out at the elections and a Bavarian "patriot" ministry was formed. Bismarck who had been trying to get the South German states to solicit for entry into the North German Confederations, had received a setback by this loss and he was certainly telling the truth when he admitted in his *Reflections and Reminiscences* that "... the gulf between North and South ... could not be more effectively bridged than by a common national war against the neighbouring nation, our aggressor for centuries."[29]

Pressure of events at home, combined with a near certainty of France's lack of any allies, for Bismarck dismissed talk of a Franco-Austrian, or a Franco-Italian agreement as "conjectural rubbish," meant that Prussia must move as quickly as possible. Negotiations between the two branches of the Hohenzollern family about the acceptance of the Spanish crown had gone on through the autumn and winter of 1869-70. Spanish emissaries had come and gone and Prince Leopold and his father had proved in some ways as irresolute as the father and son at Lisbon. The difference was that in Lisbon there was no one to push a decision, whereas in Berlin there was. Napoleon III was not decided enough to get his man in, whoever it was to be, he could only prevent a decision from being made. This left Bismarck to make the running.

On 15th March, 1870, under the guise of a private dinner party, a Crown Council was held in Berlin. Present was the possible candidate, accompanied by his father, Bismarck, the King of Prussia and Crown Prince Frederick, and Von Roon and Von Moltke, the business men of the Prussian state. All agreed the candidature should go forward, though the King reserved his position as head of the House of Hohenzollern to consider what was best for the family's interest. With this assurance that domestically there would be virtually no opposition, Bismarck had now to take a final reckoning of the odds against him in Europe.

Although it seemed fairly certain that France would have no ally in the event of a Franco-Prussian war, Bismarck had no desire to face the unexpected. Consequently the English Government had been sounded out via the Princess Victoria, married to Crown Prince Frederick, who wrote to her mother on 12th March asking what she thought of the proposed candidature. On Lord Clarendon's advice the Queen Victoria replied that it was not something on which she would comment in either sense, thus indicating to those in Berlin that England would not be drawn.[30]

Leopold's candidacy was now pressed with vigour. In Spain there were three Prussian representatives, Major von Versen, Bucher, and Theodor von Bernhard's, the latter *un homme de confiance* of Bismarck's who had armed him with money to bribe any reluctant deputies in the Cortes in Madrid. After a great deal of tortuous negotiation Bismarck managed to set it up and by June Leopold had accepted the throne with the agreement of King William of Prussia.[31]

On 25th June Napoleon III belatedly began to use his influence to produce a quick settlement of the Spanish question. He had now come to view the best solution as being a Regency for Isabella's son Alfonso, a Regency in which French influence was no doubt envisaged, but this meant that Alfonso's mother must formally abdicate. On 25th June Isabella did so. The important thing was now for France to get her solution accepted before Prussia did. This might have worked, though given the advanced state of Bismarck's plot and the vacillations of Napoleon III it is not very likely, had not the "accident" of a mistake in the ciphering of a telegram at Madrid led to the news of Leopold's candidature becoming publicly known.[32] The group which was wrongly decoded was the one giving the dates of the arrival of the Spanish representative, Salazar, from Germany. Instead of 1st July, it read 9th July, and since the Cortes was to be dissolved on 1st July this meant that there could be no reconvening until November—unless for a very special reason. In being thus forced to give reason, Salazar let the cat out of the bag.

The official breaking of the news in France produced a violent uproar. On 6th July Gramont the new Foreign Minister made a statement in the Legislative Body which was bellicose in its tenor. In spite of Napoleon III's orders to tone it down by removing certain phrases, these were re-inserted, with Ollivier's agreement, and the speech was delivered in challenging tones ending with the cry that: "we should know how to do our duty without hesitation or weakness." Since the Spanish Cortes had agreed to re-assemble on 20th July Napoleon III had little time left in which to prevent the acceptance by Leopold. This was one of the more deplorable aspects of the whole affair, that after all the months of hesitation at the end only a week was available to try and produce complicated and delicate diplomatic manoeuvres.

Given the Emperor's health (he was extremely ill and in great pain and had been told he must avoid fatigue and strain) it is quite astonishing that France won the diplomatic war in the short space of time she had. French protests and diplomatic pressure were directed towards getting Leopold to stand down. Sooner or later this meant a confrontation with Prussia, at least in the person of King William, and on 9th July Benedetti saw the King to present him France's case and to ask that he advise Leopold to give up his candidacy.

William drew a distinction between his family and his royal position. As King of Prussia he was not acting in the matter officially nor was Bismarck advising him as such. He was simply the head of a dynasty being advised by a private citizen and so he must wait to see what Leopold himself wished. Benedetti indicated that he feared this over-subtle position might be incomprehensible to French public opinion which would see Prussia as the prime mover, with her King acting as head of his state rather than head of his house.

Benedetti was pressed by his government to get a positive answer from the King, who avoided committing himself on the grounds that he had no communication from his family at Sigmaringen. Tired of a policy of delays, and fearing that if France did not move Prussia would have a military advantage, Gramont telegraphed to Benedetti on 11th July asking for an answer " . . . negative or affirmative. We must have it by tomorrow, the day after tomorrow would be too late."[33]

On 12th July the whole incident terminated when Charles Anton of Hohenzollern Sigmaringen renounced the throne on his son's behalf. Napoleon and Ollivier were delighted at this fall out of the affair since they judged it to be, quite rightly, a triumph for France. In so far as there was to be no Hohenzollern in Spain the victory was complete, but it was not enough for sections of the French Chambers and public opinion who demanded that the King of Prussia publicly associate himself with the withdrawal. This was the background to the telegram which Gramont sent to Benedetti at seven o'clock on the evening of 12th July which, while informing Benedetti officially of Prince Anton's renunciation of the throne on Leopold's behalf added: "In order that this renunciation . . . should have an effect, it seems necessary that the King of Prussia should associate himself with it and give us an assurance that he will not renew the candidature. Will you please go immediately to the King to ask for this declaration, which he will not refuse, unless he is truly motivated by some *arrière Pensée*. In spite of the renunciation which is now [publicly] known, the turbulence of opinion in such that we do not know if we shall be able to master it."[34]

The sending of this telegram was the fatal move in the whole slide to war, since it was interpreted by Benedetti in such a way as to lead him to interview the King of Prussia in the public gardens at Ems to ask for the guarantee of non-renewal and it was Bismarck's doctored account of this meeting which gave the final push into war.[35] In fairness to French policy, and to Benedetti, it must never be forgotten that the Ems incident in itself would not have produced war had not Bismarck "edited" the famous telegram.

Why had Gramont sent the telegram to the Ambassador? As Benedetti himself clearly saw, this was to open a new and very delicate phase in the negotiations, since it was now a straight duel between France and Prussia in which Spain was only a factor. In this face to face confrontation, war was a very possible outcome in case of a Prussian refusal to give a satisfactory reply.

Did the French want war? Or, to be more specific and accurate, *who* in France wanted war, and for what reasons? Although it must be stressed again that in the last report the war was made by Bismarck's fudging of the Ems telegram, yet an answer must be given as to why the French accepted the bait so readily.

In *French Opinion on War and Diplomacy during the Second Empire,* a work to which reference has frequently been made throughout this book, the point is made that the war with Prussia was clearly a popular one. It was as if all the pent-up feelings of resentment against France's apparently poor showing in Europe in the last four years simply exploded. All the observers agree on this and the Austrian-Hungarian Ambassador, Metternich, neatly summarized the position when he telegraphed to Vienna: "Here they absolutely want war, very great agitation, the cause popular, the outcome dangerous."[36]

Paris was particularly turbulent and the evening of 12th July saw the boulevards full of people, many singing the *Marseillaise* and crying: "*A Berlin, à Berlin!*" An atmosphere of feverish excitement had taken over the capital, and the Legislative Body and the Senate, both sitting late, carried out their deliberations in this atmosphere of "*Il faut en finir.*"

Why did the ministers not attempt to rein in this delirium? The answer lay partly in the fact that the situation was probably too far gone to be retrievable, but this is only a partial explanation. Far more important was the attitude of Ollivier himself, who was as much concerned with his own political position as he was about the international crisis. Not the least of the elements of tragedy in the events of

July, 1870, was that France was not only militarily but *politically* unprepared for war. The new system was too new; it was not at all clear for example where responsibility for decision-making lay and this helped to bring about the virtual collapse in the direction of policy between 12th and 14th July. The Emperor was ill and in great pain, aggravated no doubt by the intensity of the crisis, and was unable to bring his influence to bear decisively on the meetings of Ministers. It is this which has led to the charges made from various sources that it was the Empress Eugénie who was the preponderant influence at the Council of 12th July where the decision was taken which led to Gramont's telegram to Benedetti.[37]

It would seem, however, futile to try and apportion guilt or blame in a situation in which nearly all the participants were neither guiltless nor blameless, even if the sins which caused their guilt were frequently of omission rather than commission.

The most ambivalent figure of all is Ollivier. It has been argued that he was powerful and that he hoped for a moderate solution in July. Yet he did not discourage Gramont's bellicose declaration and he had committed himself as early as January by saying that any public check to France by Prussia would mean war. "We who have to render an account to parliament and the country are less able than the former government to put up with any wound to the national pride." Here was the main source of Ollivier's weakness. The former government and system which he felt he had to replace, that of *Rouhernement*, was associated with a pacific policy, almost a policy of "appeasement." Rouher had accepted Sadowa and he talked of a Germany of "three slices" which was no threat to France. Rouher had been against a diplomatic offensive against Prussia and his whole policy seemed to Ollivier to have been cowardly, timorous, and weak. It was this which made him say angrily on 6th July when the Hohenzollern crisis was really getting under way: "Prussia wishes to do us violence, but it is no longer Rouher, it is no longer La Valette who directs the policy of France."[38] Ollivier was determined not to pursue a policy like that of his predecessor and with this went the fear that any weakness and lack of control on his part would lead the Emperor to jettison him and re-install the *Vice-Empereur*. Ollivier knew that the abortive negotiations with Italy and Austria were being conducted in some measure behind his back by the Emperor, using Rouher, but he was resolved that the Emperor's indulging of himself in such intrigues should not be allowed to assist the former minister back to power.

Ollivier's weakness was his vanity and his inability to accept criticism. He had informed the Emperor in January, 1870, that: "I am happy because I believe I am saving your dynasty,"[39] and he never budged from this view. He never willingly accepted advice and so was constantly surprised when things fell out in a way in which, had he troubled to listen to others, he might have foreseen. Had Ollivier been able to sink his differences with Rouher in the crisis of 1870 he might at least have been able to control the Chambers rather than give them their head. Had he really tried, with Gramont, to work out what France's international position was, in terms of allies, he might at least have spared himself the fatal words about entering war "with a light heart."

It is no use to say that Gramont as Foreign Minister was responsible for misleading Ollivier (and others) about the state of France's nego- tiations with Austria-Hungary and Italy; Ollivier had appointed Gramont, and in any case he held the overall responsibility for the men he had chosen. Apart from this, Ollivier's difficulties in the *Corps Législatif* where he was harassed by Right and Left, meant that he was anxious for a showdown and further complicated the issue. As Allain Targé said in July: "Why did they go to war? Because they would not have remained ministers if they hadn't". To say this, however, is merely to underline the point already made about the confusion which existed as to the nature and location of responsibility in the government. The tragedy was that the Second Empire in its agonies was no longer a personal government but it was still the government of a person, and that person was Napoleon III. The Emperor's personal catastrophe lay in the fact that not only was he ill and in great physical pain but that he had become a pawn in a political game in which both Right and Left in the Chamber clamoured for war, each hoping to profit in a different way. Far from being a dynastic folly the Franco-Prussian war was a political manoeuvre urged on by Thiers and Jules Favre; Thiers, who had opposed the army reforms, and rearmament, and Favre who had denounced the follies of Imperial foreign policy. Little wonder that Rouher reminded Gambetta in 1878 during a debate in the National Assembly, "Don't you know that the war of 1870 was the work of the opposition?"

In fact the Empire had crumbled before it fell and it was not just military defeat but political confusion which was responsible for the ultimate débàcle. The Emperor dragged his sick, weary and useless way with his bewildered armies because there was nowhere else for him to go. By August he was no longer merely an encumbrance he had be- come an embarrassment. This was stated clearly by *The Times* on 12th August, 1870, which declared: "The dynasty that still reigns in

France is commonly thought of as a thing of the past." Napoleon's return to Paris was not wanted by the Right who persuaded the Empress to instruct him not to come back, nor by the Left, who in early August clamoured for an arming of the people and who already saw themselves as saviours of (Republican) France. In the end all the Emperor could hope for was death and even this was denied him. On 2nd September, bottled up in Sedan with MacMahon's "army" he sent a personal message to the King of Prussia : "Having been unable to die in the midst of my soldiers it only remains for me to surrender my sword to Your Majesty."[40] This was the literal truth. There was nothing remaining for him to do, except go to into captivity. Did he reflect at Sedan that he was only one hundred kilometres from Ham? It was just the sort of thought which might well have occurred to him. But this time there was to be no escape for him and, in fact, he never saw France again.

On Sunday, 4th September, the Republic was proclaimed in Paris and on the same day the Empress fled from Paris to England.

The Emperor later commented on the fall of the Empire that he could not believe ". . . that this nation, formerly so generous and so chivalrous, would take advantage of the moment of my misfortunes to avenge itself for imaginery injuries. No, it is not the nation which has done this . . . it is certain men—but, *mon Dieu*, what men !"

Epilogue

*"L'Assemblée nationale ... confirme la
déchéance de Napoléon III et de sa
dynastie ... et le déclare responsable de la
ruine, de l'invasion, et du démembrement de
la France."*

Assemblée Nationale, Résolution, 1st March,
1871

"It has sometimes seemed to me that the
French set up their heroes, so to speak, on
pillars of salt, so that when the first storm
strikes them, they tumble down to lie forever
in the mud. In no country in the world is the
step from the sublime to the ridiculous so
often made."

Empress Eugénie, September, 1870

AMONG the passengers disembarking from the cross-channel steamer at Dover on the afternoon of 20th March, 1871, was a smallish, ill-looking man who, as he slowly descended the gangway was greeted by the cheers and waves of a substantial crowd which had gathered at the quayside. Men waved their hats and sticks in the air and many of the ladies threw flowers. The man who stopped, obviously in amazement and distress, and who stood, with tears pouring down his cheeks, acknowledging their cheers, was Napoleon III come again to exile in England. This reception was a rare example of kindness shown to the fallen sovereign not only in his time, but subsequently.

The historian of the Second Empire is never unaware of how unpopular the period is and how much opprobrium still attaches to the name of Napoleon III—not only in France, but almost everywhere.[1] The nicknames which have pursued the Emperor for a century after his death are almost all derogative: *Badinguet, Crapulinski, Napoléon le Petit, Tom Pouie Attila, Moustachu*; none of these soubriquets, and there were many more like them, reveal any affection for the man, though it is true that the Paris working-class use of *Moustachu* was not meant to be totally offensive. Why has the Emperor continued to have a bad press even after death? *De Mortuis . . .* has rarely been applied to him and though the last fifty years have seen events and persons, both in France and in Europe, which make the Second Empire look like a paradise and the Emperor only a pantomime demon King, yet still time is found to abuse and ridicule a vanished regime and a dead man. There is, of course, nothing new or startling in this, for all regimes and many of the dead figures of history are subjected to the same treatment. Yet, the Second Empire appears to tap a particularly bilious duct in historians or indeed in anyone who finds themselves involved in a study of the period and it is for this reason that some attempt must be made to ascertain why.

The answer partly lies in the fact that the Emperor and his regime had the misfortune to attract the venom of some of the most prominent literary geniuses of the time—not only in France but also in England— and the literature inspired by the period persists long after the events and the people which provoked it, have disappeared. So, a mythology has been perpetuated which has as much basis in fact now as it had at the time it was written. It was not the least of the Empire's misfortunes that it housed a great many of France's foremost writers, musicians and painters most of whom, while denouncing the stifling atmosphere with which they were surrounded, managed to produce some very remark- able work. Of the great mass, few could be counted as partisans of the regime. Sainte-Beuve, Mérimée, Sardou, are probably the only pro- Imperialist names which mean anything to the casual observer of the mid-nineteenth century French literary scene. The list of opponents, the Goncourts, Flaubert, Baudelaire, Hugo and so on, is much greater and longer.

Perhaps one reason why the literary world was so hostile arose from the domination of the *Académie Française* by Orleanists and liberal Catholics for most of the twenty years of the Empire's existence. Guizot was the Grand Master and presided over an assemblage which never lost any occasion for spite when it came to dealing with the Emperor or the regime. Candidates known to be favoured by the Tuileries were certain not to be elected so that, for example, in 1869, Théophile Gautier was refused admission and a complete nonentity, Barbier, elected instead. In these circumstances it is surely not surprising that the regime was associated wth philistinism since often it had no choice but to avoid bestowing the kiss of death of Imperial patronage.

Undoubtedly the greatest opponent of the regime was Victor Hugo.

He had left Paris on the day of the *coup d'état* of 1851 and had gone to the Channel Islands. First at St. Helier and then at Guernsey. Here, poised between two phobias, for he also disliked England, he awaited for eighteen years the doom of his villain. He never ceased to apostrophize and condemn just as he never ceased to write.

It was not just that Hugo found endless material in the very person of Napoleon III :

> *Cassé de débauches, l'oeil terne,*
> *Furtif, les traits palis*

Hugo became the *chef d'orchestre* of the Republican Party, presenting them with new arrangements of old themes, daring variations and entire new works. Not all this work was of first rate quality, not even the greatest admirer of Hugo could claim this for *Les Châtiments,* but even when it was poor poetry, it was superb invective, rarely manifesting that it sprang from emotion recollected in tranquillity."

Hugo's hate sometimes led him to read like a travesty of the litany of the saints as in :

> *Valsez, Billault, Parieu, Drouyn, Leboeuf, Delangle!*
> *Danse, Dupin! Dansez l'horrible et le bouffon!*
> *Hyénes, loups, chacals, non prevus par Buffon,*
> *Leroy, Forey, tueurs au fer rongé de rouilles,*
> *Dansez! Dansez! Berger, d'Hautpoul, Murat, citrouilles.*

The point was certainly made and it is still taken, as though it were unthinkable that France's greatest poet could have been politically in

It was not only the politics of the Empire which revolted Hugo, it was also the lack of morality in the narrowest sense, which it seemed to exude. The Emperor and his debauchery revolted the exile who lived in a bigamous *ménage à trois* and the gayer the Empire became the more Hugo found it offensive. The *fastes de l'Empire* were an affront to the purity and sobriety of republican living which, it seemed, could pardon mistresses but never forgive the waltz at the Tuileries.

Others, like the Goncourts, rejected the Empire because it had no taste and inclined to "Caesarean socialism." Jules, the younger of the two brothers, thought that :

> *Dans l'ancien régime, tout se tient il y a un gouvernement légendaire. Un droit divin, des nobles de sang noble. Tout cela était discutable. Mais aujourd'hui on a un gouvernement démocratique, avec un Empereur en haut, au dessous les principes de '89, le culte idolâtre pour un homme, l'Eglise baisant les bottes de César! Stupide et odieux.*

The Goncourts, emotionally partisans of the *ancien régime* but politically Orleanist, were typical of many who, with infinitely less talent than themselves, haunted the Orleanist salons where *bons mots* against the regime and the Emperor and the Empress were aired and collected. The nearest the Goncourts allowed themselves to get to the Empire was through their contact with Princess Mathilde, the Emperor's cousin who had just missed being his wife, who ran what was virtually the only salon in Paris in which the regime was not overtly attacked—though Mathilde had reservations about many things which were done, and maintained until death a personal vendetta against the Empress. The Goncourts forgave her because she was a woman who *"se trouvait par hasard être une princesse"*.[2]

It was in Princess Mathilde's salon in her hôtel in the rue de Courcelles that the élite of letters met. The Princess, it was said, had missed the throne but reigned at her table. To it she invited Taine, Renan, Flaubert, Pasteur, Carpeaux, Ollivier, the Goncourts and many others whose politics were far from Imperialist. Her librarian was Théophile Gautier, but her real "lion" was Sainte-Beuve, whom she had made a Senator. It was she who pressed the Emperor for rewards and favours for her friends, in her role as *Notre Dame des Arts*, and she attempted to fill the void created by the absence of any literary and artistic circle at the Tuileries.[3]

Perhaps it would have been better for the Empire's posthumous reputation if Napoleon and Eugénie had encouraged some sort of literary and artistic côterie but in this respect they followed the general trend of courts in the nineteenth century which were distinguished by and large, for their lack of patronage of the arts in this way. Napoleon III was much more impressed by Pasteur the scientist and Victor Duruy the educationalist than he was by Courbet the artist, or musicians like Gounod, or Berlioz, for the simple reason that he was more interested in "progress" than in culture. It may be deplorable, but it was a common feature of the nineteenth century.

What is strange is that France has found it possible to forgive Napoleon I but cannot forgive Napoleon III. In August, 1968, an interesting article on Napoleon III appeared in *Le Figaro* in which the author pointed out that it was extraordinary how *Badinguet* was still reviled. Yet: "The 2nd of December was a mere bagatelle compared with the blood which Cavaignac had made to flow two years earlier. Who talks of it nowadays except some fervent historians? There have been, in history, twenty tyrants, a hundred tyrants more costly than

Napoleon III. Nevertheless it is him who is savaged. He is the national
tête de turque."

Certainly the first Napoleon cost France more in many ways than did
the third of the name. If it is true that Alsace and Lorraine were lost,
temporarily, it is equally true that Savoy and Nice were gained,
permanently. Sedan was not a victory, but neither was Waterloo. This
gives rise to the speculation that perhaps the real victory lay in choosing
the date of one's defeat. Napoleon I chose a better time to be defeated
and to die as the exiled "martyre of St. Helena". This was just the sort of
stuff which was needed in an era of romanticism, the aura of which
surrounded Napoleon's whole career. To see the flaming meteor of the
revolution extinguished in the Atlantic Ocean was a dramatic sight, and
it lost nothing in the telling in numerous versions by numerous writers
who were aided and abetted by the great Emperor himself during his
lifetime.[4]

For Napoleon III after defeat there was only imprisonment, and
exile in England. Death came from an operation in a house in Kent
which, far from being a Bonapartist shrine, is today a golf-club.
Wherever the great Napoleon's foot trod some sort of commemorative
point is made. Wherever Napoleon III's foot trod, certainly in France,
all traces have, where possible, been scrubbed away.

Perhaps the saddest comment on the end of the Empire is that French
political life could accommodate Thiers better than Napoleon III and
that today, while Napoleon III is without any monument in France,
virtually no city or town in that country is without its *Boulevard Thiers,*
or its *Avenue Thiers,* or its *Place Thiers.* Napoleon III's monument is to
be found at Farnborough Abbey, Hampshire. Even his corpse is unacceptable in France.

It is in vain that the historian tries to point out that here was a man
of heart as well as head. A dreamer and a thinker as well as a doer. A
man who hated blood and destruction to such an extent that he fatally
weakened his policies by not gearing himself to a cold hard world in
which power must be expressed in terms of force rather than in forceful
terms.

No sentimental literature sprang up about Napoleon III. No heroic
paintings hang on museum walls, no national commemorations, no
grandiose tombs. All has been denied him. Even Karl Marx thought
Bismarck's war had been from Germany's point of view "a war of
defence" and had in 1870 announced that "the French need a thrashing."

In an age dominated by the doctrine of self-help and success,
Napoleon III was a failure. He was not a man for whom Samuel

Smiles would have felt much sympathy. To many in Europe, the Prussian victory was a moral as well as a military one, whereby Catholic France had been punished for her frivolity and wickedness by upright God-fearing Protestant Prussia. Who could condemn a conquering army which celebrated its victory by singing *Nun danket alle Gott.. ?* The brutalities of the Prussians in France was overlooked except by those who wanted to see, and in truth, the brutalities of the Prussians to the French paled into insignificance beside the brutalities of French to French, as Thiers established his conservative Republic by butchering the Communards. The man who had been horrified by 2nd December, 1851, had no compunction about the 20,000 summarily executed in May, 1871

The triumph of German arms led to a triumph of German philosophy, and the French were left to go through an agony of self-doubt and re-appraisal. French historians, by and large, have always blamed their government and in particular Napoleon III, for what happened in 1870. German historians, except for a few on the far left, have never criticized Bismarck's policy and have seen Prussia always as the defender of Germany in a righteous cause. Sometimes they have even been joined by French writers in praising the Prussian minister. They have admired Bismarck for his resolutions and have forgiven him much because he introduced universal suffrage in the *Reich* which he founded. Apparently, universal suffrage in Bismarck's Germany was less tainted than it had been in Napoleon III's France—or someone would surely have recalled the seven and half million who had voted "yes" to the Empire in May, 1870. Given such a climate of opinion what hope was there for any rehabilitation of Napoleon III's reputation either as a sovereign or as a statesman? It was perhaps because of his awareness of the futility of even trying to defend himself that led the Emperor steadfastly to refuse during his exile to make any attempt to reply to the campaign of hate and vituperation which pursued him until his death. Surely it is possible now, one hundred years after the fall of the Empire and within a short time of the centenary of the Emperor's death in 1873, to begin a more serious and less partisan assessment of what the ruler and his government contributed to the course of French and European history?

References

PROLOGUE
1. Simpson, F. A., *The Rise of Louis Napoleon* (London, 1909) 6.

CHAPTER 1
1. Thomson, J. M., *Louis Napoleon and the Second Empire* (Oxford, 1965) 17.
2. Hortense to Louis Napoleon, quoted Proudhon (ed. Rochel, Paris, 1900) 344.

CHAPTER 2
1. Chateaubriand, *Mémoires d'Outres Tombe* (Pleiade Edn., vol. II, Paris, 1951) 294.
2. J. A. C. Buchon, the historian, visited Arenenberg in 1833. Here Louis Napoleon showed him a draft plan for the re-ordering of Italy, which he said had been prepared by his late brother.
Buchon, J. A. C., *Quelques Souvenirs de courses en Suisse et dans le pays de Bade*, 135.
3. c.f. Dansette, Adrien, *Louis Napoleon Bonaparte à la conquête du pouvoir* (Paris, 1961) 45-46 and 60-62.
4. Simpson, F. A., *The Rise of Louis Napoleon* (London, 1909) 64.
5. For a full account of this, see Dansette, Adrien, *Louis Napoleon Bonaparte à la conquête du pouvoir* (Paris, 1961) 51-53.
6. Interestingly, Louis Napoleon went on to say : "Arrange that my sister-in-law may think that it was I who carried off her husband; she suffers from the idea that he has hidden one action of his life from her."
The letter can be found in various places in French and English. Most accessible in F. A. Simpson's *Rise of Louis Napoleon* (1924 edition), 333.
7. The most exciting, and beautifully written account of the Odyssey of mother and son is in Simpson, F. A., op. cit., 69-76.
8. Louis, Paul, "L'Ouvrier Français de Louis XVIII à Louis Philippe", *Revue politique et Parlementaire* (Paris, 1946) 138-49.
9. c.f. Louis, Paul, op. cit. Also Dunham, A. L., *The Industrial Revolution in France 1815-1848* (New York, 1955) 178-83.
10. de Balzac, H., *Traité de la vie élégante* (Paris, 1830).
11. Charlety, S., *La Monarchie de Juillet* (Paris, 1921) 41.

12. The only serious work on the subject is the (unpublished) doctoral thesis submitted by Louis Chevalier to the Sorbonne in 1950, "Les fondements économiques et sociaux de l'histoire politique de la région parisienne, 1848-1870."

13. See Chapter IV following.

14. *Rêveries Politiques, Oeuvres de Napoléon III*, vol. I (Paris, 1869) 383. (All references to the *Oeuvres* are to the edition of 1869.)

15. Napoleon III,*Oeuvres*, 385.

16. Metternich to Apponyi. Quoted Dansette, A., *Louise Napoléon à la conquête du pouvoir* (Paris 1961), 69-70.

CHAPTER 3

1. Dansette, A., *Louis Napoléon à la conquête du pouvoir*, 92.

2. Text in Proudhon, P. J., *Napoleon III* (ed. Rochel, Paris, 1900) 370.

3. On a more intimate note, it was also the year in which the Prince became betrothed to his cousin, Princess Mathilde, daughter of ex-King Jerome, a betrothal later broken off because of the Strasbourg affair.

4. There are several accounts of the whole exploit. The classic account in English is in Simpson, op. cit., Ch. VI, and in Dansette, op. cit., 107-25. Louis Napoleon's letter to his mother describing this event can be found in Proudhon, P. J., *Napoléon III* (ed. Rochel, Paris, 1900) 377-87.

5. Vicomte de Ségur, *Histoire et Mémoires*, VII, 282.

6. The best, and most engaging, account of this affair is in Simpson, op. cit., 143-56.

7. Napoleon III, *Oeuvres*, I, 18.

8. *Fragments Historiques, Oeuvres*, I, 342.

9. *Idées*, I, 38.

10. Ibid., 51, 56.

11. Fisher, H. A. L., *Bonapartism* (London, 1909) 47.

12. *Idées*, I, 111.

13. Ibid., 116.

14. Ibid., 124.

15. Ibid., 128-29.

16. Ibid., 138.

17. Ibid., 154-55.

18. Ibid., 158.

19. *L'Idée Napoleonienne, Oeuvres*, I, 5-6.

20. Ibid., I, 7.

CHAPTER 4

1. The autograph copy of this letter is in the author's possession.

2. Speech by the Prosecutor, cited Fermé, A., *Boulogne d'Après les Documents authentiques* (Paris, 1868) 43-44.

3. For an analysis of the support which the Prince expected, see de la Fuye, M., & Babeau, E. A., *Louis Napoléon Bonaparte avant l'Empire* (Paris, 1951). The authors claim that, among others, Tsar Nicholas I was interested in the success of the enterprise (c.f. 141-43). The claim is not substantiated by

documentary evidence, but clearly is an interpretation of Nicholas's attitude to France brought about by the Near Eastern crisis.

4. The best account of the affair is to be found in Simpson, F. A., *The Rise of Louis Napoleon* (London, 1909).

5. Dorothée de Lieven to François Guizot. London, Stafford House, Midday. Friday, 7th August, 1840. *Lettres de François Guizot et la Princesse de Lieven*, vol. II (ed. J. Naville, 3 vols. 1963) 180-81.

6. Full text in Fermé, op. cit., 19-20.

7. Full text in Fermé, op. cit., 17 et seq.

8. The reference was to the *Colonne de la Grande Armée,* erected at Boulogne by Napoleon I to commemorate the encampment set up to contain the army made ready for the invasion of England in 1804-05.

9. Pierre Antoine Berryer lived to see his former client become Emperor, but never became reconciled to the Empire and maintained until its end an attitude of hostility. Indeed, he was regarded by many as the leading Legitimist politician in France during the period.

10. Beau de Loménie, E., *Les Responsabilités des Dynasties Bourgeoises,* vol. I (Paris, 1943) gives an interesting if tendentious analysis of these people.

11. For accounts of the trial see Saint-Edmé, A., *Procès de Napoléon Louis Bonaparte* (Paris, 1840).

Fermé, A., *Bologne d'après les documents Authentiques* (Paris, 1868).

Bohain, G., *Procès du Prince Napoléon Louis Bonaparte* (Paris, 1840).

12. Lebey, A., *Les Trois Coup d'États de L. N. Bonaparte* (Paris, 1906) 416.

13. Reynault, E., *Histoire de Huit Ans,* vol. I (Paris, 1857) 294-98.

14. *Oeuvres de Napoléon III,* I, 432, *Aux Mânes de l'Empereur.*

15. Ibid., 437.

16. He wrote to his cousin Prince Napoleon : From Ham on 15th November, 1841 : *"Je m'occupe toujours. Cependant mon travail sur Charlemagne n'advance pas beaucoup il y à tant de recherches à faire que par moments je me décourage."* D'Hauterive, *Napoléon III et le Prince Napoléon, Correspondance inédite* (Paris, 1925) 6.

17. *Progrès du Pas de Calais,* 28th October, 1843.

18. Ibid., various articles, e.g. 14th June, 1841, 18th October, 1843, and 4th December, 1843.

19. Letter of 28th October, 1843, to the editor of *Le Loiret.*

20. Emerit, M., *Madam Cornu et Napoléon III* (Paris, 1937) 21-22.

21. *Journal du Loiret,* 26th October, 1843, quoted Taxile-Delord, *Histoire du second Empire,* vol. I (Paris, 1869-70) 45-47.

22. Guitard, O. M., *Louis Napoléon Bonaparte* (Paris, 1939) 171. La Villette and the Faubourg St. Antoine were working-class areas in Paris, the latter being forever identified with the Revolution of 1789.

23. *L'Extinction du Paupérisme, Oeuvres,* II, 110.

24. Napoleon III, *Oeuvres,* II, 117 and 121, 122.

25. This literally means "body of wise men" but it has a technical meaning in that it can be translated as boards of arbitration between workers and employers. For this reason, the word arbitrator has been used to convey the meaning of *prud' homme.*

26. Napoléon III, *Oeuvres,* II, 123.

27. Ibid., 127.
28. Ibid., 132.
29. Ibid., 151.
30. Blanc, L., *L'Organisation du Travail* (ed. Marriott, Oxford, 1913) 14.
31. Richards, E. W., "Louis Napoleon and Central America," *Journal of Modern History*, vol. XXXIV, June, 1963.

CHAPTER 5
1. Higonnet, P. L.-R., & Higonnet, Trevor B., "Class, Corruption, and Politics in the French Chamber of Deputies 1846-1848," *French Historical Studies*, V, No. 2. A detailed analysis of this situation.
2. Marx said: "This was actually no real interest, no definite class: This was the February Revolution itself, the common uprising, with its illusions, its poetry, its imagined content, and its phrases." Marx, K., "The Class Struggle in France 1848-1850," *Selected Works* (Moscow, 1958) 1.
3. Jerrold, Blanchard, *The Life of Napoleon III*, vol. II (London, 1875) 393-94.
4. G. de Beaumont to Alexis de Tocqueville, 4th April, 1848. *Oeuvres de Tocqueville*, vol. VIII (ed. J. P. Mayer, Paris, 1967) 10.
5. The best study is that of McKay, D. C., *The National Workshops* (Harvard, 1933) but see also Duveau, G., *1848: The Making of a Revolution* (Trans. A. Carter, London).
6. Lavigne, P., *Le Travail dans les constiutions françaises 1789-1945* (Paris, 1948).
7. Duveau, G., *La Vie Ouvrière* . . . , 118-20.
8. *Collection des Affiches*, anon. (Paris, 1848).
9. Jerrold, Blanchard, op. cit., II, 407.
10. Alexis de Tocqueville to G. de Beaumont, 27th August, 1848. *Oeuvres de Tocqueville*, vol. VIII (ed. Mayer, Paris, 1969) 31.
11. Normanby to Palmerston, 27th November, 1848. (Confidential) Quoted in Simpson, op. cit., 316.
12. de Tocqueville to G. de Beaumont, 8th December, 1848. *Oeuvres*, VIII, 117.
13. For an excellent analysis of this and other features of the presidential election, see Tudesq, A. J., *L'Election Présidentielle de Louis Napoléon Bonaparte* (Paris, 1965).
14. Quoted Maurain, J., *Baroche, Ministre de Napoléon III* (Paris, 1936) 68.
15. Those who wish to pursue the struggle in the Assembly in detail can turn to any standard history of the Second Empire confident that no turn or twist will be omitted. At a fictional, and tendentious level, Zola's *Rougon Macquart* novels provide an interesting analysis of French society at the time. The first volume *La Fortune des Rougon* deals with the period 1848-52.
16. The speeches are collected in Volume III of the *Oeuvres* (1869 edition). They are illuminating in that they reveal Louis Napoleon's aptitude for catching the right mood of the audience. Frequently, in a skilful way, they link local patriotism to wider issues. General de Gaulle borrowed the technique.
17. Napoleon III, *Oeuvres*, III, 211-12.

18. For a detailed analysis of Bonapartist tactics in one region see Chevalier, Louis, *"Les fondements économiques et sociaux de l'histoire politique de la région parisienne, 1848-1870"* (doctorial thesis) (Paris, 1951).

19. Quoted Maurain, J., *Baroche*, 81.

20. There are indications that Thiers and some of the *Notables* were inclining towards the Prince de Joinville (son of Louis Philippe) as the next presidential candidate, but the manoeuvres are not at all clear. C.f. de Beaumont to de Tocqueville, *Correspondance*, September-November, 1851, de Tocqueville, *Oeuvres*, VIII, 402-19.

21. Napoléon III, *Oeuvres*, III, 272.

22. Simpson, F. A., *Louis Napoleon and the Recovery of France* (London, 1951 edition) 163.

CHAPTER 6

1. de Tocqueville, *Oeuvres*, VIII, 119.

2. Ibid., 95.

3. This period is well covered in the de Beaumont-Tocqueville correspondence already referred to. The letters in many instances are more informative than the official dispatches in the *Archives du Ministère des Affaires Étrangères: Correspondances Politiques, Angleterre*. The French Foreign Minister at this time, Bastide, was a man of moderate competence.

4. For the full text, see Mack Smith, D., *The Making of Italy, 1796-1870* (New York, 1968).

5. Quoted Simpson, F. A., *Louis Napoleon and the Recovery of France* (1951 edition), 56.

6. de Beaumont to de Tocqueville, 2nd December, 1848 (*Oeuvres*, VIII, 109-10).

7. This question is discussed in Simpson, F. A., *Louis Napoleon and the Recovery of France*, 39-42 and Palm, F. C., *England and Napoleon III* (Duke University Press, 1944) 32.

8. Senior, N. W., *Conversations with M. Thiers, M. Guizot and other Distinguished Persons*, vol. I (2 vols., London, 1878) 48-51.

9. For detail of this in documentary form, c.f. Mack Smith, D., *The Making of Italy, 1796-1870*, 166-70.

10. The classic pro-unification histories are the series written by G. M. Trevelyan. The first exposé of Victor Emmanuel came in *The Journal of Modern History*, vol. III (Chicago, 1935) 177-78 in an article by H. McGraw Smyth, "The Armistice of Novara."

Simpson (op. cit., 62-64) thinks that Louis Napoleon's warlike attitudes caused Austria to rethink the position and moderate her demands. It would seem, however, that this was not so.

11. de Tocqueville to de Beaumont, 11th May, 1849. "What I see as most worthy of condemnation in the government's actions, up to the present, is to have entrusted an operation bristling with difficulties of all sorts to a man like Oudinot." (*Oeuvres*, VIII, 128).

12. This view came in a letter to the young Edgar Ney, who was serving in Italy. Like many of Louis Napoleon's "private" statements it was undoubtedly intended for publication. (Text in Dansette, op. cit., 281).

13. de Beaumont to de Tocqueville, 30th September, 1849 (*Oeuvres*, VIII, 176-80).

14. de Beaumont to de Tocqueville, official dispatches of 13th, 14th and 21st October, 1849 (*Oeuvres*, VIII, 207-27).

15. Quoted La Fuye and Babeau, *Louis Napoléon Bonaparte avant l'Empire*, 313.

CHAPTER 7

1. Napoleon III, *Oeuvres*, III, 282-3.

2. *Le Conseil d'État sous le second Empire et la III République*, anon. (Paris, 1880).

3. c.f. Zeldin, T., *The Political System of Napoleon III* (London, 1958), where these difficulties have been analysed. This work is of great importance for the understanding of how the politics of France were structured between 1850 and 1870.

4. On the subject of post-1870 Bonapartism *vide* Rothney, J., *Bonapartism after Sedan* (Cornell, 1969).

5. Zeldin, T., op. cit., 19-21.

6. In December, 1852, after the Empire had been established, Deputies were paid 2,500 francs for each month of the Parliamentary session.

7. These "10th December Societies" had been established under the auspices of Persigny and other Bonapartist agents in France in 1848 in order to provide centres from which election campaigns could be mounted and Bonapartist propaganda disseminated. They tended to be a very curious amalgam of various brands of radical discontent and were, for this reason, not particularly favoured by governmental circles.

8. For a very complete analysis see Zeldin, T., op. cit., 28, 35.

9. La Gorce, P. de, *Histoire du Second Empire,* vol. I (Paris, 1905) 64-65.

10. Constitution of 1852. Napoléon III, *Oeuvres*, III, 293.

11. Montalembert, the liberal Catholic, passed a harsh judgement on it in 1857 : "No one will ever know what I suffered in that cellar without light and air where I spent six years struggling against reptiles." Montalembert was not re-elected in 1857.

12. La Gorce, op. cit., I, 106.

13. Maurain, *Baroche*, 128-29. Schnerb, *Rouher*, 62.

14. Senate address. See also Napoleon III's message of 22 Jan. 1853 concerning his marriage in *Oeuvres*, III, 357-360.

15. The best source for the courtship and marriage, and indeed the Empress Eugénie's life is Kurz, H., *The Empress Eugénie* (London, 1964).

16. Baron Hübner, *Neuf Ans de Souvenir . . .* , vol. I (Paris, 1904) 150.

17. Morny's family tree is worth reproducing :

    Louis XV—Adelaide Filleul
      Adelaide Filleul (1761)=Alexandre de Flahault
      (Mistress of Talleyrand)
        Auguste-Charles Joseph de Flahault (1785)
        Lover of Queen Hortense Bonaparte,
        (mother of Napoleon III)
          Auguste-Charles Joseph Demorny (1811)

18. Zeldin, T., *Political System of Napoleon III*, 66.

19. Maurain, *Baroche*, 156.

20. Ibid. Rouland to Baroche, 22nd July, 1857. Rouland was a conservative deputy, had been Minister of Public Instruction in 1856. Significantly, he become a Senator and governor of the Bank of France in the 1860's, when the real battle between "conservative" and "progressive" Bonapartists was being fought.

21. La Gorce, *Second Empire*, II, 207.

22. Thiers to Duc d'Aumale, 6th January, 1861. Quoted Zeldin, *Political System of Napoleon III*, 107.

23. Maurain, *Baroche*, 159n.

24. Schnerb, *Rouher*, 80.

25. Prince Napoleon to the Emperor. *Correspondance de Napoléon III et du Prince Napoléon* (ed. d'Hauterive, Paris, 1925) 141.

26. Full text in Napoléon III, *Oeuvres*, V, 73.

27. The reference to William III is from the *Fragments Historiques*, c.f. Chapter IV, 51-52.

28. Zeldin, T., *Emile Ollivier* (Oxford, 1963) 59.

29. Zeldin, *Ollivier*, 62.

30. Ibid. 66.

31. E. Ollivier, *L'Empire Libéral*, vol. V (Paris, 1895-1918) 95.

CHAPTER 8

1. Rémond, R., *La Vie Politique en France*, vol. II (1848-1879) (Paris, 1969) 223-25
Also Prélot, M., "La Signification Constitutionelle du Second Empire," *Revue Française de Science Politique, III* (January-March 1953).

2. The most recent work on the subject is Kulstein, D., *Napoleon III and the Working Class* (California State College, 1969). The author is, in general, hostile to the Empire and considers that the educational approach was a failure. (c.f. 194-95 passim.)

3. Duveau, G., *La Vie Ouvrière pendant le Second Empire*, notes, 101 that this was so in 1852. It was equally true of subsequent elections.

4. See Chapter V.

5. Duveau, op. cit., 391.

6. For examples of this type of intervention see Duveau, op. cit., 391 passim and also Huillier F. L., *La Lutte Ouvrière à la Fin du Second Empire* (Paris, 1957) especially 68 ff.

7. The most recent analysis of the working class pamphleteers is in Kulstein, op. cit., 126-35.

8. For an analysis of the policy of public works see Girard, L., *La Politique des Travaux publics du Second Empire,* (Paris, 1952) particularly Part IV.

9. For details of the *Affaire Mirès*, and for a very good analysis of the type of transaction which led to his downfall, see Cameron, Rondo E., *France and the Economic Development of Europe* (Princeton, 1961) 285-88 and 291 ff.
See also Girard, L., *Travaux Publics . . .*, 267-69.

10. For a full account of the collapse of the *Crédit Mobilier*, see Cameron,

Rondo E., op. cit., pp. 190-95. Also Pradalié, G., *Le Second Empire* (Paris, 1969), 53-6. An interesting analysis of the banking questions is "The Old Bank and the New : The Financial Revolution of the Nineteenth Century", by D. Landes in *Essays in European Economic History 1789-1914* (ed. F. Crouzet, W. H. Chaloner, and W. M. Stern, London, 1969).

11. The most readily available account of the so-called "Fould Letter," which is actually a statement before the budgetary commission of the *Corps Législatif* for 1861, is to be found in Girard, L., *Travaux publics...*, 264-75.

12. Girard, op. cit., 275.

CHAPTER 9

1. The question of Franco-Russian relations at this period are best covered in Puryear, V., *England, Russia and the Straits Question 1844-1856* (Archon Books, Connecticut, 1931, re-published 1965) (see especially note on p. 26 which is borne out by the author's checking of the *Correspondance Politique Russie*, 178 and 179, in Ministère des Affaires Etrangères, Paris).
Also valuable is Lobanov-Rostovsky, A., *Russia and Europe, 1825-1878* (Ann Arbor, Michigan, 1954) ch. IV and Florinsky, M., *Russia: A History and an Interpretation* (New York, 1960) Ch. XXXII.

2. c.f. Chapter IV above.

3. For the full text see Kertesz, G. A., *Documents in the Political History of the European Continent 1815-1939* (Oxford, 1968) 91-94.

4. See Jennings, L. C., "Lamartine's Italian Policy in 1848 : a re-examination," *Journal of Modern History*, vol. 42, 3rd September, 1970.

5. Kertesz, op. cit., 13.

6. Napoleon III, *Oeuvres*, I, 153-55.

7. Nicholas seems to have read the pamphlet in the winter of 1852, after much pressure from the anti-Bonapartist group at St. Petersburg. c.f. Palm, *England and Napoleon III*, 139.

8. The whole of this highly-important subject is dealt with in Puryear, *England, Russia and the Straits Question*, 40ff.

9. See Duroselle, J. B., "Michel Chevalier, Saint-Simonien," *Revue Historique*, ccv, 1956.
Apopolis, E., "Les idées politiques de Michel Chevalier, 1842-1846." *Revue d'Histoire Moderne et Contemporaine*, XII, 1965.
Also Blanchard, M., *Le Second Empire* (Paris, 1950).

10. It is interesting that the leading Russian authority, E. V. Tarle thinks Palmerston made the policy and that Aberdeen was a puppet. C.f. Tarle, E. V., *Krimskaya Voina*, cited Seton-Watson, H., *Russian Empire 1801-1917* (Oxford, 1967).

11. For the most recent analysis of Austrian attitudes, see Macartney, C. A., *The Hapsburg Empire* (London, 1968) 482-84.

12. This is a well-known dispute. For those with interest to pursue it in detail, the best accounts are in Puryear (op. cit.) and Temperley, H. V., *England and the Near East: The Crimea* (London, 1936). See also Taylor, A. J. P., *The Struggle for Mastery in Europe 1848-1918* (1954) 49-50, and for a new light on Stratford and the fleet movements of 1853, see Corley, T. A. B., *Democratic Despot, A Life of Napoleon III* (1961) 387-89.

13. For full text see Albrecht-Carrié, R., *The Concert of Europe, 1815-1914* (1968) 160-62.

14. Hübner (Austrian Ambassador in Paris) to Buol, 10th October, 1853, cited Hallberg, C. W., *Franz-Josef and Napoleon III* (1955) 50.

15. Napoleon III, *Oeuvres,* III, 373-79.
Case, L., *French Opinion on War and Diplomacy during the Second Empire,* thinks that Napoleon III's letter was a sop to the large sections of French public opinion which were either hostile or indifferent to the possibility of war. The Emperor himself said : "Public opinion looks for moderation in a sovereign." 25.

16. Napoléon III, *Oeuvres,* III, 382-86.

17. Macartney, C. A., *The Hapsburg Empire 1790-1918,* 482-83.

18. Hallberg, C. W., *Franz Josef and Napoleon III,* 79.

19. Ibid.

20. Mosse, W. E., *The Rise and Fall of the Crimean System* (London, 1963) 12-17.

21. For an example of what the Prince meant by Napoleon III's "crude notions" see Smith, W. H. C., "Napoleon III, England and Iberia," *Bulletin des Études Portugaises* (Paris, 1966) XXVII, 167 ff.

22. Lord Malmesbury; *Memoirs of an ex-Minister,* vol. II (London, 1884) 12.

23. For an analysis of this situation, and in particular Morny's part, see Grothe, G., *Le Duc de Morny* (Paris, 1967) 165-71.

24. On the question of the Emperor's attitude to public opinion, see Case, *Public Opinion on War and Diplomacy.*

25. *M.A.E. Correspondence Politique, Angleterre,* 703. Persigny to Walewski, 15th and 20th November, 1855.

26. For a detailed account see Puryear, V, J., op. cit.
For a lucid and brief account, see Mosse, W. E., op. cit.

27. La Gorce, op. cit., I, 455.

28. Quoted Mosse, op. cit., 22-23.

29. Quoted Hallberg, *Napoleon III and Franz-Josef,* 105.

CHAPTER 10

1. Sorel, Albert, *Lectures Historiques* (Paris, 1894).

2. The key clause read : "*Les stipulations del a paix serait complétées par un traité d'alliance entre l'Austriche, la France et la Grand Bretagne, garantissant l'intégrité de l'Empire Ottoman, et rétablissant comme casus belli toute infraction portée par la Russie aux stipulations de la dite paix.*" This clause was whittled down until it emerged in a final and weakened form on 15th April, 1856. c.f. text in Albrecht-Carrié, *Concert of Europe* (London, 1968).

3. For a full analysis of this event, see Mosse, *The Rise and Fall of the Crimean System.*

4. Mosse, op. cit., 104.

5. Morny, *Une Ambassade en Russie. 1856* (Paris, 1892) 169

6. Morny, op. cit., 137-38.

7. Quoted in Grothe, Gerda, *Le duc de Morny* (Paris, 1967) 193-94.

8. For a full account of the Russian railway operation see Cameron, Rondo,

France and the Economic Development of Europe 1800-1914 (Princeton, 1961) 275-83.

9. For an analysis of Russian economy see Portal, R., *Études d'Histoire Moderne et Contemporaine* V (1953) for a *dépouillement* of an article by Zlotnikov, "Ot Manufaktury k fabrika" (de la Manufacture à la Fabrique), *Voprosiy Istorii* 11-12 (Moscow, 1946).

10. The best account of the negotiations is in Boutenko, V., "Un projet d' Alliance Franco-Russe en 1856," *Revue Historique* (1927) 315 ff.

11. See Yale, W., *The Near East* (Ann Arbor, 1958) 76-78.

12. De Thouvenel had noticed in 1856 that the Bulgars hoped for a Russian victory: "The entire *rayat*, since the beginning of the war have shown themselves in favour of Russia; our successes plunge them into gloom." M.A.E. Paris, A.P., 255, Papiers Thouvenel.

13. See Henry, Paul, *Napoléon III et les Peuples.* (Gap, 1943).

14. For a full account of this question in the period 1851-1861 see Smith, W. H. C., "Napoleon III, England and Iberia," in *Bulletin des Études Portuguaises* 27 (Paris, 1956) also the same author, *Anglo-Portuguese Relations 1851-1861* (Lisbon, 1970).

15. A full account of this project is in Mosse, op. cit., Chapter IV.

16. Queen Victoria, *Letters,* III, Albert to Clarendon, 21st May, 1857.

17. Martin, Theodore, *Life of the Prince Consort,* IV (London, 1878) 110.

18. P.R.O. F.O. 27. France. Cowley to Lord Clarendon, Confidential, 12th May, 1857.

19. For a full acccount of this, see Pack, M., *The Bombs of Orsini* (London, 1958).

20. For an account of the sharp encounter between the Emperor and the *Conseil d'État* see Maurain, *Baroche*, 173-74.

21. Cavour to La Marmora, 24th July, 1858, in *Carteggio Cavour-Nigra dal 1858 al 1861*, vol. I (Bologna, 1961 edition) 114.

22. This letter from Cavour to the King is of great interest and importance. It will be found in Mack Smith, *The Making of Italy,* 238-47.

23. There are several sources of information on this incident. That of Prince Napoleon himself, which was edited by E. d'Hauterive in 1928 "La Mission du Prince Napoléon à Varsovie," needs to be treated with caution since it is much too self-congratulatory.

Apart from a review by Feygin and Schule in *Revue des Deux Mondes,* July, 1928, which points out inaccuracies, there are several letters from Napoleon III to his cousin which indicate his irritation with the Prince's performance at Petersburg. C.f. d'Hauterive, *Correspondance de Napoleon III,* 119-22. The best account is in an article by Tapié, V., "Le Traité Secret de 1859 entre la France et la Russie" in *Études d'Histoire Moderne et Contemporaine,* V (1953) 116-47.

24. The English diplomats seem to have spread the rumour. Hübner in his diary under date of 1st January says: "Lord Chelsea, first secretary at the British Embassy, had nothing better to do than go to the *Union Club* and spread an inexact account of the incident. By evening, Paris was in a state of consternation." Hübner, *Neuf Ans de Souvenirs . . .*, II, 244.

25. For Cavour's plans see telegram to General Durando in Mack Smith, *The Making of Italy*, 260.

26. Napoleon III to Prince Napoleon, not dated but probably 24th/25th January, d'Hauterive, op. cit., 130. Even more explicit is the letter of 26th January, ibid., 131-33.

27. Napoléon III, *Oeuvres*, v, 36-37.

28. For an account, see Odo Russell to Lord Malmesbury, 8th March, 1859. Blakiston, N., *The Roman Question* (London, 1962) 7-10.

29. Ibid., 11-14.

30. Martin, T., *Life of the Prince Consort*. IV, 405.

31. Odo Russell to Malmesbury 9th April, 1959. Blakiston, *Roman Question*, 15-16.

32. This is argued by Hallberg, *Franz-Joseph and Napoleon III*, 176 ff.

33. See Mack Smith, *The Making of Italy*, 272 ff. Cavour's agitation is revealed by the correspondence quoted.

34. The confusion at Vienna is dealt with by Craig, G. A., *War, Politics and Diplomacy* (London, 1966) in the essay on "Command and Staff Problems in the Austrian Army 1740-1866," 16-19. See also Hallberg, *Franz-Joseph and Napoleon III*, 182-92.

35. For this development see Case, *French Opinion on War and Diplomacy*, Chs. III and IV.

36. Cameron, Rondo, *France and the Economic Development of Europe* (Princeton, 1961) 435-48.

37. Text of Villafranca in Mack Smith, *The Making of Modern Italy*, 287. Smith should be consulted for this entire period, in particular the letters of Cavour which are quoted.

38. Victor Emmanuel to British Military Attaché (Cadogan), 14th July, 1859. Quote Mack Smith, op. cit., 288-91.

39. Quoted Hallberg, op. cit., 213.

40. For a lucid analysis of this period see Macartney, *The Hapsburg Empire*, Chp. 11.

41. For the most recent analysis, see Barker, N. N., *Distaff Diplomacy: The Empress Eugénie and the Foreign Policy of the Second Empire* (University of Texas, 1967) 106-7. See also Kurz, H., *The Empress Eugénie* (London, 1964) 176-78.

42. Hallberg, op. cit., 272.

CHAPTER 11

1. For an excellent summary of this subject see Humphreys, R. A., "The States of Latin America," *New Cambridge Modern History*, Vol. X (Cambridge, 1967).

2. c.f. expedition of 1838-39.

3. Dawson, D., *The Mexican Adventure* (London, 1935) 9-16.

4. Dawson, op. cit., 8.

5. Farmer, Paul, "The Second Empire in France," *New Cambridge Modern History*, Vol. X.

6. For other examples of popular reaction, see Case, L. M., *French Opinion* . . ., 143-55.

7. Cited in Latreille and Rémond, *Histoire du Catholicisme en France,* III (Paris, 1962) 322.

8. Schefer, C., *La Grande Pensée de Napoléon III* (Paris, 1939) 32.

9. Schefer, op. cit., 55-57.

10. Schefer, op, cit., 100.

11. See, for example, de la Torre, Ernesto, Vilar, *La Intervención francesa y el triunfo de la Republica* (Mexico, D. F., 1968) 14.

12. See Canovas, Augustin Cue, *Mexico ante la Intervención* (1861-64) (Mexico, D. F., 1966) 88-89.

13. Corneille, A., *La Seine Inférieure, industrielle et Commerciale* (Rouen, 1873) 170. See also *Annuaire Statistique* (1938) 138.

14. "L'Economie du Nord est et la Résistance à l'Empire" by F. Mauro. Essay in *La Intervención franseca y el Imperio de Maximiliano* (Ed. Arnaiz y Freg A. and Bataillon, C., Mexico D. F., 1965).

15. The full text is in Niox, G. L., *L'Expèdition du Mexique 1861-1867* (Paris, 1874) 212-16.

16. The most interesting account of how Napoleon III took up the idea of monarchy is in Corti, E., *Maximillian and Charlotte of Mexico,* vol. I (New York, 1928) 99-103. C.f. also Schefer, op. cit., 114-19, who is much more perceptive.

17. For this topic c.f. Chapter XV below.

18. The text of this letter may be found as an appendix to Corti, *Maximillian and Charlotte...* I, and also in Brock, C. H., *Prelude to Tragedy* (Philadelphia (University of Pennsylvania), 1966). Appendix F. This latter work is an exhaustive analysis of the negotiations leading to the signing of the October Convention, 1861.

19. C.f. Dawson, *Mexican Adventure,* 126-27.

20. Bourne, K., *Britain and the Balance of Power in North America 1855-1908* (London, 1967) 255. Dr. Bourne's book is of great importance in that it shows how British policy had developed in Central America c.f. particularly Ch. 6.

21. Text in Temperley, H., & Penson, L., *Foundations of British Foreign Policy* (London, 1938) 295.

22. Quoted Bourne, op. cit., 255.

23. Miller, R. R., "Matias Romero : Mexican Minister to the U.S. during the Juarez-Maximilian era," in *Hispanic American Historical Review* 45 (1965).

24. The whole of this topic is examined in Case, Lynn M., *French Opinions on the United States and Mexico 1860-1867* (1936, reprinted 1969).

25. For the whole question of French attitudes to the Civil War, see Case, L. M. and Spencer, W. F., *The United States and France: Civil War Diplomacy,* University of Pennsylvania, 1970.

26. See pamphlet by Quinet, Edgar, *L'Expédition du Mexique* (London, 1862).

27. Napoléon III, *Oeuvres,* V, 227-28.

28. The best succinct account of this period in the Far East is Hudson, C. F., "The Far East," *Cambridge Modern History* (1967) vol. X, Ch.

XXVI. Another version is in Panikkar, K. M., *Asia and Western Dominance* (London, 1959) 92-106.

29. In this see Thomson, R. S., "The Diplomacy of Imperialism : France and Spain in Cochin-China 1858-1863," *Journal Modern History XII* (1940) 334-56.

30. Quoted Cady, J., *The Roots of French Imperialism in the Eastern Asia* (Cornell, 1954) 206. Cady's work is the best guide to this topic.

31. Hansard, *Parliamentary Debates,* 3rd series CLVII, 769-70.

CHAPTER 12

1. See Chapter V, 65 above.

2. See Bobr-Tylingo, S., "Napoleon III et le problème Polonais, 1830-1859," *Revue internationale d'histoire politique et constitutionelle* (Paris, July 1955). Also Mosse, W. E., *The Rise and Fall of the Crimean System,* 17.

3. See Chapter XI, above 184-5.

4. See Emerit, M., "La Crise Syrienne et l'expansion économique française en 1860". *Revue Historique,* ccvii, Paris 1952.

5. Metternich to Rechberg (Foreign Minister), 24th January, 1863. Quoted Bobr-Tylingo, S., *Napoléon III, l'Europe et la Pologne en 1861-64* (Rome, 1963) 14.

6. See Taylor, A. J. P., *The Struggle for Mastery in Europe* (Oxford, 1954) 134 ff. Also Mosse, W. E., *The European Powers and the German Question,* 110 ff.

7. Golz to Bismarck. 15th February, 1863. Quoted Bobr-Tylingo, op. cit., 33-34.

8. Blayau, N., *Billault, Ministre de Napoléon III* (Paris, 1969).

9. Bobr-Tylingo, op. cit., 29-30.

10. Historians have varied in their approach. A. J. P. Taylor in his *Struggle for Mastery . . .* , 136, is sceptical. W. E. Mosse, *The European Powers and the German Question*, appears, 114, to take it seriously as does N. N. Barker, *Distaff Diplomacy*, 108 and appendix. T. B. Corley, *Democratic Despot*, thinks, 256, that the ideas were in fact Napoleon's and that the Empress was giving them an airing. The document appears in Oncken, H., *Die Rhein politik Kaiser Napoleons III 1863-1870*, I (1926) 4, a book which has less to do with Napoleon III than it has with justifying German policy since 1870 on the grounds that it was a necessary defence against French aggression.

11. Hallberg, *Franz-Josef and Napoleon III,* 322-24.

12. Cameron, Rondo E., *France and the Economic Development of Europe,* 415-16.

13. Quoted Bobr-Tylingo, op. cit., 131.

14. For the implications of these elections see Zeldin, *Political System*, Ch. VIII.

15. Blanqui to Lacambre, 16th April, 1863. Quoted Dommanget, M., *Blanqui et l'opposition révolutionnaire à la Fin du Second Empire* (Paris, 1960) 44-45.

16. C.f. various reports in Case, L., *French Opinion on the United States and Mexico 1860-1867* (reprinted Archon Books, 1969) 333-35 *et al.* See also Bobr-Tylingo, op. cit., 134-36.

17. For this episode c.f. d'Hauterive, *Correspondance de Napoléon III et du Prince Napoléon*, 235-49.

18. Russell to Cowley, 3rd July (sic), 1863. P.R.O. F.O. 27/1480 Confidential.

19. c.f. Hatton, Ragnhild, "Charles XV in 1863," *Historisk Tidskrift* (second series, vol. XXIX. (Stockholm 1966). I am most grateful to Professor Hatton for drawing my attention to these negotiations.

20. Blayau, N., *Billault*, 360-61.

21. Schnerb, R. *Rouher*, 179.

22. C.f. Hatton, R., op. cit.

23. Napoléon III, *Oeuvres*, V, 201-02.

24. Ibid., 209-13.

25. Palmerston to Russell, 8th November, 1863. Quoted Taylor, A. J. P., *Struggle for Mastery in Europe*, 141.

26. La Gorce, *Second Empire*, IV, 546-47. Reports an extremely interesting conversation between Bismarck and Gramont.

27. Hansard, 3rd series, CLXXII, 1252.

28. Ibid., CLXXVI, 731.

29. Ollivier, E., *L'Empire libéral*, VII, 475.

30. Renouvin, P., *Histoire des Relations Internationals*, V, 1815-1871, 358-59.

31. Drouyn de Lhuys to Benedetti. 30th March, 1866. Quoted Fletcher, W. A., *The Mission of Vincent Benedetti to Berlin, 1864-1870* (Hague, 1965) 57.

32. Case, L., *War and Opinion*, 199 ff.

33. Clark, C. W., *Franz-Joseph and Bismarck* (New York, 1934) 437-38.

34. Engels to Marx, 25th July, 1866. Quoted Rubell, M., *Karl Marx devant le Bonapartisme*, 126.

35. Vandam, A., *Undercurrents of the Second Empire* (New York, 1896) 316. The Prussian Ambassador, Goltz, found Napoleon "shaken" and "broken."

36. Schnerb, R., *Rouher*, 186. Also Maurain, J., *Baroche*, 311-12.

CHAPTER 13

1. Blayau, N., *Billault, Ministre de Napoléon III* (Paris, 1969) 385.

2. Fletcher, *The Mission of Vincent Benedetti . . .*, 111.

3. Schnerb, R., *Rouher*, 195.

4. Ibid., 191.

5. Taylor, A. J. P., *Struggle for Mastery in Europe*, 175.

6. Taylor thinks it was the revival of the Eastern Question in the shape of the Cretan revolt of 1860 which finally sundered Russia and France, but the breach was surely irreparable before that.

7. Case, L., *Public Opinion . . .*, 221.

8. *Annuaire Statistique, 1938*, also Bouvier, Furet and Gilet, *Le Mouvement du profit en France au XIX Siècle* (Paris) 407 and 423.

9. See Chapter VIII above.

10. Giraud, L., *Travaux Publics . . .*, 363, 364.

11. Kulstein, D., *Napoleon III and the Working Class*, 162 ff and Dom-

manget, M., *Blanqui et l'Opposition révolutionnaire à la fin du Second Empire* (Paris, 1960) 60-62.

12. Schnerb, R., *Rouher*, 201.
13. D'Hauterive, *Correspondence inédite* . . . , 278-285.
14. *Papiers et Correspondance de la Famille Impériale* (Paris, 1870) 132-46.
15. Napoléon III, *Oeuvres*, V, 278-79.
16. Fletcher, *Benedetti* . . . , 163.
17. Case, L., *French Opinion* . . . , 233.
18. Taylor, A. J. P., *Struggle for Mastery* . . . , 183.
19. The clearest and most succinct account of what the reforms meant is in Howard, M., *The Franco-Prussian War* (London, 1961) 24 ff.
20. Schnerb, R., *Rouher*, 221-22.
21. Hibberd, C., *Garibaldi and his Enemies* (London, 1965) 354-56.

CHAPTER 14
1. Bellet, R., *Presse et journalisme sous le Second Empire* (Paris, 1967) Part 1 and also 312-13.
2. L'homme, J., *Economie et l'Histoire* (Paris, 1967) 143.
3. Weill, G., *Histoire du Mouvement social en France 1859-1924* (Paris, 1924) 15.
4. Napoléon III, *Oeuvres*, 314.
5. Taylor, A. J. P., *Struggle for Mastery* . . . , 194-96.
6. Craig, Gordon, "A Study in the Application of Non-intervention : Great Britain and the Belgian Railways Dispute 1869," *War, Politics and Diplomacy* (London, 1966).
7. The best account of this election is Zeldin, T., *The Political System of Napoleon III*, Chapter X.
8. Ponteil, F., *Les Classes Bourgeoises*, (Paris, 1968) 319.
9. Prince Napoleon, *Note sur les élections générales de 1869*, "Remise à l'Empereur." In d'Hauterive, *Correspondance* . . . , 386-95.
10. Zeldin, T., *Emile Ollivier* (Oxford, 1963) 117 and Schnerb, *Rouher*, 260.
11. d'Hauterive, *Correspondance* . . . , 394-95.
12. Duguit, L. & Monnier, H., *Les Constitutions de la France* (Paris, 1915) 308-14.
13. Maurain, J., *Baroche*, 483.
14. Napoleon to Prince Napoleon, 4th March, 1870. d'Hauterive, *Correspondance*, 303.
15. L'Huillier, F., *La Lutte Ouvière à la fin du Second Empire* (Paris 1957) 74.
16. Duveau, G., *La Vie Ouvrière* . . . , 392.
17. Quoted in Zeldin, T., *Emile Ollivier*, 155.

CHAPTER 15
1. Cameron, Rondo E., *France and the Economic Development of Europe*, 89-91.
2. Smith, W. H. C., "Napoleon III, England and Iberia," *Bulletin des Études Portugaises* XXVII (Paris, 1966). For Anglo-Portuguese relations

generally in this period see the same author's, *Anglo-Portuguese Relations 1850-1861* (Lisbon, 1970).

3. M.A.E. Paris, *Correspondance Politique, Portugal*, 181. French Minister in Lisbon (Marquis de Lisle) to Count Walewski, 5th November, 1855.

4. Smith, W. H. C., *Anglo-Portuguese Relations* (Ch. IV on finance).

5. M.A.E. Paris, *Correspondance Politique, Portugal,* 181 de Lisle to Drouyn de Lhuys, 27th November, 1854.

6. M.A.E. Paris, *Mémoires et Documents, Espagne,* 366. Memorandum by Drouyn de Lhuys, May, 1855.

7. See Chapter X above.

8. For this incident see Smith, W. H. C., *Anglo-Portuguese Relations,* Ch. VI. For the point about the nature of the cargo, see *Archives Nationales* (Paris), *Contentieux, Portugal,* 390, *Charles et Georges.* Report of the *Procurer Impérial.*

9. M.A.E. Paris, *Correspondance Politique, Portugal,* 195-96. Various dispatches of May, June, July, 1859 see also Smith, W. H. C., op. cit.

10. M.A.E. Paris, *Correspondance Politique, Portugal,* 196. de Guitand (*chargé d'affaires* to Thouvenel. Various dates in May, June and July, 1860.

11. M.A.E. Paris, *Mémoires et Documents, Espagne,* 366, Memorandum by Vicomte de Grouchy to Drouyn de Lhuys, 26th December, 1862.

12. Cameron, Rondo E., *France and the Economic Development* ... 248 ff.

13. M.A.E. Paris, *Correspondance Politique, Portugal,* 201. Various dispatches, in particular that of 26th February, 1866.

14. *Archives Nationales,* Series AB XIX, 173.

15. M.A.E. Paris, *Correspondance Politique, Espagne,* 870. Mercier to de Moustier, 8th May, 1868.

16. M.A.E. Paris, *Correspondance Politique, Espagne,* 871. Telegram to Minister for Foreign Affairs, 28th September, 1868.

17. Smith, W. A., "Napoleon III and the Spanish Revolution of 1868," *Journal of Modern History* XXV (1953). The writer thinks that Napoleon III was never seriously behind a Portuguese candidature but he relies too heavily on the evidence of the Spanish historian A. Pirala, *Historia Contemporanea.*

18. M.A.E. Paris, *Correspondance Politique, Espagne,* 871, 30th October and 9th November, 1868, report from Madrid. 1st December cipher telegram from Emperor to Mercier.

19. P.R.O. London. F.O. 63. Clarendon to Murray (in Lisbon), *V. Confidential,* 13th April, 1869. (The dispatch is marked : "Seen by Gladstone and the Queen".)

20. M.A.E. Paris, *Correspondance Politique, Angleterre.* Auvergne to La Valette. 17th March, 1869. This dispatch was sent on to Madrid marked, "strictly confidential".

21. M.A.E. Paris, *Correspondance Politique, Espagne,* 873. Bartholdi (French Minister) to La Valette, 1st May, 1869.

22. M.A.E. Paris, *Correspondance Politique, Portugal,* 203. Maynard to Auvergne, 25th September, 1869.

23. P.R.O. London F.O. 361/1 (Clarendon Papers), Lord Howden to Lord

Lyons, Bayonne, 2nd June, 1870. Lyons sent the letter to Lord Clarendon on 9th June.

24. Corley, T. A. B., *Democratic Despot,* thinks Napoleon wanted to keep Fernando because he was liable to be succeeded by his daughter, whose husband was Leopold of Hohenzollern, 322. This is feasible, but ignores the Portuguese King's *penchant* for an Iberian union which would have made King Luis a more likely successor.

25. P.R.O. London F.O. 361/1 (Clarendon Papers) Clarendon to Layard (in Madrid), 15th March, 1870.

26. Steefel, L., *Bismarck, the Hohenzollern Candidacy, and the Origins of the Franco-German War of 1870.* (Cambridge, Mass., 1962) 12-13.

27. Count Vincent Benedetti, *Ma Mission en Prusse* (Paris, 1871) 307.

28. Windell, G. G., *The Catholics and German Unity, 1866-1871* (1954) 231.

29. Von Bismarck, O., *Reflections and Reminiscences* (Eng. Trans.), Vol. II (London, 1898) 88-89.

30. Mosse, W. E., *The European Powers...,* 302-03. Mosse thinks Clarendon was very negligent in not advising the Queen to be more careful in her reply to Berlin, presumably by intimating that England would not be wholly aloof? In any event, Queen Victoria's comments were written on 16th March after the decisive council had been held in Berlin.

31. There is a good summary of this very complicated period in Fletcher, W. A., *The Mission of Vincent Benedetti,* 238-41.

32. On this question see Lord, R., *Origins of War of 1870,* Steefel, L. D., *Bismarck The Hohenzollern Candidacy...*and above all Bonnin, G., *Bismarck and the Hohenzollern Candidature for the Spanish Throne* (Trans. I. Massey) (London 1957). Bonnin proves conclusively that this deciphering was a deliberate mistake.

33. Quoted Fletcher, *Benedetti,* 248.

34. Quoted de la Gorce, P., *Histoire ...,* VI, 267.

35. Fletcher, W. A., *Benedetti,* 254-59. This is the most recent account of this incident and contains full references in the notes.

36. Case, L., *Public Opinion ...* Ch. X is devoted to the episode of the background to the Franco-Prussian war and is of great value.

37. This whole question has been more recently dealt with in Barker, N. N., *Distaff Diplomacy* (University of Texas, 1967) 197-200. In dealing with the Hohenzollern candidacy this work is weakened by the fact that the author has relied on the published *Origins Diplomatiques de la guerre de 1870-1871.* She seems unaware of the discrepancies which exist between the published and unpublished documents, which were carefully edited. For example, she thinks that Mercier de l'Ostende's correspondence from Madrid is fragmentary for the spring of 1870. In fact it is to be found in the *Correspondance Politique, Espagne,* from No. 875 onwards.

38. Schnerb, R., *Rouher,* 272.

39. Zelchin, T., *Emile Ollivier,* 122.

40. A superb account of the war is Howard, M., *The Franco-Prussian War* (London, 1961).

EPILOGUE

1. For a recent view see Spitzer, A. R., "The Good Napoleon III," *French Historical Studies,* Vol. II, no. 3, 1962.

2. *Lettres de Jules Goncourt, Les Frènes Goncourt, André Billy,* (Paris, 1954) 239.

3. For the life of Princess Mathilde see Richardson, Joanna, *Princess Mathilde* (London, 1969).

4. See Smith, W. H. C., "L'Historiographie Anglaise et Napoléon Ier", *Journal des Savants,* Paris, Avril-Juin, 1969.

Bibliography

I·N a work of this nature a large number of secondary sources are bound to be used. Many of them will be well known to students of the period who will have used Robert Schnerbs' bibliographical article "Napoleon III and the Second Empire" published in the *Journal of Modern History*, VIII, 1936, but it is hoped that this bibliography may prove valuable to those less familiar with the topics who may wish to extend or deepen their knowledge. The primary sources listed below have been consulted by the author with varying degrees of application since many of the documents in, for example, the fields of finance, industry, and commerce are of real value only to the economic historian who has the requisite training to make full use of them.

I. UNPUBLISHED DOCUMENTARY SOURCES

FRANCE

A. Ministère des Affaires Etrangères, Paris (referred to in the text as M.A.E.)
Correspondance Politique, Angleterre, Espagne, Portugal. This series contains the official letters and despatches between the French Embassies and the Quai d'Orsay.
Fonds Divers
Espagne, 366. 1849-1874.
Portugal, 27.1855-1881.
Papiers Privés
Papiers Thouvenel
Papiers Walewski

B. Archives Nationales, Paris
Second Empire.
Série F : F7. Finance., F.12. Commerce, Industrie., F.30 Finance (projets).

Série A(rchives) P(rivées).
Papiers Persigny, 44 A.P.
Papiers Rouher, 45 A.P.
Papiers Montholon, 115 A.P.
Papiers Mangin, 149 A.P.
Papiers Pelissier, 235 A.P.
Papiers Fould, 247 A.P.
Papiers Thouvenel, 255 A.P. and Microfilms M I. 192. Série AB XIX 159-178. Papiers Trouvés au Palais des Tuileries Septembre 1870. Cartons.
173-176. This is a very heterogeneous collection and on it was based the published volumes of papers belonging to the Imperial family.
3038. Papiers Lavallette.

C. Bibliothèque, Thiers, Paris.
Papiers Baroche, 960-1245.

ENGLAND

Public Record Office, London (referred to in the text as P.R.O.)
P.R.O. F.O. 27. France.
F.O. 519. Cowley Papers.

II. PUBLISHED DOCUMENTARY SOURCES

Les Origines Diplomatiques de la Guerre de 1870-1871, 29 Vols. Paris 1910-1930. This collection requires to be used with care since many of the documents have been heavily edited.
Papiers et Correspondance de la famille impériale. Paris, 1870.
Papiers sauvés des Tuileries, 2 Vols. Paris 1870-1872. The main purpose behind the publication of these two collections was to discredit the Imperial regime. The series finished as a result of the burning down of the Palace of the Tuileries by the Communards in 1871.
Oeuvres Complètes d'Alexis de Tocqueville (ed. J. Mayer) Correspondance avec Gustave de Beaumont.
Napoleon III et le Prince Napoléon, Correspondance inédite. Ed. E. d'Hauterive. Paris, 1925.

III. PUBLISHED HISTORICAL WORKS

Aaronson, T., *The Fall of the Third Napoleon*, London, 1970.
Anon. *Biographie de Napoléon-Louis Bonaparte.* Pamphlet, n.d., probably October 1836.
d'Auvergne, E., *Napoleon III*, London, 1929.
Barker, N. N., *Distaff Diplomacy*, University of Texas, 1967.

——, "Austria, France, and the Venetian Question, 1861-1866," *The Journal of Modern History*, xxxvi, 1964.

——, "Empress Eugénie and the Mexican venture," *The Historian*, 1960.

——, "France, Austria, and the Mexican Venture, 1861-1864," *French Historical Studies* III, 1963.

——, "Napoleon III and the Hohenzollern Candidacy for the Spanish Throne," *The Historian*, xxix, 1967.

Bastid, P., *Les Institutions Politiques de la Monarchie Parlementaire Française*, Paris, 1954.

Beau de Loménie E., *Les Responsabilités des Dynasties Bourgeoises,* Paris, 1943.

Blakiston, N. (Editor), *The Roman Question.* Extracts from the dispatches of Odo Russell from Rome 1858-1870, London, 1962.

Blanchard, M., *Le Second Empire*, Paris, 1957.

Bonnin, G. (Editor), *Bismarck and the Hohenzollern Candidature for the Spanish Throne*, London, 1957.

Bratianu, G., *Napoléon III et les Nationalités*, Bucharest, 1934.

Cameron, Rondo E., *France and the Economic development of Europe,* Princeton University Press, 1961.

Canovas, Augustin, *Mexico ante la Intervenciòn (1861-1864)*, Mexico D.F.,1960.

Case, L. M., *French Opinion on War and Diplomacy during the Second Empire*, University of Pennsylvania, 1954.

——, *French Opinion on the United States and Mexico, 1860-1867,* 1936 (reprinted 1969).

——, with W. F. Spencer, *The United States and France: Civil War Diplomacy*, University of Pennsylvania, 1970.

Charles-Roux, F., "Alexandre II, Gortchakoff et Napoleon III", Paris, 1913.

Chastenet, J., "Emile Ollivier et les conséquences d'une situation Fausse," *Revue des Travaux de l'Académie des Sciences morales et politiques* Paris, 1945.

Chevallier, J. J., *Histoire des Institutions politiques de la France 1789-1945*, Paris, 1958.

Chrétien, P., *Le duc de Persigny (1808-1872)*, Toulouse, 1943.

Clark, C. W., *Franz-Joseph and Bismarck before 1866*, Havard University Press, 1934.

Corley, T. B., *Democratic Despot. A life of Napoleon III.* This is an important book containing an excellent "guide to the Sources."

Corti, E. C., *Maximilian and Charlotte of Mexico*, New York, 1928.

Cousteix, P., "Les Financiers sous le Second Empire," *1848, Revue des Révolutions Contemporaines*, Vol. 43, July, 1950.

Dansette, A., *Deuxieme République et Second Empire,* Paris, 1942.

——, *Louis Napoleon à la conquête du Pouvoir,* Paris, 1961.

——, *Histoire Religieuse de la France Contemporaine,* Paris, 1965.

Delord, T., *Histoire du Second Empire,* 6 Vols., Paris, 1869-1875.

Dommanget, M., *Blanqui et l'Opposition Révolutionnaire à la fin du Second Empire,* Paris, 1960.

Doutenville, J., "La Politique extérieure de Napoleon III," *Revue des Études Napoleoniennes,* xxi, 1923.

Dunham, A. L., *The Industrial Revolution in France,* 1815-1848, New York, 1955.

Duveau, G., *La Vie Ouvrière sous le Second Empire,* Paris 1946.

Emerit, M., *Lettres de Napoleon III à Madame Cornu,* 2 Vols., Paris. 1937.

——, "La crise Syrienne et l'expansion économique française en 1860," *Revue Historique,* Avril-Juin, 1952.

——, "Les sources des idées sociales et coloniales de Napoleon III," *Revue d'Alger,* 1945.

Fisher, H. A. L., *Bonapartism,* London, 1908.

Fletcher, W. A., *The Mission of Vincent Benedetti to Berlin, 1864-1870,* The Hague, 1965.

Forbes, A., *Life of Napoleon III*, London, 1898.

Friedjung, H., *The Struggle for Supremacy in Germany,* 1859-1866, (An abridged translation of the German original.), London, 1935.

Fuye, de la, M. and Babeau, E. A., *Louis Napoléon Bonaparte avant l'Empire,* Paris, 1951.

Girard, L., *La Deuxième République,* 1848-1851, Paris, 1968.

——, *La Politique des Travaux Publics du Second Empire,* Paris, 1952.

——, "Problèmes politiques et constitutionels du Second Empire," *Les Cours de la Sorbonne,* Paris, 1964.

——, "Le Second Empire et l'unité Italienne," Atti del Convegno Internazionale sul tema: Il Risorgimento e Europa. *Accademia Nazionale dei Lincei,* ccclxi, Roma, 1964.

Gonnard, P., *Les Origines de la légende Napoléonienne,* Paris, 1906.

Gorce de la, P., *Histoire du Second Empire,* 7 Vols., Paris, 1894-1905.

Grothe, G., *Le duc de Morny,* Paris, Fayard, 1967.

Guedalla, P., *The Second Empire,* London, 1922.

Guest, I., *Napoleon III in England,* London, 1952.

Hallberg, C., *Franz-Josef and Napoleon III, 1852-1864,* New York, 1955.

Hatton, R., "Charles XV in 1863," *Historisk Tydskrift*, Second Series, Vol. xxix. Stockholm, 1966.

Hales, E. E. Y., *Pio Nono*, London, 1954.

Henry, P., *Napoléon III et les Peuples*, Gap, 1943.

L'Héritier, M., "Les documents austro-allemands sur les origines de la guerre de 1870," *Revue d'Histoire Moderne*, II, 1913.

Higonnet, P. and T. B., "Class, corruption, and politics in the French Chamber of Deputies, 1846-1848," *French Historical Studies*, V. No. 2, 1961.

Houston, D. W., "Emile Ollivier and the Hohenzollern Candidacy," *French Historical Studies*, IV, 1965.

Hyde, H. Montgomery, *Mexican Empire*, London, 1946.

Jeloubovskaia, E., *La chute du Second Empire et la naissance de la Troisième Republique*, Moscow, 1959.

Jennings, L. C., "Lamartine's Italian policy in 1848; A re-examination," *The Journal of Modern History*, Vol. 42, 1970.

Jerrold, Blanchard, *Life of Napoleon III*, 4 Vols., London, 1874-1882.

Johnson, D., *Guizot*, London, 1963.

Kurz, H., *The Empress Eugénie*, London, 1962.

Latreille, A. and Rémond, R., *Histoire du Catholicisme en France*, Vol. III. Paris, 1962.

Lord, R. H., *The Origins of the War of 1870*. Harvard University Press, 1924.

Malmesbury, Earl of, *Memoirs of an ex-Minister,* 2 Vols. London, 1884.

Mastellone, Salvo, *La Politica Estera del Guizot,* Florence, 1957.

Maurain, J., *Baroche, Ministre de Napoleon III*, Paris, 1936.

——, *La Politique Ecclesiastique du Second Empire*, Paris, 1930.

Mosse, W. E., *The European Powers and the German Question,* Cambridge, 1958.

——, *The Rise and Fall of the Crimean Alliance,* London, 1857-1871, London, 1963.

Napoléon III, *Oeuvres,* 5 Vols. Paris, 1869. These volumes contain the major pamphlet works of Napoleon III, *e.g.* the *Idées Napoléoniennes,* and also all the major public speeches.

Niox, G. L., *L'Expédition du Mexique, 1861-1867,* Paris, 1874.

Ollivier, E. L., *L'Empire Libéral,* 18 Vols. Paris, 1895-1916.

Oncken, H., *Die Rheinpolitik Kaiser Napoleons III,* 1863-1870, 3 Vols. Stuttgart, 1926.

Pagès, G., *La Politique Extérieure de Napoleon III*, Paris, 1933.

Palat, Général., *Les Origins de la guerre de 1870; La Candidature Hohenzollern,* Paris, 1912.

Palm, F. C., *England and Napoleon III.* Duke University Press, 1944.

Payne, H., *The Police State of Louis Napoleon Bonaparte*, 1851-1860. University of Washington Press, Seattle, 1966.

——, "Preparation of a coup d'état (1849-1851)" in *Studies in Modern European History* (in honour of F. Charles Palm), New York, 1956.

Péreire, G., *Oeuvres d' I. et E. Péreire. Documents sur l'origine et le développement des Chemins de Fer.* T. III. 1833-1870, Paris, 1913.

Perreux, A., *Les Conspirations de Louis Napoléon—Strasbourg. Boulogne*, Paris, 1926.

Pierrard, P., *La Vie ouvière à Lille sous le Second Empire*, Paris, 1965.

Pimient, R., *La Propagande Bonapartiste en 1849.* Paris, 1911.

Pingaud, A., "La Politique extérieure du Second Empire," *Revue Historique*, CLVI, 1927.

——, "Un projet de désarmament en 1870," *Revue de Paris*, XXI, 1914.

Pinkney, D., "Migrations to Paris during the Second Empire," *Journal of Modern History*, 1953.

——, *Napoleon III and the Rebuilding of Paris.* Princeton University Press, 1958.

Ponteil, F., *Les institutions de la France de 1814-1870.* Paris P.U.F., 1965.

——, *Les Classes Bourgeoises et l'Avènement de la Démocratie*, Paris, 1968.

Portal, R., "L'économie russe avant 1870," *Etudes d'Histoire Moderne et Contemporaine*, V, 1953.

Pradalié, G., *Le Second Empire (Que sais-je?* series), Paris, 1957.

Rain, P., "Les relations Franco-russes sous le Second Empire," *Revue des Etudes Historiques*, LXXXIX.

Renouvin, P., *Le dix-nèuvième siécle I, de 1815 à 1871.*

——, Tome, V. of *Histoire des Relations Internationales*, Paris, 1954.

Rémond, R., *La Droite en France de la Première Restauration à la Vᵉ Republique*, Paris, 1963.

——, *La Vie Politique en France 1848-1879*, T.2. Paris, 1969.

Richards, E. W., "Louis Napoleon and Central America," *Journal of Modern History*, Vol. XXXIV. June, 1962.

Rothan, G., *Souvenirs diplomatiques: l'Europe et l'avènement du Second Empire*, Paris 1870.

Rubel, Maximilien., *Karl Marx devant le Bonapartisme.* Paris, 1960.

Schefer, C., *La Grande Pensée de Napoleon III.*

——, *Les origines de l'expedition du Mexique*, Paris, 1939.

Schnerb, Robert., *Rouher et le Second Empire*, Paris, 1949.

——, "Napoleon III and the Second French Empire." *Journal of Modern History*, Vol. VIII. 1936. (Bibliographical article of great value.)

Simpson, F. A., *The Rise of Louis Napoleon*, 3rd Edition, 1950.

——, *Louis Napoleon and the Recovery of France*, 3rd Edition, 1951.

Smith, W. A., "Napoleon III and the Spanish Revolution of 1868," *The Journal of Modern History*, XXV, 1953.

Smith, W. H. C., *Anglo-Portuguese Relations 1850-1861*, Lisbon, 1970.

——, "L'Historiographie anglaise et Napoleon Ier," *Journal des Savants*, Paris, Avril-Juin, 1969.

——, "Napoleon III, England and Iberia," *Bulletin des Etudes Portugaises*, 27, Paris, 1966.

Sorel, E., *Lectures Historiques*, Paris, 1894.

——, *Histoire diplomatique de la guerre Franco-Allemande*, 2 Vols. Paris, 1875.

Spitzer, Alan R., "The Good Napoleon III," *French Historical Studies.* Vol. II, No. 3, 1962.

Steefel, L., *The Schleswig-Holstein Question*, Harvard University Press, 1932.

Tapié, V., "Le Traité Secret de 1859 entre la France et la Russie," *Etudes d'Histoire Moderne et Contemporaine*, V, 1953.

Taylor, A. J. P., *The Struggle for Mastery in Europe, 1848-1918*, Oxford, 1954.

Thirria, H., *Napoleon III avant l'Empire*, Paris.

Thompson, J. M., *Louis Napoleon and the Second Empire*, Oxford, 1954.

Thouvenel, H., *Nicolas Ier. et Napoleon III*, Paris, 1891.

Tudesq, H., "La Légende Napoléonienne en 1848," *Revue Historique*, 1957.

Valsecchi, F., "Considerazioni sulla politica Europea di Napoleone III," *Rivista Storica Italiana*, 62, 1950.

Vilar, Ernesto de la Torre, *La Intervencion francesa y el triumfo de la Republica*, Mexico, D. F., 1968.

Windell, G. C., *The Catholics and German Unity 1866-1871*, University of Minnesota Press, 1954.

Zeldin, T., *Emile Ollivier and the Liberal Empire of Napoleon III*, Oxford, 1963.

——, *The Political system of Napoleon III*, London, 1958.

——, "English Ideas on French Politics during the 19th Century," *Historical Journal*, 1959.

——, "Government Policy in the French General Election of 1849," *English Historical Review*, 1959.

Index